CRITICAL INSIGHTS

The Tales of
Edgar Allan Poe

CRITICAL INSIGHTS

The Tales of
Edgar Allan Poe

Editor
Steven Frye
California State University, Bakersfield

Salem Press
Pasadena, California   Hackensack, New Jersey

Cover photo: The Granger Collection, New York

Published by Salem Press

© 2010 by EBSCO Publishing
Editor's text © 2010 by Steven Frye
"The *Paris Review* Perspective" © 2010 by Nathaniel Rich for *The Paris Review*

∞The paper used in these volumes conforms to the American National Standard for Permanence of Paper for Printed Library Materials, Z39.48-1992 (R1997).

Library of Congress Cataloging-in-Publication Data
The tales of Edgar Allan Poe / editor, Steven Frye.
   p. cm. — (Critical insights)
Includes bibliographical references and index.
ISBN 978-1-58765-616-3 (alk. paper)
1. Poe, Edgar Allan, 1809-1849. Tales. I. Frye, Steven.
PS2618.T32T35 2010
813′.3—dc22

                                               2009026318

PRINTED IN CANADA

Contents_____

The Tales and Their Author_____

Critical Contexts_____

Critical Readings_____

Resources

About This Volume _____

Steven Frye

This collection of essays contains a rich variety of perspectives on the tales of one of the most important American writers of the nineteenth century, an author whose work has influenced subsequent literary artists in multiple traditions. The first section of the volume contains a series of essays, recently written, that balance text, context, and influence in order to orient readers to the aesthetic features of Edgar Allan Poe's short fiction, as well as to chart the various strands of his influence in America and abroad. The second section contains a comprehensive array of important essays, republished here, that have served to define Poe studies in the last three decades. These critical treatments, written by many of the foremost scholars in the field, address a host of essential issues, from genre and experimentation to race and sociopolitical concerns. In addition, the volume contains a chronology of the author's life, a comprehensive list of his works, and a brief biography by Charles E. May, as well as a bibliography, an index, and a perspective from *The Paris Review* provided by Nathaniel Rich. I have also written a brief introduction to the volume dealing primarily with Poe's contribution to literary aesthetics, especially as it relates to subsequent art movements and his own concept of the tale.

In the "Critical Contexts" section that begins the collection, Jeff Grieneisen and Courtney Ruffner account for the author's influence, as well as his continuing relevance and popularity, through an exploration of Poe's experimental work with various genres. Susan Amper offers a wealth of historical context to explore his contribution to the early development of the short story, as well as his initial pre-modern forays into psychological issues. Emphasizing Poe's influence on Charles Baudelaire, Matthew Bolton explores his use of point of view in transforming the relation of writer and reader, which initiates a formal practice in the short story that continued into the twentieth century. Finally, Santiago Rodríguez Guerrero-Strachan considers Poe's fantastic tales, particularly in the blending of genres and a confluence of varying styles and elements of tone.

The "Critical Readings" section presents republished essays from eminent scholars specializing in Poe and in American Romantic narrative broadly construed. John Cleman, J. Gerald Kennedy, J. O. Bailey, Robert Shulman, and Elena V. Baraban deal with issues of normal and abnormal psychology, as they explore Poe's inquiry into the power and limitation of human reason. J. Woodrow Hassell, Jr., Ronald Bieganowski, and Cynthia S. Jordan analyze the role of genre, aesthetics, and style, often as they relate to a dense interiority of character. In the volume's final essay, Maurice S. Lee considers the racial implications of Poe's tales, particularly as they bear upon genre formation and aesthetic practice. In each of these fine treatments, Edgar Allan Poe emerges as an author densely rooted in literary tradition, consciously concerned with recasting previous forms, all in the context of an incisive inquiry into the human mind and its relationship to the perceivable world.

Virtually any genre or thematic concern in Poe's short fiction is addressed by one or more of the essays in this volume. I join my colleagues in expressing the hope that the reader will gain a renewed appreciation for the formal intricacy, psychological intensity, and social relevance of Edgar Allan Poe's tales.

THE TALES
AND
THEIR
AUTHOR

On Poe's Tales_____

Steven Frye

Though many associate Edgar Allan Poe with his poems and his tales, his influence in the realm of formal literary aesthetics is vast and difficult to measure. In his brief but brilliant career as a writer and magazine editor, he wrote numerous reviews and prefaces that, taken together, formulate a complex but coherent conception of artistic practice and purpose, one that served to illuminate the Romanticism of his era and provide an impetus for a worldwide reconsideration of literary art and its nature. This was especially notable in the "aesthetic movement" in France under Charles Baudelaire, Stéphane Mallarmé, and Paul Verlaine, and in Britain under Oscar Wilde. It was also observable in the French Symbolist poets, including Paul Valéry, as well as in the rise of New Critical Formalism in the early twentieth century. But Poe's aesthetic concepts were by no means removed from the act of creation. Principally, he was a writer of short stories and poetry, and his work in literary criticism emerged from his extensive reading and his own painstaking labor with the pen. In the preface to *Tales of the Grotesque and Arabesque* (1840), he explores the nature of the Gothic tale as it emerges from Germany, but in the end he concludes that at its best the Gothic portrays a "terror of the soul."

Poe's use of the term "terror" must be pondered carefully. In some of his best tales, such as "The Fall of the House of Usher," "Ligeia," "The Cask of Amontillado," and "The Tell-Tale Heart," Poe's notion of "terror" rarely involves a fear of physical destruction from without, but instead articulates the immanent dread of something morally repellant from within. A voracious reader working within a densely textured intellectual milieu, he perhaps derives this concept from Ann Radcliffe's concepts of "horror" and "metaphysical dread," which involve the fear of something internal to character, as well as trepidation when confronted with the mysteries of origin and the incomprehensibilities of the universe itself. Horror is very much at play in "The Tell-Tale

Heart." Metaphysical dread is the protagonist's curse in "The Pit and the Pendulum." In the works of Ann Radcliffe, Mary Shelley, Nathaniel Hawthorne, Herman Melville, and Edgar Allan Poe, physical destruction is perhaps the most benign of human concerns. Poe's essential preoccupation is profoundly humanistic, insofar as his tales reflect a near obsession with the power and the reach of human perception, the capacity and limitations of reason, the impulse to self-destruction, the impish delight in brutality and malevolence, all of which involve an exploration and portrayal of madness. In many of his tales, modern psychologists might note a number of identifiable pathologies. But for Poe these categories would not suffice, since his characters involve a realistic blend of normative states of mind and perception with varying degrees of delusion and misperception, all of which are presented as natural though by no means universal features of human consciousness as it encounters the world.

Poe deals with these issues primarily in the context of the Gothic romance, which he saw as a genre uniquely suited to these concerns. Distinctive from the social novel that was equally popular in America, this Gothic tradition appeared in high and low forms, both of which involved varying degrees of popularity. Beginning as a literary genre in 1765 with Horace Walpole's *The Castle of Otranto: A Gothic Story*, the term "gothic" owes its roots in history to the Vandals, Visigoths, and Ostrogoths who decimated the Roman Empire and brought on the Dark Ages. But the blending of barbarian and Latin peoples that occurred in the middle of the first millennium resulted in a complex medieval Christian culture, and in art history the term "Gothic" is used to describe the architectural forms that emerged in cathedrals throughout Europe, which are characterized by elaborate narrative motifs and iconography that embody the essentials of the Christian tradition. Central to this sweeping narrative, seen in stained glass and intricate stone figures, is the perpetual conflict between the forces of light and darkness, good and evil, the Trinitarian God and the malevolent forces that oppose him.

In the Gothic romances that emerge in the wake of the neoclassical period, this tension is enriched by authors such as Poe when the dualistic conflict of opposing forces becomes internal, circumscribing the mind and identity of the gothic hero/villain. Rationality and irrationality, passion and hatred, love and rapacious sexuality merge in the thoughts of protagonists in an explosive confluence of competing impulses that are in the end fundamentally real. In "The Cask of Amontillado," Montresor is tortured by memory and guilt, but his murderous acts and the mysterious jealousy remain with him, making his contrition at best questionable. In "Ligeia," the unnamed narrator's love for Ligeia is blended in memory with a psychological stress exacerbated by opium fantasy, which may either delude him or raise him to realms of apprehension that extend beyond the natural world. In "The Fall of the House of Usher," both the narrator and Roderick Usher descend into a shared delusion, and the ambiguous rendering of events may or may not be a genuine experience of realms transcending normative experience and sense perception. Even in detective stories such as "The Purloined Letter" and "The Murders in the Rue Morgue," which are notable examples of a genre Poe is credited with creating, there is a quality of Gothic dread and darkness. Detective Dupin's remarkable ability to unravel the mystery is linked to a seemingly intuitive capacity to understand hidden and mysterious motives that mere logic and empirical inquiry cannot apprehend. Yet for all of the horror, darkness, and psychological intensity of these tales, Poe displays a remarkable sense of humor, which appears in "How to Write a Blackwood Article," his satirical parody of stories published in *Blackwood's Magazine*. His comic voice is unambiguously rendered in "The Man That Was Used Up" and "Lionizing." But Poe's sense of the comic was deeply rooted in his intuitive apprehension of human psychology, and he understood that the comic and the satirical modes emerge from an innate fear of meaninglessness and oblivion, a highly conjectural epistemic and existential prospect he by no means celebrates. Even in Gothic tales he employs a form of romantic irony, drawn in part from the aesthetics of Friedrich Schlegel and August Wilhelm Schlegel, that blends the comic and the horrific in grotesque renderings of the human scene.

But the intensity of Poe's psychological concerns, orchestrated brilliantly through his use of the Gothic romance, works paradoxically within the context of a varied but ultimately coherent aesthetic model in which the literary artist works painstakingly to inspire a deep response in the reader. In the end, it is not the psychology of character but the psychology of aesthetic response that most concerns him. The "terror of the soul" experienced by protagonists must rise from the page and evoke a kind of pain/pleasure response in those who perceive the organic unity in the tale or poem. In "The Poetic Principle" (1850), he describes a related experience as the apprehension of "Supernal Beauty," a quality one might broadly associate with the Sublime. This emotional experience must never be subjugated to "the Heresy of the Didactic," the neoclassical notion that ideas or thematic maxims are the primary purpose of the work. It is the short form, the lyric poem or the tale, that allows for this response. In his 1842 review of Nathaniel Hawthorne's *Twice-Told Tales*, he elevates the tale above all fictional forms, because in the crystalline unity of the tale the reader apprehends the intensity of situations, the concentration of language, and the compelling densities of the human dilemma. Out of this experience emerge what might be termed the twin virtues of identification and empathy, which for Poe are the ingredients of an understanding that transcends maxims and printable truths. For all of the apparent darkness of Poe's tales, his emphasis is on the mind's capacity to rise beyond, if only for a moment, the mundane realities of material existence. Like his near contemporary Herman Melville, who illuminates his fictional practice in his poem "Art," Poe articulates his aesthetic in verse form. Published in 1831, "Israfel" speaks of an angel of music whose heartstrings are those of a lute. The poet sings in praise of the angel Israfel's song, which embodies a transcendence intimated by the heart but which is imperfectly rendered in our world, through the dark, refracted murmur of human language. Music becomes the metaphor for art in its highest form. As a medium borne of careful composition yet received in pure emotion, the Supernal Beauty in song gives a deep and inexpressible meaning to perception and experience, and the notes and phrases of the lute bring the writer to a profound understanding of his purpose:

> To thee the laurels belong,
> Best bard, because the wisest!
> Merrily live, and long!
> The ecstasies above
> With thy burning measures suit—
> Thy grief, thy joy, thy hate, thy love,
> With the fervor of thy lute—
> Well may the stars be mute!

Poe knows that the power of the angel's song is beyond the reach of words. But in all of his work, his hope is to still the stars and to lift the soul to reverie. Thus the best of his tales, written primarily though not exclusively in the varied permutations of the Gothic romance, are serious inquiries into the complexities of the mind and the nature of perception, but more important they are evocative expressions of those densities, and when read carefully they inspire as well as teach, which accounts for their continuing resonance over time.

Biography of Edgar Allan Poe_____

Charles E. May

Early Life

Edgar Allan Poe was born January 19, 1809, in Boston, Massachusetts. His mother, Elizabeth Arnold Poe, was a talented actress from an English theatrical family. Because Poe's father, David Poe, Jr., a traveling actor of Irish descent, was neither talented nor responsible, the family suffered financially. After apparently separating from David Poe, Elizabeth died in Richmond, Virginia, in 1811. The young Edgar, though not legally adopted, was taken in by a wealthy Scottish tobacco exporter, John Allan, from whom Poe took his middle name.

For most of his early life, Poe lived in Richmond with the Allans, with the exception of a five-year period between 1815 and 1820 that he spent in England, where he attended Manor House School, near London. Back in America, he attended an academy until 1826, when he entered the University of Virginia. He withdrew less than a year later, however, because of various debts, many of them from gambling; Poe did not have the money to pay, and his foster father refused to help. After quarreling with Allan about these debts, Poe left for Boston in the spring of 1827; shortly thereafter, perhaps because he was short of money, he enrolled in the United States Army under the name "Edgar A. Perry."

In the summer of 1827, Poe's first book, *Tamerlane, and Other Poems*, published under the anonym "A Bostonian," appeared, but it was little noticed by the reading public or by the critics. In January, 1829, he was promoted to the rank of sergeant major and was honorably discharged at his own request three months later. In December, 1829, Poe's second book, *Al Aaraaf, Tamerlane, and Minor Poems*, was published, and it was well received by the critics. Shortly thereafter, Poe entered West Point Military Academy, possibly as a way to get into his foster father's good graces.

After less than a year in school, Poe was discharged from West Point by court-martial for neglecting his military duties. Most biographers agree that Poe deliberately provoked his discharge because he had tired of West Point. Others suggest that he could not stay because John Allan refused to pay Poe's bills any longer, although he would not permit Poe to resign. After West Point, Poe went to New York, where, with the help of some money raised by his West Point friends, he published *Poems by Edgar A. Poe, Second Edition*. After moving to Baltimore, where he lived at the home of his aunt, Mrs. Clemm, Poe entered five short stories in a contest sponsored by the *Philadelphia Saturday Courier*. Although he did not win the prize, the newspaper published all five of his pieces. In June, 1833, he entered another contest sponsored by the *Baltimore Saturday Visiter* and this time won the prize of fifty dollars for his story "Ms. Found in a Bottle." From this point until his death in 1849, Poe was very much involved in the world of American magazine publishing.

Life's Work

During the next two years, Poe continued writing stories and trying to get them published. Even with the help of a new and influential friend, John Pendleton Kennedy, a lawyer and writer, Poe was mostly unsuccessful. Poe's financial situation became even more desperate when, in 1834, John Allan died and left Poe out of his will. Kennedy finally persuaded *The Southern Literary Messenger* to publish several of Poe's stories and to offer Poe the job of editor, a position that he kept from 1835 to 1837. During this time, Poe published stories and poems in the *Messenger*, but it was with his extensive publication of criticism that he began to make his mark in American letters.

Although much of Poe's early criticism is routine review work, he began in his reviews to consider the basic nature of poetry and short fiction and to develop theoretical analyses of these two genres, drawing upon the criticism of A. W. Schlegel, in Germany and Samuel Taylor Coleridge, in England. Poe's most important contribution to criticism is his discussion of the distinctive generic characteristics of short fiction in a famous review of Nathaniel Hawthorne's *Twice-Told Tales* (1837). Poe makes such a convincing case for the organic unity of short fiction, argues so strongly for its dependence on a unified effect, and so clearly shows how the form is more closely allied to the poem than to the novel that his ideas have influenced literary critics ever since.

In 1836, Poe married his thirteen-year-old cousin, Virginia Clemm, a decision that, because of her age and relationship to Poe, has made him the subject of much adverse criticism and psychological speculation. In 1837, after disagreements with the owner of the *Messenger*, Poe moved to New York to look for editorial work. There he completed the writing of *The Narrative of Arthur Gordon Pym* (1838), his only long fiction, a novella-length metaphysical adventure. Unable to find work in New York, Poe moved to Philadelphia and published his first important short story, a Platonic romance titled "Ligeia." In 1839, he joined the editorial staff of *Burton's Gentleman's Magazine*, where he published two of his greatest stories, "The Fall of the House of Usher" and "William Wilson."

In 1840, Poe left *Burton's* and tried, unsuccessfully, to establish his own literary magazine. He did, however, publish a collection of his stories, *Tales of the Grotesque and Arabesque* (1840), as well as become an editor of *Graham's Magazine*, where he published his first tale of ratiocination, "The Murders in the Rue Morgue." In this landmark story, he created the famous detective Auguste Dupin, the forerunner of Sherlock Holmes and countless other private detectives in literature and film. A biographical sketch published at that time described Poe as short, slender, and well proportioned, with a fair complexion, gray eyes, black hair, and an extremely broad forehead.

In 1842, Poe left *Graham's* to try once again to establish his own literary magazine, but not before publishing two important pieces of criticism: a long review of the poet Henry Wadsworth Longfellow, in which he established his definition of poetry as the "Rhythmical Creation of Beauty," and his review of Hawthorne, in which he defined the short tale as the creation of a unified effect. Between 1842 and 1844, after Poe moved to New York to join the editorial staff of the *New York Mirror*, he published many of his most important stories, including "The Masque of the Red Death," "The Pit and the Pendulum," "The Black Cat," and two more ratiocinative stories, "The Mystery of Marie Rogêt" and "The Gold Bug." It was with the publication of his most famous poem, "The Raven," in 1845, however, that he finally achieved popular success.

In February of 1845 Poe left the *New York Mirror* to join a new weekly periodical, *The Broadway Journal*, where he continued the literary war against Longfellow begun in a review written for the *Mirror*. The series of accusations, attacks, and counterattacks that ensued damaged Poe's reputation as a critic at the very point in his career when he had established his critical genius. Poe's collection of stories, *Tales*, was published in July, 1845, to good reviews. Soon after, Poe became the sole editor and then proprietor of *The Broadway Journal*. In November, he published his collection, *The Raven, and Other Poems*.

The year 1846 marked the beginning of Poe's decline. In January, *The Broadway Journal* ceased publication, and soon after Poe was involved in both a personal scandal with two female literary admirers and a bitter battle with the literary establishment. Moreover, Poe's wife was quite ill, a fact that necessitated Poe's moving his family some thirteen miles outside the city to a rural cottage at Fordham. When Virginia died on January 30, 1847, Poe collapsed. Although he never fully recovered from this series of assaults on his already nervous condition, in the following year he published what he considered to be the capstone of his career, *Eureka: A Prose Poem*, which he presented as an examination of the origin of all things.

In the summer of 1849, Poe left for Richmond, Virginia, in the hope, once more, of starting a literary magazine. On September 24, he delivered a lecture, "The Poetic Principle," at Richmond, in what was to be his last public appearance. From that time until he was found semiconscious on the streets of Baltimore, Maryland, little is known of his activities. He never recovered, and he died on Sunday morning, October 7, in Washington College Hospital.

Dictionary of World Biography: The 19th Century. Pasadena, CA: Salem Press, 1999.

Bibliography

Bittner, William. *Poe: A Biography*. Boston: Little, Brown, 1962. This volume is a reliable study of Poe's life and is suitable for general readers.

Brown, Arthur A. "Literature and the Impossibility of Death: Poe's 'Berenice.'" *Nineteenth-Century Literature* 50 (March, 1996): 448-463. Argues that Poe's stories of the dead coming back to life and of premature burial dramatize the horror of the impossibility of dying. In "Berenice," our attention to the details of the tale reproduces the narrator's obsession with that which speaks of death and does not die and thus implicates us in his violation of the still-living Berenice in her tomb.

Buranelli, Vincent. *Edgar Allan Poe*. 2nd ed. Boston: Twayne, 1977. This study of Poe's life and works offers an excellent introduction. The book includes a chronology of his life and an annotated, select bibliography.

Burluck, Michael L. *Grim Phantasms: Fear in Poe's Short Fiction*. New York: Garland, 1993. Considers the question of why Poe focused primarily on portraying weird events in his stories. Discusses the gothic conventions Poe used to achieve his effects. Argues that neither drugs nor insanity are responsible for Poe's gothic tales, but rather they were a carefully thought out literary tactic meant to appeal to current public taste and the general human reaction to fear.

Carlson, Eric, ed. *Critical Essays on Edgar Allan Poe*. Boston: G. K. Hall, 1987. This supplement to Carlson's 1966 volume (below) offers a cross section of writing about Poe from the 1830's to the 1980's. Many of the essays deal with short stories, illustrating a variety of interpretive strategies.

_____, ed. *The Recognition of Edgar Allan Poe*. Ann Arbor: University of Michigan Press, 1966. This selection of critical essays from 1829 to 1963 is intended to illustrate the development of Poe's literary reputation. It includes a number of the most important earlier essays on Poe, including Constance Rourke's discussion of Poe as a humorist. Also includes several essays by French and British critics.

Crisman, William. "Poe's Dupin as Professional, the Dupin Stories as Serial Text." *Studies in American Fiction* 23 (Autumn, 1995): 215-229. Part of a special section on Poe. Argues that the Dupin stories bear out his mesmeric revelation that the mind forms one continuum with inert substance. Poe's emphatic insistence on the role of the material and the materialistic in his detective tales makes them important psychological statements.

Frank, Lawrence. "'The Murders in the Rue Morgue': Edgar Allan Poe's Evolutionary Reverie." *Nineteenth-Century Literature* 50 (September, 1995): 168-188. Claims that Poe's story explores the implications of the nebular hypothesis and did not reinforce the prevailing orthodoxy; rather it may have been in the service of an emerging Darwinian perspective.

Hoffman, Daniel. *Poe Poe Poe Poe Poe Poe Poe*. Baton Rouge: Louisiana State University Press, 1998. A perceptive study of Poe's personality and work. As the title suggests, Hoffman finds many Poes, a man and artist of many masks. He traces the coherence of the poet's work through the unity of his images.

Howarth, William L. *Twentieth Century Interpretations of Poe's Tales*. Englewood Cliffs, NJ: Prentice-Hall, 1971. This volume contains fifteen essays on Poe's stories, several offering general points of view on his fiction but most offering specific interpretations of tales such as "The Fall of the House of Usher," "Ligeia," "William Wilson," "The Black Cat," and "The Tell-Tale Heart." Includes a chronology of Poe's life, a bibliography, and a helpful index to the stories discussed.

Hyneman, Esther K. *Edgar Allan Poe: An Annotated Bibliography of Books and Articles in English, 1827-1973*. Boston: G. K. Hall, 1974. The quantity and variety of writings on Poe make it exceedingly difficult to compile complete lists. This volume, supplemented by *American Literary Scholarship: An Annual* for coverage of subsequent years, will provide an ample resource for most readers.

Irwin, John T. *The Mystery to a Solution: Poe, Borges, and the Analytical Detective Story*. Baltimore: The Johns Hopkins University Press, 1994. An analytical/theoretical discussion of Poe's and Borges's contributions to the detective story. Argues that Borges doubles Poe's three most famous detective stories—"The Murders in the Rue Morgue," "The Purloined Letter," and "The Mystery of Marie Rogêt"—in three of his own stories.

Kennedy, J. Gerald. *A Historical Guide to Edgar Allan Poe*. New York: Oxford University Press, 2001. Considers the tensions between Poe's otherworldly settings and his representations of violence, delivers a capsule biography situating Poe in his historical context, and addresses topics such as Poe and the American publishing industry, Poe's sensationalism, his relationships to gender constructions, and Poe and American privacy. Includes bibliographic essay, chronology of Poe's life, bibliography, illustrations, and index.

Martin, Terry J. *Rhetorical Deception in the Short Fiction of Hawthorne, Poe and Melville*. Lewiston, NY: Edwin Mellen Press, 1998. An original reading of "The Murders in the Rue Morgue." Martin seeks to identify this story and those by Hawthorne and Melville as "a significant subgenre of the modern short story."

May, Charles E. *Edgar Allan Poe: A Study of the Short Fiction*. Boston: Twayne, 1991. An introduction to Poe's short stories that attempts to place them within the nineteenth century short narrative tradition and the context of Poe's aesthetic theory. Suggests Poe's contributions to the short story in terms of his development of detective fiction, fantasy, satire, and self-reflexivity. Includes passages from Poe's narrative theory and three essays by other critics illustrating a variety of critical approaches.

Peeples, Scott. *Edgar Allan Poe Revisited*. New York: Twayne, 1998. An introductory critical study of selected works and a short biography of Poe. Includes bibliographical references and index.

Pillai, Johann. "Death and Its Moments: The End of the Reader in History." *MLN* 112 (December, 1997): 836-875. Argues that Poe's "The Tell-Tale Heart" establishes its modernity by both affirming and denying its status as a narrative of historical events; contends the story declares its fictive nature in its relation to history, which it purports to transcend or slide past; concludes it is the hermeneutical relation of the narrative voice of the tale to the narrative voice of criticism that determines the story's paradoxical temporality.

Quinn, Arthur Hobson. *Edgar Allan Poe: A Critical Biography*. Baltimore: The Johns Hopkins University Press, 1998. A comprehensive biography of Poe, with a new introduction by Shawn Rosenheim, devoted to fact and describing how Poe's life and legend were misconstrued by other biographers.

Silverman, Kenneth. *Edgar A. Poe: Mournful and Never-Ending Remembrance*. New York: HarperCollins, 1991. The first major biography of Poe in fifty years, a close reading of the writer's life and work.

Sova, Dawn B. *Edgar Allan Poe, A to Z: The Essential Reference to His Life and Work*. New York: Facts On File, 2001. A thorough encyclopedic reference guide to the life and works of Poe.

Thoms, Peter. *Detection and Its Designs: Narrative and Power in Nineteenth-Century Detective Fiction*. Athens: Ohio University Press, 1998. A study of early detective fiction from readings of Poe's Dupin stories to Arthur Conan Doyle's *The Hound of the Baskervilles*.

Whalen, Terence. *Edgar Allan Poe and the Masses: The Political Economy of Literature in Antebellum America*. Princeton, NJ: Princeton University Press, 1999. A brilliant study of Poe that provides an inventive understanding of his works and his standing in American literature.

the PARIS
REVIEW

The *Paris Review* Perspective _____

Nathaniel Rich for *The Paris Review*

Edgar Allan Poe has had as awkward a path to literary immortality as any American writer. His writing sold so poorly during his own lifetime that, at the time of his death, he was best known for his book reviews. It was not until eight years after his death, when Baudelaire translated his stories and wrote an admiring essay about him, that Poe became, in French translation, one of the best-loved American writers abroad. So it was through the somewhat elevated personage of Monsieur E. A. Poe that Edgar Poe, a drunkard left for dead in a Baltimore gutter at the age of forty, was reincarnated.

Poe's popularity has been assured for more than a century now, but his status as a serious writer, at least in the States, has long been uncertain. For all his foreign admirers—a group that includes not just Baudelaire but Stéphane Mallarmé and Paul Valéry, as well as Fyodor Dostoevsky—he has had numerous detractors among prominent writers in the English-speaking canon. William Butler Yeats called "The Pit and the Pendulum" "an appeal to the nerves by tawdry physical affrightments"; Aldous Huxley assailed Poe's "vulgarity" and "bad taste"; T. S. Eliot described his control of language as "slipshod"; and D. H. Lawrence, of all writers, called his style "meretricious"—a criticism that Lawrence no doubt heard from his own critics.

They are not entirely wrong. Poe writes in a baroque, leaden prose that is slowed by frequent repetition and embellishment. Consider the opening line of "The Fall of the House of Usher," which is packed with as many connotations of gloom as any sentence written in the English language:

> During the whole of a dull, dark, and soundless day in the autumn of the
> year, when the clouds hung oppressively low in the heavens, I had been
> passing alone, on horseback, through a singularly dreary tract of country;
> and at length found myself, as the shades of the evening drew on, within
> view of the melancholy House of Usher.

The reader can hardly be surprised to learn, in the following line, that
the narrator is pervaded by "insufferable gloom"—even though the
narrator "knows not how it was" that he became so afflicted. The methodical recurrence of dreariness reaches its apotheosis in Poe's poetry; think of the incantation of "Nevermore" in "The Raven," or the
maniacally repetitive "The Bells," in which the word "bells" appears
sixty-one times in four stanzas.

Yet this technique is not without effect. The embellishment and the
tortuous prose give Poe's tales a lush, Gothic aura, which does not
frighten the reader so much as lull him into a kind of quiescent melancholy. It is for the same reason that Poe set so many of his stories in
manor houses in the European countryside, or at sea, or in antiquity.
The reader is put at a safe distance from the action. When Poe finally
reveals the perversity that lies at the heart of every tale—a corpse coming back to life, an accidental suicide, the presence of a malicious appa-
rition—the melancholy spell is broken, and the terror rushes at the
reader with startling immediacy and strangeness.

After all, the lasting appeal of all of Poe's great works—not just his
tales of horror, but his detective stories, satires, science-fiction fantasies, and humor pieces—derives from his brilliant instinct for the perverse: man's secret desire to turn against what he knows to be right,
proper, and good. "Perverseness," as Poe wrote, "is one of the primitive impulses of the human heart."

His best expression of this impulse comes in "The Black Cat." The
story's narrator tortures and then murders Pluto, his adorable pet cat,
for no other reason than that the innocent animal loved him devotedly:

One morning, in cool blood, I slipped a noose about its neck and hung it to the limb of a tree;—hung it with the tears streaming from my eyes, and with the bitterest remorse at my heart;—hung it *because* I knew that it had loved me, and *because* I felt it had given me no reason of offence;—hung it *because* I knew that in so doing I was committing a sin—a deadly sin that would so jeopardize my immortal soul.

Poe's mastery of perversity was not, as his critics suggest, the product of a vulgar and slipshod mind—far from it. Although he died more than one hundred years before the first *Paris Review* Writers at Work interview, Poe would have been the ideal interview subject, for unlike most of the writers of his time he exhibited a unique candidness about his own writing process. In an essay called "The Philosophy of Composition," published in *Graham's Magazine* in 1846, Poe went so far as to prophesy the original motivation behind the *Review*'s interview series:

I have often thought how interesting a magazine paper might be written by any author who would—that is to say who could—detail, step by step, the processes by which any one of his compositions attained its ultimate point of completion. Why such a paper has never been given to the world, I am much at a loss to say—but, perhaps, the autorial [*sic*] vanity has had more to do with the omission than any one other cause. Most writers—poets in especial—prefer having it understood that they compose by a species of fine frenzy—an ecstatic intuition—and would positively shudder at letting the public take a peep behind the scenes, at the elaborate and vacillating crudities of thought.

From Poe's writing about his own craft, we know that he was a dedicated outliner and reviser, and that the plot was the last thing he determined:

> I prefer commencing with the consideration of an *effect*. . . . I say to myself, in the first place, "Of the innumerable effects, or impressions, of which the heart, the intellect, or (more generally) the soul is susceptible, what one shall I, on the present occasion, select?" Having chosen a novel, first, and secondly a vivid effect, I consider whether it can be best wrought by incident or tone—whether by ordinary incidents and peculiar tone, or the converse, or by peculiarity both of incident and tone.

Taking "The Raven" as a test case, he goes on to explain how, in writing that poem, he proceeded, step by step, to its completion "with the precision and rigid consequence of a mathematical problem."

In a short editorial called "The Poet's Vision," Poe gives his best—and most revealing—definition of artistry: "An artist *is* an artist only by dint of his exquisite sense of Beauty—a sense affording him rapturous enjoyment, but at the same time implying, or involving, an equally exquisite sense of Deformity." Poe remains our most exquisite poet of deformity.

Bibliography
Poe, Edgar Allan. *The Portable Poe*. New York: Penguin, 1977.

CRITICAL
CONTEXTS

A Debt Owed, a Debt Paid:
Poe's Literary Cultural Heritage_____

Jeff Grieneisen and Courtney Ruffner

In the world of literature, we have witnessed a shift in what is published and how those published works are received. Since the 1950's, literary criticism has swept through the reading world and has influenced the way we read texts, from structural analysis and economics to political/social theories of reading. This may seem obvious, and it leads to another obvious conclusion: namely, the literary community continues to redefine the very texts that comprise it, and the "canon" is under constant revision. In light of these changes—changes that occur at a much faster rate these days—we must ask: What constitutes a work of "significance," and how do we determine where an author fits in the various traditions of world literature? These legitimate questions keep literature fresh, allowing the reader to explore works in historical and cultural contexts, the idea being that any work that does not withstand the test of time in a global sense must make way for work that does.

If we apply these tenets to the work of Edgar Allan Poe, we will find that he does, indeed, withstand the test of time. Namely, his work represents the foundation of psychoanalysis, arguably the most universally understood (and misunderstood) cliché of a theory both inside and outside of academe. As part of his legacy, Poe's work in the tales represents a rebellion that draws in new readers; more important, the tales stand as primary examples of explorations into the unconscious that have resonated with readers for more than a century. With the recent rise in medical literature as a topic in creative writing, including nonfiction, poetry, and prose, Poe's tales continue to resonate and provide a structure for reading physical and emotional illness. Often described as a Gothic writer, Poe moved beyond the low Gothic tradition—with its settings castles, atmosphere of mystery, women in distress, etc.—to include the real work of medical inquiry. Of course, his work in sleuthing, often referred to as his tales of ratiocination, adds an element of realism to the Gothic and helps to create Poe's status as a pioneer of the detective story.

It is in these genre foundations of Poe that any exploration of his cultural currency must begin; however, we cannot end there. Instead, we must allow the reputation of Poe and his work its due as the tales are continually reconfigured, successfully, by readers seeking simultaneously an escape into the terrifyingly exotic and a grounding in the reality of psychological diagnosis and emotional logic. In order to flesh out his cultural/historical legacy, we need to outline a general sense of his influence, and then treat his tales as they appear categorically: detective, madness, and "love story," each with a sense of timelessness and persistent historical relevance.

Perhaps one of the most significant measures of a writer's work is his or her reputation among contemporaries abroad. Even though many contemporaries in America did not appreciate his work, Poe was hailed as a genius in circles of French intellectuals. Raymond Foye announces that "France's greatest poetic geniuses took Poe seriously, while he was generally misunderstood and derided in literary America" (77). Poe's influence spread into France, primarily through Baudelaire, who, in five of his volumes, translated a number of Poe's works. Writing shortly after Poe's death, Baudelaire states, "Edgar Poe and his country were not on the same level. The United States is a gigantic infant, naturally jealous of the older continent" (81). In France, Baudelaire introduced Poe to writers such as Stéphane Mallarmé and Paul Valéry. Valéry, taking up the defense begun by Baudelaire seventy years earlier, notes that "Poe's universal fame is dimmed or dubious only in his native country and in England" (112). Thus, even in the 1920's, Poe's reputation is defended most staunchly by French writers.

Poe's reputation in America was damaged by reports, both accurate and exaggerated, of his problems with alcohol and his scandalous life. Baudelaire notes that an American will "freely admit his [Poe's] genius, perhaps he [an American] will even display pride; but, in a sardonic and superior tone, he will speak of the depraved life of the poet"

(81). This reputation was most damaging to Poe during his lifetime, but in more contemporary responses, it seems to be the very facet that draws a number of readers to his work.

In part, his reputation abroad may have come from his adherence to some of the traditions of European and British writers. According to the brief but complete biography by Kay Cornelius, "the romantic qualities of Edgar Allan Poe's writing link him to the literary movement that began in Europe and Great Britain in the 18th century and spread to the United States" (24). She further notes that among the Romantics, Poe "identif[ied] himself most personally with Lord Byron and Percy Bysshe Shelley" (25). In addition to continuing with the themes and styles of the Romantics, he is often credited with continuing the Gothic traditions begun in eighteenth-century England, and further, he knew that, in terms of writing for profit, "people liked the vicarious thrills that come from reading tales of horror while being quite safe from direct experience with the unspeakable" (Cornelius 28). The literary elites contemporary with Poe were often harsh in their criticism. William Butler Yeats and Aldous Huxley found Poe's writing to be "vulgar," and the Transcendentalists were unforgiving in their estimation of Poe's abandonment of their optimism. Yet for all of the detractors, Poe also had his influence in America and beyond the Euroamerican tradition. His theories of the tale are credited with influencing such writers as Nathaniel Hawthorne, Fyodor Dostoevsky, and Henry James.

The generalized notion of his influence is the result of his theories of the tale. Denouncing the novel as a form that invites the reader to step away, and thus be taken out of the story, the tale is brief enough to be read through at one sitting. To create the effect that Poe deemed necessary to the tale, he ascertained that the effect of what he called unity must be perfected, wherein all details contribute methodologically to the singular effect of the tale. In addition to this structural mantra, Poe utilized a number of subjects and puzzled through a number of concepts that stand, even to this day, as a major force of his reputation (even among his detractors).

Harold Bloom, often unflattering in his discussion of Poe's writing style, nonetheless admits that "there is a dreadful universalism pervading Poe's weird tales" and that even from his own first reading of Poe at the age of ten, "Poe induced [in Bloom] nasty and repetitious nightmares that linger even now" (4). In his discussion, Bloom insists that Poe's writing, per se, is not his talent but rather the tale, itself, which is "stronger than the telling" (4). As a continuation of myth, the stories that survive are valuable as "a hymn to negativity" (14). Yet this ignores the very real cultural heritage of Poe's work in the tales as they fall into three general types: the detective tales or tales of ratiocination, the psychological gothics or madness tales, and the "love stories." It is, therefore, prudent, to examine the cultural and historical significance of Poe's tales in terms of the three commonly known types.

Tales of Ratiocination

One of Poe's major contributions to literature through the tales is the very genre he invented: the detective story. Considered to be his best tale of ratiocination, "The Purloined Letter" published in 1844 is the third in his series of detective stories centered on the character of Dupin, a private investigator. Poe's interest in these tales as solvable mysteries has a correlation with his other interests, such as inner workings of the mind and doubling, or the doppelgänger motif, and the readers would have recognized these tales as both fictionalizations of news reports and resonances of other popular forms of entertainment. Catherine Nickerson notes that the popularity of detective fiction in "film, radio, and television [is] connected to the acceleration of real and perceived crime, violence, and surveillance over the course of the nineteenth and twentieth centuries" (745). With the growth of cities and industrialization, visible crime increased. In fact, according to Nickerson's observation, the readership of the nineteenth century would have been following stories of criminality, and with this, the shifting legal system's response to these changes. Of particular note is John Cleman's observation that the insanity defense was among the fastest-growing controversies in the first half of the nineteenth century. Cleman quotes an 1843 argument presented by Daniel McNaughton who argues that "the [insanity] defense was undermining civil order . . . perception [of the people was] that to be acquitted on the basis of insanity was to avoid punishment" (66). Further, the "increased use of medical testimony in court to determine insanity . . . [further established] the study of the mind on a scientific basis" (66). This insanity defense was in part defined by defense attorney Peter A. Browne as "partial insanity" (qtd. in Cleman 68), a term that Poe would call "monomania" in reference specifically to his tales of madness in the form of the psychological gothic.

Monomania is not really of key importance to the detective tales, however, but the scientific exploration that resolves the crime is. Poe would have been aware of monomania, and thus unsavory, or "savage" behavior on the part of otherwise rational people. This behavior would be the driving force behind the commission of crime, perhaps, but more important, the historical legacy of the detective tales is in the examination of the sense of logic/reason. Andrea Goulet notes that detective fiction "may actually provide a critique of reason, itself, by exposing libidinal—even savage—energies that subtend it . . . what makes a detective successful . . . is what makes him most like the criminal he pursues" (50). Thus, the realistic detective and his blend of rational inquiry and understanding of the mind of the other represents a resolution and "bringing to justice" of the criminal.

Poe's protagonists in the detective tales employ contemporary techniques (in terms of the time of his writing) to solve unsolvable crimes. Moreover, Dupin, who is not a policeman, outwits not only the "criminal" but also the policeman on the case, and thus he criticizes the rational mind that ignores the psychology and emotion of human interaction. Dupin explains to the narrator that the Prefect will necessarily fail in his pursuit of the stolen letter because he cannot measure the intellect, ideas, or ingenuity of the thief. By contrast, Dupin relates that "the Prefect and his cohort fail so frequently, first, by default of this identification, and, secondly, by ill-admeasurement, or rather through non-admeasurement, of the intellect with which they are engaged" (Poe "Purloined" 216). Dupin demonstrates the mistake of overlooking the obvious clues by narrating the example of playing the game of puzzles on the map, where the adept player selects the largest of words that stretch across the map, unlike the novice who seeks to "win" by naming the most minutely indicated name. The importance of correct "admeasurement" is indicated by the children's game of "even and odd," where the astute player is aware of whether his opponent is or is not a "simpleton." Similarly, Dupin solves the case by matching the intellect of his opponent, Minister D——, and viewing the crime from the perspective of his rival. He has, in effect, measured that his "opponent" (if we are to call Minister D—— his opponent) is a "simpleton."

In addition to the subject matter of the mysteries, future writers, notably in Sir Arthur Conan Doyle's Sherlock Holmes series, would mimic the structure of Poe's detective tale. Poe introduces "the device of the baffled friend" and the announcing of the surprise solution at the end of the story (Cornelius 33). Poe's narrator would become Watson in the Holmes series, as Holmes ultimately reveals the end-of-story announcement (the solution) to Watson and allows the reader to eavesdrop. Again, following Poe's own dictum of the theory of unity, each element of the tale leads to the ultimate conclusion: Poe's one-upmanship of his nemesis, Minister D——.

In more contemporary interpretations, "The Purloined Letter" has been treated by critics in terms of its doubling, secrecy, and punishment. Liahna Klenman Babener observes that "the double principle informs the basic action of the story, the major event of which is Dupin's retrieval of the purloined letter and consequent triumph over the resourceful D——" (324). She discusses instances of doubling in Dupin's return to Minister D——'s apartment, the folded or "doubled" letter that Dupin lays in place of the authentic letter, and most significant, the doubling of Dupin as the shadow of D——, which might indicate that "Poe's persistent duplication suggests . . . that the two characters somehow constitute a single person" (332). The use of the double, Babener continues, "expose[s] a deep affinity between Dupin and his archrival, one which equates them morally and calls into question the customary ethical norms of the detective tale" (333). Ultimately, this doubling reveals that the self is at once the "hunter and the hunted," according to Babener, or that Poe, through the mystery, explores the way in which the mind works to rationalize. The text is a criticism of purely mathematical figuring in favor of the mind that can recognize the mind of another. Thus, the contemporary legacy of Poe in "The Purloined Letter" is born of the observation that we do not learn anything of poor, murdered Marie Rogêt, the contents of the letter, or the woman who hires the Prefect. Instead, the primary focus is what Shawn Rosenheim calls play, "which, for Poe, is always the testing of 'one mind against another'" (386). Another facet of Poe's legacy in detective tales follows us all the way into the popular culture of detective work, including the cartoon series *Scooby Doo* and novels such as Agatha Christie's *Murder on the Orient Express*.

Madness Tales

Perhaps Poe's most famous tales are his psychological Gothic tales or the madness tales. One can hardly take an introduction to literature course in college without reading (or having already read in high school) Poe's 1843 "The Tell-Tale Heart" or his 1846 "The Cask of Amontillado." The psychological gothic tales, much more than the detective tales, utilize many elements of the Gothic tradition. Yet as Cornelius indicates, they are "free from hackneyed devices [used by others of this time] like ghosts, vampires and werewolves. Instead, his heroes are usually exceptionally well-educated men who struggle with their sanity and the loss of their beautiful, ethereal women" (28). In a work like "The Tell-Tale Heart," Poe strives to create a definition of "moral insanity." This he derives in part from analysts such as J. C. Prichard, who in 1835 defined moral insanity as madness consisting in a morbid perversion of the natural feelings, affections, inclinations, temper, habits, and moral disposition and natural impulses without any remarkable disorder or defect in the intellect or knowing and reason. (qtd. in Vaknin n. pag.)

Poe was puzzling through the very notion of insanity as it related to the growing examination of mental illness and the self. According to Cleman, Dr. Isaac Ray, a nineteenth-century American psychiatrist and founder of forensic psychiatry, "argued that the moral (affective) and rational (intellectual) functions of the brain were physically separate" (69). By this observation, Poe believed that the rational man could have immoral thoughts and commit immoral actions. The question of the day, among those inquiring into science and medicine, was that of the dimensions, definitions, and intersection of (im)morality and (in)sanity.

Poe's psychological gothic tales present, among other considerations, the unreliable narrator. When considering the legacy of insanity and the definition of monomania, we might read "The Cask of Amontillado" not as a confession, as has often been the case, but rather "as self-defense, an attempt to provide a rational account of apparently irrational events and behavior" (Cleman 70). Generations are drawn into the story precisely because readers can never know why Montresor entombs Fortunato, beyond some vague reference to "a thousand insults." This continual search for reason changes with the growing discourse on sanity/insanity and reason/unreason. It is precisely the unnamed insults and the physical setting of entombment that draw psychoanalysts to the story. If we can only grasp Montresor's justification or see into his mind, then we can finally understand the frightening labyrinth of the mind, in general. Ultimately, it seems that the only explanation is monomania: a singular obsession from which the narrator cannot turn away. In fact, this "abnormal predominance of some one faculty over all the others" (Foye 37) fits Poe's definition of "genius," and therefore, the narrator is a genius who suffers only from a lack of what we might call moral center.

If Fortunato and Montresor fill the role of a single entity doubled, as we considered Dupin and Minister D——, then this tale, too, is naturally positioned for psychoanalysis. Robert Shulman notes that

> the usual psychological study of Poe treats the fiction as an unconscious manifestation of the author's problems or as an unconscious confirmation of orthodox Freudian categories, [*sic*] it seems to me that in his best stories Poe has a genuine understanding of the unconscious processes and imaginative powers. (245)

Shulman's approach in 1970 was not to read the tales as a natural consequence of Poe's criticism, and thus as the unconscious that Poe could never recognize, but rather to examine the works themselves in order to appreciate the real sense that Poe explored the processes of the mind convincingly in his fictions. Contemporary readers are drawn to this sense of the unconscious, precisely because the average person cannot begin to fathom the critical, technical aspects of it. Instead, readers turn to the story for escape, for enjoyment, or out of morbid curiosity while watching Poe unfold "that basically irrational strategy by which the mind attempts to preserve itself from its own forces of madness, disease, and disintegration by rigidly isolating itself" (248).

What makes "The Cask of Amontillado" so convincing as a revenge tale may be Montresor's masterful understanding of his foe. As in the detective tales, the protagonist "wins" by matching the wits of his enemy. Montresor does not force Fortunato into the catacombs, but rather plays on Fortunato's ego. He repeatedly insists that Fortunato not descend into the vaults for fear that the "nitre" and dampness would aggravate his cough. Readers love the foreshadowing in Fortunato's own declaration, "I shall not die of a cough (Poe "Cask" 276), and Montresor's ironic toast, "and I [drink to] your long life" (276).

This understanding of the foe, coupled with monomania, fits Poe's definition of genius, and through that genius, we listen to Montresor's account, fifty years later, of his entombment of his challenger. From the opening, the reader is put in the position of auditor, addressed as "You, who so well know the nature of my soul" (274), thus being drawn closer to the narrator. The combination of an impending but unknown method of vengeance and the familiarity set up by the narrator act to pull the reader in.

Love Stories

Much as Bloom states that Poe's work is important in its allegory, we can view the psychological gothic tales as allegorical tales that employ and enrich the Gothic tradition, and further illustrate the madness that Poe uses to draw in the reader as he does in his other tales. In Poe's 1842 "Eleonora," we find the autobiographical situation of love for a first cousin enacted in a mystical, enchanting land that falls to ruin following the death of his lover. Again, the reader is challenged to validate the authenticity of the narrator's tale, as he states

> . . . we will say, then, that I am mad. I grant, at least, that there are two distinct conditions of my mental existence—the condition of a lucid reason, not to be disputed, and belonging to the memory of events forming the first epoch of my life—and a condition of shadow and doubt, appertaining to the present, and to the recollection of what constitutes the second great era of my being. (649)

While "Eleonora" may not enjoy the same fame as the Dupin tales and the horror tales, scholars consider it to hold a significant place in the Poe's canon. Among those noted scholars, Richard P. Benton notes the Platonic allegory of the story, where Eleonora represents Aphrodite or Venus, who, according to Benton, was recognized by Plato as being "not one but two, a concept which proposes to us that there are Twin Venuses or Twin Aphrodites" (294). Much as Poe presents the insane/genius narrators, he uses the doubling for which he is famous to puzzle through the notion of love. Specifically, Benton argues, Eleonora represents the innocent, heavenly love while Ermengarde represents earthly love.

The struggle for Poe to reconcile these two forms reinforces his struggle to reconcile his infamous "doppelgänger" figure (described by David Grantz as the "divided self"). Unlike protagonists in his other tales, Poe's protagonist in "Eleonora" ends with absolution: Eleonora, or the narrator's visions of Eleonora, declares "thou art absolved, for reasons which shall be made known to thee in Heaven" (653). In this way, some critics deem that Poe has used this "love story" to illustrate the stages of development into adulthood much like the allegorical Oedipus riddle to which he refers. While in youth, he has his "earthly love" in Eleonora, but upon leaving the wild, Eden-like setting, he meets his courtly love in Ermengarde, and in a self-psychological forgiveness, he re-creates the voice of the deceased love of his youth. Some further argue that Poe used this tale to forgive himself for his own marriage to his thirteen-year-old cousin, Virginia Clemm.

Poe's use of the supernatural in "Eleonora," among other works, was praised as early as 1910. The early twentieth-century audience would have been quite aware of the tradition of spirits in the British and German Gothic tradition, but, as Arthur Hobson Quinn notes, "the supernatural in American literature belongs, then, mainly to the nineteenth century" (115). Of "Eleonora," he observes that the effect Poe seems to create by using the supernatural is "artistic" because "the mood is spiritual" (121). Specifically, "Eleonora" utilizes the supernatural aspect in terms of the "description of the spirit world and the relations of human beings with it" (120). However, unlike many of Poe's other works, terror seems to be abated. The supernatural speaks either from beyond the grave, if we are to trust the narrator, or, if we are not (as he clearly tells us not to trust the second phase), then from the narrator's own mind. He draws us to the questions of eternity and human relationships that will be revealed in heaven. Here, for perhaps the first time in a Poe tale, we have a narrator truly at peace.

Poe's 1839 publication of "The Fall of the House of Usher" is a tale that blends elements of the madness tales with those of his "love stories." In the preface to the anthology *The Unknown Poe*, Raymond Foye observes:

> Poe was among the first to attempt a methodological investigation of the unconscious mind. If there was one thing Poe insisted upon, it was *theory* [Foye's emphasis], and his psychological theories (in his *Marginalia*, essays, and reviews) are vital. By focusing on them, we transform those "innocent" tales of mystery and imagination into blueprints of unconscious mental processes (vii).

As an example, Foye cites the often-cited example of "Usher" representing the unconscious, complete with Roderick and Madeline acting as "two halves of a single self" and the furnishings, passageways, and central fissure acting as a "pre-Freudian model of the unconscious mind" (vii). Further, Foye cites Richard Wilbur's observation that "Poe is the first writer of the Modernist Age to discover our century's most characteristic subject: the disintegration of personality" (viii). This is as a result of Poe's use of the Gothic tale to reveal mental states, but more so, in his "bridg[ing] to a contemporary psychological treatment of characters and events" (viii).

Much like Poe's other tales, "Usher" lends itself to psychoanalysis, which is how it has been read for decades. In this tale, the very house is seen as symbolic of its owner, Roderick Usher, as a structure on the verge of collapse and with a vague fissure that the narrator perceives immediately. The story's only impact, one might argue, is the exploration into terror and madness, as here, Poe does not present a mystery to be solved. Instead, the story commences with the terror mediated through the narrator. Unlike the narrators of most psychological Gothic tales, the narrator of "Usher" seems reliable from the beginning but eventually descends into a question of reliability as he cannot know whether "[his] excited fancy had deceived [him]" (243).

One common reading is to interpret Roderick Usher as the autobiographical Poe, based on their relationship with a relative (Roderick's sister and Poe's cousin) and on Usher's physical resemblance to Poe: "lips somewhat thin and very pallid, but of a surpassingly beautiful curve; a nose of a delicate Hebrew model but with a breadth of nostril unusual in similar formations; a finely moulded chin . . . an inordinate expansion above the regions of the temple" (234). In contrast, an unusual approach to reading this story was presented in a pedagogical article on "The Fall of the House of Usher." In terms of myth and archetype common to discussions of the story, students frequently haven't read enough to make meaningful identifications and comparisons (Howes 30). Howes begins discussion of the story by examining the features of the interpolated texts and uses the poem "The Haunted Palace" and the story "Mad Trist" to define the "allegorical romance" genre of "Usher" before the class continues explicating the story. To the contemporary audience of teachers, this would seem to strengthen the identification of Poe with the allegory, moreover proving that, in at least one instance, Poe's work adheres quite well to his own theory of "unity."

While Poe's work is situated well with the work of the traditional Gothic, in the spirit of Walpole's *The Castle of Otranto*, Ann Radcliffe's *The Italian*, or Matthew Lewis's *The Monk*, Poe adds to the Gothic the element of the unreliable narrator in his tales. Sometimes controversial, his tales are, according to Bloom, "a permanent element in Western literary culture" (3) precisely because the psychological and scientific explorations within them lend themselves to continual reinterpretation. This is the mark of a superb tale.

What tends to draw undergraduate literature students to Poe is the legend. Much as they enjoy Sylvia Plath and Anne Sexton as "forbidden" or "misunderstood" authors who would commit suicide, students read Poe as an exotic, early version of the Emo/grunge characters that they fancy as themselves. He was tortured and misunderstood, and he died mysteriously. They love to cite the irony of his obscurity in life and success after death.

These readers, often new to literature, feel as though they can iden-tify with Poe—a man of complex psychology and emotion. Such stu-dents are often familiar with "The Raven" and the more popular of his tales: "The Tell-Tale Heart," "The Cask of Amontillado," "The Black Cat," and "The Fall of the House of Usher." Into these tales they read psychoanalytic complexities that dovetail with their introduction to psychology courses. Unconscious desires revealed (or interpreted) de-light them, as they feel they have accomplished something and have successfully joined the world of literary criticism. They "get it." Poe's works create this connection precisely because they are complex enough to warrant close rereading, tantalizing enough to capture inter-est through revenge and murder, and accessible as solidly written "uni-fied" stories.

Works Cited

Babener, Liahna Klenman. "The Shadow's Shadow: The Motif of the Double in Edgar Allan Poe's 'The Purloined Letter.'" *The Purloined Poe: Lacan, Derrida, and Psychoanalytic Reading*. Ed. John P. Muller. Baltimore: Johns Hopkins University Press, 1988. 323-344.

Baudelaire, Charles. "From Edgar Poe: His Life and Works." Trans. Raymond Foye. *The Unknown Poe: An Anthology of Fugitive Writings*. San Francisco: City Lights, 1980. 78-91.

Benton, Richard P. "Platonic Allegory in Poe's 'Eleonora.'" *Nineteenth-Century Fiction* 22, no. 3 (1967): 293-297.

Bloom, Harold. Introduction to *Edgar Allan Poe: Modern Critical Series*. Ed. Har-old Bloom. New York: Chelsea House Publishers, 1985. 1-14.

Cleman, John. "Irresistible Impulses: Edgar Allan Poe and the Insanity Defense." *Edgar Allan Poe: Bloom's BioCritiques*. Ed. Harold Bloom. Philadelphia: Chel-sea House Publishers, 2002. 65-77.

Cornelius, Kay. "Biography of Edgar Allan Poe." *Edgar Allan Poe: Bloom's BioCritiques*. Ed. Harold Bloom. Philadelphia: Chelsea House Publishers, 2002. 5-41.

Foye, Raymond, ed. *The Unknown Poe: An Anthology of Fugitive Writings*. San Francisco: City Lights, 1980.

Goulet, Andrea. "Curiosity's Killer Instinct: Bibliophilia and the Myth of the Ra-tional Detective." *Yale French Studies* 108 (2005): 48-59.

Grantz, David. "The Primal Origins of Poe's Doppelgänger as Reflected in Roderick Usher." *The Poe Decoder* (August 23, 2008). Available at http://www.poedecoder.com/essays/fissure/.

Howes, Craig. "Teaching 'Usher' and Genre: Poe and the Introductory Literature Class." *The Journal of the Midwest Modern Language Association* 19, no. 1 (1986): 29-42.

Nickerson, Catherine. "Murder as Social Criticism." *American Literary History* 9, no. 4 (1997): 744-757.

Poe, Edgar Allan. "The Cask of Amontillado." *The Complete Tales & Poems of Edgar Allan Poe*. New York: Vintage, 1975.

_____. "Eleonora." *The Complete Tales & Poems of Edgar Allan Poe*. New York: Vintage, 1975.

_____. "The Fall of the House of Usher." *The Complete Tales & Poems of Edgar Allan Poe*. New York: Vintage, 1975.

_____. "The Purloined Letter." *The Complete Tales & Poems of Edgar Allan Poe*. New York: Vintage, 1975.

_____. "The Tell-Tale Heart." *The Complete Tales & Poems of Edgar Allan Poe*. New York: Vintage, 1975.

"Poe and Humor." *The Edgar Allan Poe Society of Baltimore*. October 11, 1997. Available at http://www.eapoe.org/geninfo/POEHUMOR.HTM.

Quinn, Arthur Hobson. "Some Phases of the Supernatural in American Literature." *PMLA* 25, no. 1 (1910): 114-133.

Rosenheim, Shawn. "'The King of Secret Readers': Edgar Poe, Cryptography, and the Origins of the Detective Story." *English Literary History* 56, no. 2 (1989): 375-400.

Shulman, Robert. "Poe and the Powers of the Mind." *English Literary History* 37, no. 2 (1970): 245-262.

Vaknin, Sam. "The History of Personality Disorders." *American Chronicle*. July 11, 2006. Available at http://www.americanchronicle.com/articles/11384.

Valéry, Paul. "On Poe." *Situation de Baudelaire*. Trans. James Lawler. *The Unknown Poe: An Anthology of Fugitive Writings*. San Francisco: City Lights, 1980. 112-115.

Introduction to Poe Criticism_____

Susan Amper

Overview: Poe and the Evolution of Criticism

Literary criticism is not a single, clearly definable enterprise. Invariably works of literature are involved, but how the critic deals with these texts and what assumptions, perspectives, and goals he or she brings vary from critic to critic and have changed course many times over the years. Understanding critics' ideas about Poe's tales requires some basic understanding of these "schools" of critical thought.

Some might challenge the use of the word "evolution" in relation to literary criticism, inasmuch as that word implies a progression to a more advanced state. To some, the succession of literary theories seems less like progress—in the sense of scientific progress in understanding the atom—than mere swings in intellectual fashion. At least from a present-day perspective, however, it does seem like progress to recognize that books and their meanings are not frozen; seeing the simultaneous existence of different ways to view works of literature brings us closer to the heart of the literary experience.

In regard to Poe in particular, our understanding has come a long way. Research on Poe tells us that there is a great deal more to Poe than first meets the eye. It certainly provides a picture of Poe's work very different from what most readers conceive. Research has revealed, indeed, a bewildering tangle of contradictions in his work, which leaves us with astonishingly little consensus about what Poe is all about. Most scholars would agree that his work is, by design, perplexing. As such it offers an inviting opportunity to young scholars of today and tomorrow to carry on the effort to come to terms with this towering but enigmatic author.

Poe in His Own Time

Poe was a fairly well-known writer in his day, but not one of the superstars. Although criticism today focuses largely on his tales, he was better known as a poet and probably best-known as a magazine editor and critic. Toward the end of his short life, he traveled about giving lectures on the poets and poetry of America, literary politics, and the function of criticism. As a reviewer, he was renowned for his talent and taste for devastating pans, which earned him the sobriquet "Tomahawk Man."

Poe started his writing career as a poet and turned to story writing mainly for financial reasons (though his tales also earned very little, in those days before copyright laws). He never stopped writing poetry, however, and in 1845 published "The Raven," which was sensationally popular. Prior to that time, when Henry Wadsworth Longfellow brought out a collection of American poems that did not include Poe's work, and again when Rufus Griswold's *The Poets and Poetry of America* came out with only three of Poe's poems, Poe complained bitterly about this treatment. It seems that Poe's reputation was high enough that he could reasonably claim unfairness but not so high that editors felt obliged to make more room for him in the first place.

The short story at this time was just in the process of being invented. Indeed, Poe is credited, probably more than any other single writer, with creating and defining the genre. His tales were widely recognized for their power and artistry. One criticism, however, was repeatedly leveled at him during his career, and it has dogged him ever since: his Gothic sensationalism.

As early as 1836, reviewers were lamenting what was then referred to as Poe's "Germanism." One critic of the day described Poe as "too fond of the wild—unnatural and horrible." Why, this critic complained, "will he not disenthrall himself from the spells of German enchantment and supernatural imagery?" (Thomas and Jackson 202). T. W. White, the editor of *The Southern Literary Messenger*, a prominent literary journal of the time, expressed the view of many. White generally admired Poe's work but repeatedly complained about his use of "too much German horror" and his blending of the "shadows of the tomb with the clouds of sunshine of life" (qtd. in Ingram 117).

In 1839 *The Southern Literary Messenger* rejected what is today considered one of Poe's masterpieces, "The Fall of the House of Usher." An editor, writing on behalf of White, told Poe:

> He doubts whether the readers of the *Messenger* have much relish for tales of the German School although [your tale is] written with great power and ability. . . . I doubt very much whether tales of the wild, improbable and terrible class can ever be permanently popular in this country. (Harrison, 48: vol 17)

Poe's Gothicism was passé, the editor believed; people preferred the more modern, realistic style of Charles Dickens.

Time has proven the editor quite mistaken in his estimation of Americans' tastes, for horror stories never disappeared, and in the movie industry they are perhaps the most consistently popular genre of all. But a note about the editor's comments may be in order for readers new to Poe. Some readers view Poe's Gothic tales reflexively as expressions of their author's tortured state of mind. This idea seems "natural." His tales are so macabre, so focused on death, decay, and tortured minds, that readers believe the obsessions reflect those of Poe. White, who knew Poe personally, thought no such thing. His point was not that Poe was personally obsessed with dark, subconscious terrors but that Poe was choosing to write in an unpopular genre. For White, the darkness and decay and terror were part of the Gothic genre, not Poe's personality.

Nevertheless, the idea that Poe's tales are the reflection of his own psychological torments has a long history. The viewpoint was given its early shape by one very influential obituary, written by an acquaintance and bitter rival of Poe, Rufus Griswold. Writing under a pseudonym, Griswold published, two days after Poe's death, an obituary of him in the *New York Tribune*. He wrote that the news of Poe's death would cause "poignant regret among all who admire genius" but that few would grieve personally because of the kind of man Poe was. He explicitly claimed that Poe himself was like the characters he created. Describing Poe as one of literature's "most brilliant and erratic stars," Griswold largely created the idea of Poe as an artistic genius tormented to madness. Griswold expanded his profile in an introduction he wrote to what was for a time the definitive edition of Poe's works. Griswold's viewpoint was disputed by others who knew Poe but was widely repeated and became popularly accepted.

Reception in Europe

The picture of Poe as the Romantic artist was enshrined by Charles Baudelaire, one of the greatest French poets of the nineteenth century. Baudelaire discovered Poe's writings in 1852, three years after Poe's death, and began translating his works and writing articles about him. In *Histoires extraordinaires* (1856) Baudelaire characterized Poe as the *poète maudit* ("accursed poet"), who suffered in the materialistic and commercial society of America yet was able to create the finest literature of his age. Baudelaire himself died broke and unrecognized, but he profoundly influenced the next generation of French poets, who enthusiastically seconded his appreciation of Poe. The French Symbolist movement, led by Stéphane Mallarmé, believed that the role of art was to give expression to the wild confusion of the poetic mind, reveling in symbolic language and literary artifice. Poe was their avatar.

Admiration for Poe was expressed by other prominent European literary figures as well. In an 1861 introduction to three of Poe's tales newly translated into Russian, Dostoevsky declared that the "vigor of [Poe's] imagination" distinguished him from every other author (61). In England, Algernon Charles Swinburne, Oscar Wilde, and Dante Gabriel Rossetti lauded Poe. These writers, from Baudelaire on, are often considered to be the first modernists, and their praise recast Poe (whom the editor of *The Southern Literary Messenger* had dismissed as retrograde) as a forefather of modernist writing.

The Europeans' respect for Poe made its way back to America, but the process took time. In 1893, when a well-known literary magazine polled its readers on the top ten books by American authors, Poe was scarcely even mentioned. In 1900, when the Hall of Fame for Great Americans was unveiled, designed to proclaim America's place in world civilization, Ralph Waldo Emerson, Nathaniel Hawthorne and Henry Wadsworth Longfellow were included; Poe was not. As scholars and other literary figures, including the Irish playwright George Bernard Shaw, criticized the omission, Poe's reputation in his homeland began to ascend. (He was voted into the Hall of Fame in 1910.)

In 1923, the English novelist D. H. Lawrence included an essay on Poe in his very influential book *Studies in Classic American Literature*. Two years later, the American poet William Carlos Williams published an essay presenting Poe as a pioneer of serious American literature. (Williams suggested, as Shaw had done, that Poe's lack of stature in his native land was a measure more of the defects of the American reading public than Poe's true literary worth.) From that period onward, although Poe's literary merit has been denigrated by a continuing stream of critics, his eminent position in the literary canon has not been shaken.

Psychoanalyzing Poe

Much of what was written about Poe from the 1920's through the 1940's continued to focus on his presumed psychopathology. Lorine Pruette's "A Psychoanalytic Study of Edgar Allan Poe," John Robertson's *Edgar A. Poe: A Psychopathic Study*, and Joseph Wood Krutch's *Edgar Allan Poe: A Study in Genius* adopted the widely held view of Poe as an aberrant personality. Their attempts to uncover the nature and source of his aberration helped to perpetuate the perception. The most important of the psychoanalytic studies was that of Marie Bonaparte, published in French in 1933 and in English in 1949.

Bonaparte was a friend of Sigmund Freud and adopted his viewpoint about the nature of the unconscious. Like many critics working from psychoanalytic paradigms, in effect she treats Poe as a patient, examining his life and his work for clues to his psyche. She analyzes his tales as a psychoanalyst would parse a patient's dreams: searching out the hidden symbolism that reveals Poe's inner conflicts. Taking up "The Black Cat," for example, she argues that the narrator, whom she identifies with Poe, displaces his hatred of his mother onto the all-black cat, which he mutilates and kills for biting him. He is able, for a time, to regard the second cat as a *good* mother, because this one has a large splotch of white on its breast. The splotch, by its color and location, represents a mother's milk; moreover, the second cat is found in a tavern (where one drinks), atop a barrel of liquor.

Bonaparte's work is controversial. On one hand, she is praised for her keen insight into the symbolic imagery in Poe's tales. On the other hand, she is faulted, first, for her complete adherence to Freud's theories (which today few analysts accept in their entirety) and, second, for her identification of Poe the man with his tales. The latter is an important issue, in terms of both Poe's work in particular and our ideas about how to think about literature.

Bonaparte takes Poe's tales as expressions of himself. Poe writes the tale; Bonaparte explains what it reveals about him. But while dreams may be the products of the dreamer's unconscious, is not a short story largely a conscious creation? Poe thought about how to draw his character, what setting to place him in, what would happen to him, and what he would say about these things. How ought we to think about the end product: in terms of what it tells us about Poe, or what Poe is trying to tell us about the world?

An example may clarify this idea. Nathaniel Hawthorne, in tales such as "The Birthmark" and "Rappaccini's Daughter," writes of men who exhibit fears of women and end up killing them. Yet few critics or general readers consider these tales as expressing Hawthorne's personal psychology. Rather, Hawthorne is seen as designing his tales in such a way that they expose these tendencies to our view. How is Poe different? He, too, has invented male characters who show fears of women and ultimately kill them. Why do readers think that Poe is merely *expressing* his own feelings, while Hawthorne is *exposing* a human condition? One possible difference is that Hawthorne's third-person narrators point out their male characters' insecurities. Poe's first-person narrators do not. It is, however, widely agreed in the study of fiction that first-person narrators should not be identified with their authors, any more than a character in a play should be identified with his or her author.

Other critics also turned their attention, as Bonaparte did, to the way Poe's stories symbolically depict unconscious struggles, but with an important difference. Instead of seeing the tales as expressions of Poe's own insecurities and inner torments, the stories are read as expositions of the human unconscious in general. This was the view D. H. Lawrence took. Poe's tales of terror, for Lawrence, trace the disintegration of the human psyche. In Roderick Usher and in the narrator of "Ligeia," for example, Lawrence detected the image of vampires, who in their desire to know their female counterparts suck out their very life.

Some scholars, while agreeing that Poe's stories represented symbolic struggles, conceived these struggles in different ways. Some viewed them, as Baudelaire had, in terms of the artistic temperament, either in conflict with itself or in opposition to external forces. Poe's canonical tales of terror supported readings along these lines. Roderick Usher is an artist; Ligeia is a brilliant philosopher. Critics also pointed to Poe's longest work of fiction, *The Narrative of Arthur Gordon Pym*, which invites reading as the record of a visionary quest through the realms of intellectual experience to some kind of denouement, whether tragic or ecstatic.

Whether the conflict was construed as superego versus id or imagination versus reason, these discussions share a common assumption: that the tales present their conflicts essentially in earnest. In the second half of the twentieth century, that perspective began to be displaced.

New Approaches

In attempting to explicate Poe's symbolism, the criticism of the late nineteenth and early twentieth centuries focused largely on theme—the idea of fiction being that it is designed to express an idea. Over time, literary scholars grew disenchanted with this conception, feeling that it limited readers' experience of literature. To say that a certain story or poem "means" a certain thing was called "reductive." If one boils down a work of literature to its meaning, critics argued, all that is left is the meaning. One thereby misses what makes it art. The poet Archibald MacLeish summed up the new viewpoint in his oft-quoted lines, "A poem must not mean / But be."

In the 1920's there flourished in Russia a school of literary criticism known as formalism. Russian Formalists sought to analyze the text-in-itself, paying particular attention to its linguistic properties, as opposed to the historical or cultural conditions in which it was created. New Criticism, which peaked in England and the United States in the 1940's and 1950's, resembles formalism in its focus on the text itself. New Critics called on readers to view poems and works of fiction as self-contained works of art, focusing on the way they are constructed, their unifying principles. New Criticism gradually gave way to structuralism, which shares, however, an emphasis on *how* works of literature convey meanings.

Surprising Discoveries

When critics started analyzing how Poe's tales are constructed, a fundamental shift began. Like the house of Usher with its barely detectable fissure running from top to bottom, Poe's tales themselves seemed on close inspection to be divided against themselves. The tales of terror are prime examples. Horrifying they certainly are, but they are not *simply* horrifying. We experience them also as complicated, puzzling, and at times almost comic. At some points they read like metaphysical essays and at others like cheap novels. Poe scholars set to work to explain these contradictions.

One dividing line, discussed in an important article by James Gargano, "The Question of Poe's Narrators," cuts between the stories and their narrators. Almost always Poe's tales are narrated in the first person, by participants or at least on-the-scene observers. But what the stories tell us, Gargano argues, is quite different from what the narrators are saying. Poe's tales present the narrators' accounts, but in a way that allows the reader to see much more—including the failure of the narrators to see. The narrator of "William Wilson" is overwhelmed and blind to what is happening to him, but the reader understands that the man is in denial. The young man in "The Tell-Tale Heart" convinces himself that he is sane because he has rationally planned the old man's murder; we see that fear and guilt have driven him insane. Montresor in "The Cask of Amontillado" believes he has cleverly avenged a wrong done to him; we see that he has inflicted a far greater injury on himself.

For Gargano, Poe's tales depict a moral universe. The narrators act, and speak, in blindness to this moral order but cannot escape it. G. R. Thompson, in his important book *Poe's Fiction: Romantic Irony in the Gothic Tales*, agrees that the tales reveal the blindness of their narrators. He views Poe, as many do, in the context of the Romantic tradition, which argues that man's trust in reason is folly. Poe mocks rationalism, Thompson argues, by exposing his narrators' incomprehension of what is happening to them. Thompson notes the self-parody that can be seen in Poe's seemingly serious horror stories as further examples of the author's "ironic" stance.

A valuable body of literature has emerged, analyzing specific tales in terms of the disparities between the narrators' versions of events and the interpretations that readers may reach. Thus Gargano argues that the inability of the narrator of "The Black Cat" to understand the events he relates exposes his lack of moral vision ("Perverseness"). Benjamin Franklin Fisher believes that "The Assignation" reveals the limitations of its narrator in appreciating the Romantic ideal ("Flights"). Marc Leslie Rovner sees William Wilson as too obtuse to understand his moral circumstances.

Poe as Parodist

While the discovery of the contradictions in Poe's tales led Thompson and others to see irony, some saw parody and hoax. Clark Griffith argued that the Gothic horror tale "Ligeia" contained a disguised mockery of Transcendentalism. Richard P. Benton described the seemingly Romantic "The Assignation" as a hoax in which Poe parodies Thomas Moore's account of Lord Byron's affair with an Italian countess. Robert Regan saw "The Masque of the Red Death" as playing on Nathaniel Hawthorne's "Legends of the Province House." Stories that most readers have taken and continue to take seriously were now often identified as hoaxes or parodies. Griffith read "Ligeia" as covertly parodying the Gothic tradition; Fisher took a similar view of "The Fall of the House of Usher" ("Germanism"); James M. Cox saw burlesque in both of those stories and "William Wilson" as well.

To readers new to Poe, the idea that his seemingly dark and horrifying tales could be read as humorous is incredible. It is worthwhile, therefore, to consider the basis for such claims. In essence, the reasons are two.

The first is Poe's often abominable writing, a long-standing issue in the study of Poe. If he is such a great writer, the question is asked, why are his tales filled with passages that are overwrought, clichéd, or silly? For some, the answer is, Poe is *not* a great writer. Poe's contemporary, the poet James Russell Lowell, mocked Poe as "three-fifths genius and two-fifths sheer fudge." The aristocratic Henry James declared that "an enthusiasm for Poe is the mark of a decidedly primitive stage of reflection." American-born English poet T. S. Eliot sneered that Poe had "the intellect of a highly gifted young person before puberty." English writer Aldous Huxley said that Poe was "cursed with incorrigible bad taste." He considered Poe's writing "vulgar," like wearing a "diamond ring on every finger." The highborn Irish poet William Butler Yeats also thought "vulgar" the best word. When a friend sent Yeats a copy of Poe's poems that he had illustrated, Yeats wrote back to tell the illustrator he was wasting his talents. The gifted poet described Poe's work as "vulgar and commonplace" and a few sentences later "insincere and vulgar." Such invective continues to the present day.

Poe's defenders often try to look beyond his flaws. The critic Allen Tate, who holds a generally favorable opinion of Poe, nevertheless confesses that "Poe's serious style at its typical worst makes the reading of more than one tale at a sitting an almost insuperable task." Tate notes how overripe Poe's tales can be: the "Gothic glooms, the Venetian interiors, the ancient wine-cellars (from which nobody ever enjoys a vintage but always drinks 'deep')—all this, done up in a glutinous prose." But, says Tate, Poe is worthy and readable if one is able to see through to "the power underlying the flummery."

Many scholars are unwilling to accept Poe's excesses as defects. Instead, they seek to explain them as part of a deliberate design. Michael Allen, in a book published in 1969, argues that Poe designed his stories to appeal simultaneously to two different audiences. Allen's analysis has been very influential and is worth understanding for the way it places Poe in the context of the literary marketplace of his time and the way it deals with the contradictions that readers encounter in Poe's tales.

Allen argues that if one wishes to understand Poe's work, one must consider the most successful literary magazine of Poe's time, *Blackwood's*. Any magazine editor, as Poe was, would have spent time searching for the key to its success. That key, Allen went on, was the ability of *Blackwood's* to attract two distinct audiences: the unsophisticated "many" and the elite "few." For the many, *Blackwood's* offered plentiful helpings of sensationalism, literary gossip, and fiction; to the highbrows it provided sophisticated burlesques, bits of curious and esoteric learning, serious criticism, and a pervasive tone of superiority. Poe understood the magazine's strategy and applied it to his own work. The result was a combination of lowbrow sensationalism, esoteric commentary, and sophisticated parody all within a single tale. Allen's analysis accounts neatly for the contradictions—or the unevenness, as some would call it—that critics were pointing out in Poe's tales. Allen's focus on the economic considerations Poe faced, his need to win readers, inspired others, including Jonathan Elmer, to explore the implications of Poe's role or roles in the literary marketplace.

Such analysis as Allen's leaves some readers unsatisfied. It accounts for the defects in Poe's tales, but the defects remain defects. We crave a "reading" of a tale in which the pieces fit together to serve an artistic purpose, not just a commercial one. Poe himself championed this idea, which he called "unity of effect." In order to be regarded as great, should a writer not be in control of the effects his or her works have on readers? If we say that Poe is an able writer, and if readers commonly experience parts of his tales as meretricious, vulgar, or silly, then we should be able to account for these reactions in terms of the overall design of the tale—especially when the passages are so conspicuous, so pervasive, so seemingly central to our experience. Viewing the tales as parodies or hoaxes answers this need.

Poe the Humorist

A second factor that disposes many Poe scholars to see humor where the general reader sees only gloom and horror is the overall context of Poe's work. Many readers know Poe from a handful of tales: "The Fall of the House of Usher," "The Tell-Tale Heart," "The Black Cat," "The Cask of Amontillado," and perhaps two or three others. It comes as a surprise to such readers that of Poe's more than sixty tales, about half are openly comical.

"The System of Doctor Tarr and Professor Fether" tells of a man who visits a mental hospital known for its revolutionary methods. The man is invited to stay for dinner by his hosts, who grow wilder through the evening until it is finally revealed that these are in fact the inmates, who have overpowered their keepers and taken over the asylum. In "The Duc de L'Omelette," a French duke dies and goes to hell. He maneuvers the devil into a game of cards and escapes damnation by defeating him—palming a king while the devil takes a drink of wine.

"Why the Little Frenchman Wears His Hand in a Sling" is told in dia-
lect by Sir Patrick O'Grandison Barronitt, who finds himself in com-
petition with a Frenchman for the affections of the "purty widdy
Misthress Tracle." Seated together on a sofa, the men pursue the
woman through surreptitious handholding. The passion with which Sir
Pathrick feels his attentions returned convinces him that he has won,
until the woman steps away, and he realizes that it is the Frenchman's
hand he holds. Infuriated, he crushes the Frenchman's hand, thereby
answering the question posed in the title. The list of such tales goes on
and on.

Perhaps more provocative than Poe's burlesques is his taste for
hoax. What is now called "The Balloon Hoax," purports to tell the
story of the first transatlantic balloon crossing. It was published in the
New York Sun without any indication that it was fiction. "The Facts in
the Case of M. Valdemar" presents itself as the factual, eyewitness account of a professional hypnotist, who tells of hypnotizing his dying
friend to see whether the trance could arrest his death. The patient remained unchanged for seven months, the author says, until the decision
was made to awaken him from the trance. When this was done the man
instantly rotted away to a liquid mass. So preposterous is the ending
that one cannot imagine that Poe would think anyone would believe it,
yet many did.

By contrast, "Von Kempelen and His Discovery" is a deliberate
hoax. In offering some details about its fictitious subject, the narrator
writes as though the basic news of Von Kempelen and his recent amazing discovery—how to turn lead into gold—were already well known
to the world. "The Premature Burial," "The Unparalleled Adventure of
One Hans Phall," "The Journal of Julius Rodman," and many other
tales may also be regarded as hoaxes. Indeed, scholars themselves dis-
agree, so difficult is it to know when Poe is kidding.

In this regard, two parodies are particularly significant. When "Silence—A Fable" was first published, it appeared under a title, "Siope—
A Fable [in the manner of the Psychological Autobiographists]," that

clearly announced its parodic intent. But when readers took the tale seriously, Poe removed the subtitle (Regan 281). "Metzengerstein," too, was originally intended as a parody, but many readers took it as a genuine tale of the supernatural. Poe made one attempt to smarten his readers up: republishing in 1836, he added the subtitle "A Tale in Imitation of the German" (Thompson "Metzengerstein" 46 and n. 57). When readers persisted in taking the tale seriously, however, he removed the subtitle, and in subsequent republications even toned down or deleted some of the most ridiculous passages.

No reader should decide that Poe's horror tales are *not* parodies until he or she reads "How to Write a Blackwood Article." In this unquestioned parody, a silly woman calling herself Psyche Zenobia, seeking to elevate the literature being turned out by the society of which she is a member, turns for advice to the editor of Britain's prominent literary magazine. He provides a list of rules for constructing tales "full of taste, terror, sentiment, metaphysics, and erudition." Clearly Poe is having fun at *Blackwood's* expense. The second part (sometimes printed separately under the title "A Predicament") presents Zenobia's attempt to translate *Blackwood's* advice into fiction. It tells of a woman visiting a cathedral, who gets her head stuck between the hands of the clock in the tower. The tale is ridiculous, yet it reads with the same breathless horror as Poe's "serious" tales of terror. Moreover, the parody was published within a month of "Ligeia" and only one year before "The Fall of the House of Usher." It seems incredible that a writer could ridicule a style so mercilessly one month and then employ it in complete seriousness the next.

Against the background of Poe's total output, it is easy to see why many Poe critics are more inclined than general readers to see parody and hoaxing in tales like "Usher." Indeed Poe's hoaxing has become a central focus of Poe scholars, who have addressed it from a variety of perspectives. It is not simply that hoaxing helps explain otherwise confusing features (and presumed faults) in Poe's work. More and more, Poe's hoaxing seems an essential part of what he is about. Many of the essays in Shawn Rosenheim and Stephen Rachman's collection, *The American Face of Edgar Allan Poe*, examine aspects of what the editors call "Poe's charlatanism" (xii).

Deconstruction

As awareness of the depth of Poe's hoaxing grew, along came another development in the evolution of literary criticism. Poststructuralism and its close cousin deconstructionism can be seen as continuing the attack on the idea that literature is all about conveying ideas. The formalists had said, in effect, "Don't just think what a work of art 'means' or 'says'; look at how it is constructed and how it creates the effects it creates." Deconstructionists said, "Look at how stories and poems *avoid* saying what they mean." Where you think you see unity and coherence in a work, look closer, and you will find over and over elements in the text that qualify, undercut, or contradict the "coherent" meaning you have constructed. These qualifications are not accidents or mistakes: they are part of the essence of the literary enterprise.

Deconstructionists searching for texts to analyze found in Poe's work a veritable bonanza. In addition to all the parody and hoaxing along the lines already discussed, Poe offered a trove of works that took hoaxing and blocked meaning as their very subject. One article sought to explain the nature of "Diddling," contemporary slang for what today we would call a scam or a con. The plot of "Mystification," a word that to Poe meant the deliberate attempt to baffle someone, turned upon a piece of writing of a type called amphigory, which appears to be meaningful but proves to be nonsense. Deconstructionists also pored over "The Gold Bug," with its secret writing, and "The Purloined Letter," about a piece of writing that is concealed, disguised, turned inside out. "The Purloined Letter" was the subject of a famous article by Jacques Lacan, a rejoinder by Jacques Derrida, and a staggering volume of subsequent commentary by others.

Another key text for deconstructionists was *The Narrative of Arthur*

Gordon Pym, a novel of baffling indeterminacy, filled—even more than is usual for Poe—with narrative lapses and contradictions, along with forged notes, hieroglyphic writing, and other explicit references to the problematic nature of the written word. Scholars taking up the tale include John Carlos Rowe, John Irwin, Dennis Pahl, and G. R. Thompson.

Finally there is "The Man of the Crowd," about a man who, looking out the window of a coffeehouse, picks a man out of the crowd and determines to know, as it were, the secret of his character. He follows and observes the man all night until dawn the next day, finally concluding that he will never learn what he wants to know. He ends the story (as he began it) with what he says is a comment made about a certain book: "it does not permit itself to be read." The line, made-to-order as a motto for those interested in the way that texts block the construction of coherent meaning, has been quoted and discussed, at a conservative estimate, in hundreds of scholarly papers over the past three decades.

Deconstructionist writings are often complex, diffuse, and difficult to follow. They consider the works they examine mainly in terms of what these works reveal about literature itself, rather than in terms of traditional literary themes that seem closer to ordinary life. Much deconstructionist writing is also heavily self-referential, leaving many readers wistful for literary analysis that speaks about something outside itself and "real." At the same time, deconstruction does seem singularly in tune with Poe's work, which consistently challenges our most basic assumption that literature involves an attempt by the writer to "communicate." If such is the case, why does Poe again and again give us writing that appears expressly designed to mystify us?

Works Cited

Allen, Michael. *Poe and the British Magazine Tradition*. New York: Oxford University Press, 1969.

Benton, Richard P. "The Interpretation of 'Ligeia.'" *College English* 5 (1944): 363-372.

Bonaparte, Marie. "The Black Cat." *Partisan Review* 17 (1950): 834-860.

_____. *The Life and Works of Edgar Allan Poe: A Psycho-analytic Interpretation*. Trans. John Rodker. 1949. London: The Hogarth Press, 1972.

Carlson, Eric, ed. *The Recognition of Edgar Allan Poe*. Ann Arbor: University of Michigan Press, 1966.

Cox, James. "Edgar Poe: Style as Pose." *The Virginia Quarterly Review* 44 (1968): 67-89.

Derrida, Jacques. "The Purveyor of Truth." Trans. Alan Bass. *The Purloined Poe: Lacan, Derrida, and Psychoanalytic Reading*. Eds. John P. Muller and William J. Richardson. Baltimore: Johns Hopkins University Press, 1987. 173-212.

Dostoevsky, Fyodor. "Three Tales of Edgar Allan Poe." 1861. Trans. Vladimir Astrov. *The Recognition of Edgar Allan Poe*. Ann Arbor: University of Michigan Press, 1966. 60-62.

Eliot, T. S. *From Poe to Valéry*. New York: Harcourt, Brace and Co., 1948.

Fisher, Benjamin Franklin, IV. "The Flights of a Good Man's Mind: Gothic Fantasy in Poe's 'The Assignation.'" *Modern Language Studies* 16 (1986): 53-60.

_____. "Playful 'Germanism' in 'The Fall of the House of Usher.'" *Ruined Eden of the Present: Hawthorne, Melville and Poe: Critical Essays in Honor of Darrel Abel*. Eds. G. R. Thompson and Virgil L. Lokke. West Lafayette: Purdue University Press, 1981. 355-374.

_____. "To 'The Assignation' from 'The Visionary' (Part Two): The Revisions and Related Matters." *Library Chronicle* 40 (1976): 221-251.

Gargano, James. "'The Black Cat': Perverseness Reconsidered." *Texas Studies in Language and Literature* 2 (1960): 172-178.

_____. "The Question of Poe's Narrators." *College English* 25: 1963, 177-181.

Griffith, Clark. "Poe's 'Ligeia' and the English Romantics." *University of Toronto Quarterly* 24 (1954): 8-25.

Griswold, Rufus Wilmot. "Death of Edgar Allan Poe." 1849. *New York Tribune*, October 9. *The Recognition of Edgar Allan Poe*. Ed. Eric Carlson. Ann Arbor: University of Michigan Press, 1966. 28-35.

Huxley, Aldous. "Vulgarity in Literature." 1930. *Music at Night and Other Essays*. New York: Harper & Row, 1958.

Ingram, John. *Edgar Allan Poe: His Life, Letters, and Opinions*. London: John Hogg, 1880.

Irwin, John T. *American Hieroglyphics: The Symbol of Egyptian Hieroglyphics in the American Renaissance*. New Haven, CT: Yale University Press, 1980.

James, Henry. "Charles Baudelaire." *French Poets and Novelists*. London: Macmillan, 1878.

Krutch, Joseph Wood. *Edgar Allan Poe: A Study in Genius*. 1923. New York: Penguin, 1971.

Lacan, Jacques. "Seminar on 'The Purloined Letter.'" Trans. Jeffrey Mehlman. 1972. *The Purloined Poe: Lacan, Derrida, and Psychoanalytic Reading*. Eds. John P. Muller and William J. Richardson. Baltimore: Johns Hopkins University Press, 1988. 28-54.

Lawrence, D. H. *Studies in Classic American Literature*. 1923. New York, Penguin, 1971.

Lowell, James Russell. *A Fable for Critics: The Complete Poetical Works of James Russell Lowell*. New York: G. P. Putnam, 1891.

Pahl, Dennis. *Architects of the Abyss: The Indeterminate Fictions of Poe, Hawthorne, and Melville*. Columbia: University of Missouri Press, 1989.

Poe, Edgar Allan. *Complete Works of Edgar Allan Poe*. Ed. James A. Harrison. 17 vols. New York: G. P. Putnam, 1902.

_____. *Histoires extraordinaires*. 1856. Trans. Charles Baudelaire. Paris: Livre de Poche, 1972.

Pruette, Lorine. "A Psycho-analytical Study of Edgar Allan Poe." *American Journal of Psychology* 31 (October 1920): 370-402.

Regan, Robert. "Hawthorne's 'Plagiary': Poe's Duplicity." *Nineteenth-Century Fiction* 25 (1970): 281-298.

Robertson, John. *Edgar A. Poe: A Psychopathic Study*. New York: G. P. Putnam, 1923.

Rosenheim, Shawn, and Stephen Rachman. Introduction to *The American Face of Edgar Allan Poe*. Eds. Shawn Rosenheim and Stephen Rachman. Baltimore: The Johns Hopkins University Press, 1995. ix-xx.

Rovner, Marc Leslie. "What William Wilson Knew: Poe's Dramatization of an Errant Mind." *Poe at Work: Seven Textual Studies*. Ed. Benjamin Franklin Fisher IV. Baltimore: The Edgar Allan Poe Society, 1978. 73-82.

Rowe, John Carlos. *Through the Custom-House: Nineteenth-Century American Fiction and Modern Theory*. Baltimore: Johns Hopkins University Press, 1982.

Tate, Allen. "Our Cousin, Mr. Poe." *The Man of Letters in the Modern World: Selected Essays, 1928-1955*. London: Meridian Books, 1957. 132-145.

Thomas, Dwight, and David K. Jackson. *The Poe Log: A Documentary Life of Edgar Allan Poe, 1809-1849*. Boston: G. K. Hall & Co., 1987.

Thompson, G. R. "Poe's 'Flawed' Gothic: Absurdist Techniques in 'Metzengerstein' and the *Courier* Satires." *ESQ* 60 (1970): 38-58.

_____. *Poe's Fiction: Romantic Irony in the Gothic Tales*. Madison: University of Wisconsin Press, 1973.

Williams, William Carlos. *In the American Grain*. New York: New Directions Publishing, 1956.

Yeats, William Butler. "To W. T. Horton." 3 September, 1899. *Letters of W. B. Yeats*. Ed. Allan Wade. New York: Macmillan Company, 1955.

"Hypocrite Lecteur":
The Reader as Accomplice in Poe's Short Stories____

Matthew J. Bolton

At the conclusion of "To the Reader," the first poem in Charles Baudelaire's 1861 volume *Fleurs du Mal* (*Flowers of Evil*), a narrator who has been speaking of himself suddenly shifts his focus elsewhere, calling, "*–Hypocrite lecteur,–mon semblable,–mon frère!*" (227). Stanley Kunitz translates the line as "—Hypocrite reader, you—my double! My brother!" (2). Until the poem's last line, the reader may have considered himself only an onlooker and a listener. True, the narrator uses the first-person plural, as in "Our sins are strenuous, cowardly our repentances" (2), but that plural possessive need not include the reader. "Our" and "we" have a generic rather than a specific sense of inclusion. The narrator must be referring to himself and other sinners like him, the reader thinks, people who may be observed from a safe remove. The direct address that closes the poem, however, makes the reader into something other than an observer: an accomplice. If the reader has thought to exclude himself from the "we" and the "our" of the poem, then he is not merely a sinner but a hypocrite. The tone and intensity of the poem's last line is a striking departure from the conventional mode in which an author addresses his reader. Gone is the sense of civility, deference, and formality that one might expect to find at the start of a collection of poems. Gone, too, is the line that separates fiction from life and spectacle from spectator. The reader is not Baudelaire's honored guest or patron, but a fellow sinner, one who is too self-deluded to realize that he and the haunted poet could pass for brothers. The direct address that begins *Fleurs du Mal* is less invocation than accusation.

Baudelaire's direct address signals just how radically the relationship between narrator and reader had changed by the second half of the nineteenth century. In his 1802 preface to *Lyrical Ballads*, William Wordsworth defined the poet as "a man speaking to men" (Wu 360).

The first-person voice, be it in poetry or fiction, was a mode in which a narrator could communicate directly with the reader. A generation later, by the time Baudelaire published *Fleurs du Mal*, this relationship had been transformed. T. S. Eliot recognized the importance of Baudelaire's line by using it to conclude the first part of *The Waste Land* (1922). It is fitting that the *hypocrite lecteur* formulation should figure prominently in what might be the most important English-language poem of the twentieth century, for it was English and American literature that pointed Baudelaire toward his new understanding of the confessional mode. Few authors did more to recast the conventions of first-person confessional narration than Edgar Allan Poe, whose work Baudelaire spent seventeen years translating into French. Poe's short stories mark a fundamental change in the relationship between a first-person narrator and his or her reader. Baudelaire can level an accusation at his reader only because Poe had already made the case for the reader's guilt.

The novelists and poets of the Romantic period tend to write from the viewpoints of narrators whose sympathies are similar to their own. In the case of Wordsworth, for example, it may be difficult to make any clear distinction between the poet and his narratorial persona. Poe, on the other hand, gives voice to narrators whose attitudes are as alien and abhorrent as their crimes. Many of his most famous stories have as their narrators madmen and murderers. These speakers are the reader's only point of access to the world of the story; the events of that world are filtered through the attitudes and perceptions of a homicidal narrator. As a result, the reader is constantly reassessing what he has been told, reordering events into a more logical and objective pattern. Poe's criminals are classic examples of what critic Wayne Booth terms "the unreliable narrator." Operating under the assumption that his story will be received sympathetically, the narrator confesses to the reader a ghastly crime. But only a very naïve reader will accept the narrator's account of this crime. A more savvy one understands that he is in possession of two stories, the self-justifying version of events that the narrator tells and the damning reality that this self-justification inadvertently reveals. Much of the effectiveness of Poe's stories lies in this dramatic revaluation of the dynamics of telling a story and of listening to one. Poe's stories are double-voiced, animated by a constant tension between two orders of reality. Russian Formalist Mikhail Bakhtin described double-voiced narration as "another's speech in another's language, serving to express authorial intentions but in a refracted way" (324). Poe's voice is not to be confused with that of his narrators, for the author sees what the narrator cannot: the monstrous nature of the crimes that are being confessed. Whereas the poets and novelists of the previous generation saw direct address as a way of clearly communicating from author to reader, Poe subverts the conventions of first-person narration, speaking from behind masks that at once hide and reveal the stories they tell. The reader, as Baudelaire would later make explicit, is implicated in the dark materials of Poe's story. Poe's transformation of the narrator's relationship with his reader represents one of the major developments of nineteenth-century literature. Poe and several of his contemporaries, including Nathaniel Hawthorne and Herman Melville, laid the groundwork for the metafictional devices that would be so important to twentieth-century literature.

Poe's most effective short stories are told by consummate narcissists, men whose disconnection from reality is as frightening as the crimes they have committed. The narrators of "The Black Cat," "The Tell-Tale Heart," and "The Cask of Amontillado" have much in common: each has murdered an innocent person and hidden his or her body behind the walls or under the floorboards of the narrator's house. Each casts his story in the form of a direct address, admitting what he has done to an unspecified "you" who may be a stand-in for the reader or may be the reader himself. Yet reading the three stories in the order that Poe wrote them shows a measured progression from a narrator who makes a confession of guilt to one who is mounting a defense of his own sanity in order to assuage his guilt, to one who seems to feel no guilt at all. This process reworks the role of the reader, for if the reader of "The Black Cat" is essentially a criminal's confessor, the reader of "The Cask of Amontillado" is his accomplice-after-the-fact. There is an arc across the three stories that points the way toward Baudelaire's indictment of the *hypocrite lecteur.*

The narrator of "The Black Cat" makes a confession on the night before he is to be executed, declaring "to-morrow I die, and to-day I would unburthen my soul" (63). The short story records this confession; it purports to be the actual text that the condemned man set down on paper. There is no question that the narrator is guilty of the crimes for which he has been convicted. In his prologue he lays out his reason for confessing: "My immediate purpose is to place before the world, plainly, succinctly, and without comment, a series of mere household events" (63). He hopes that "some intellect more calm, more logical, and far less excitable than my own" might better explain the events that have befallen him (63). Having detailed his reasons for making a confession, the narrator launches into the story itself. Bedeviled by alcoholism, the man abuses both his wife and his menagerie of pets. When his favorite black cat avoids him one night, he punishes it by cutting out its eye; eventually, he hangs the animal from a tree. Some months later, he finds a similar cat—missing eye and all—and adopts it. This new animal terrifies the narrator, particularly since what was once a white spot on its coat has gradually resolved itself into the shape of a gallows. When the cat gets underfoot one night, the enraged narrator takes an ax to it. His wife intercedes on behalf of the cat, and the narrator "buried the ax in her brain" (68). He hides the body behind the walls of his basement, skillfully setting the bricks back in place. When the police come to investigate his wife's disappearance, they are fooled by the false wall. It is the narrator himself who raps on the wall of his basement, declaring "These walls—are you going, gentlemen?—these walls are solidly put together" (69). There is an answering cry from behind the wall, and the police knock it down to discover the hidden corpse. Too late, the narrator realizes he "had walled the monster up within the tomb!" (70).

At first glance, one might take this confession as just what the narrator represented it to be: "a series of . . . events" told "plainly, succinctly, and without comment" (63). The condemned man may be mad, and is certainly a murderer, but that does not necessarily make him an unreliable narrator. Yet there are a half-dozen places where the narrator's reason and reliability fail to pass muster, and where the reader, if he is successfully to navigate "The Black Cat," must be "more calm, more logical, and far less excitable" than the condemned man. The first few lines encode the narrator's inherent unreliability:

> For the most wild, yet most homely narrative which I am about to pen, I neither expect nor solicit belief. Mad indeed would I be to expect it, in a case where my very senses reject their own evidence. Yet, mad am I not— and very surely I do not dream. But tomorrow I die . . . (63).

The narrator's insistence that he is not mad produces the opposite effect; in proclaiming his own sanity, he calls that sanity into question. Like Lady Macbeth, the guilty narrator "protests too much." The specter of madness hovers over the entire story, and indeed precipitates the narrator's confession in the first place. He hopes that a calm and logical reader will be able to provide a rational explanation for the series of events that have befallen him. The most rational explanation by far is to deem the narrator delusional. The narrator himself skirts this truth when he notes "my very senses reject their own evidence." Rereading the account under the hypothesis that the narrator is delusional, one realizes that no outside party can verify the strange coincidences and eerie events around which the story revolves. The narrator's wife, for example, points out the white spot on the second cat's coat, but it is only the narrator himself to whom this spot appears to take the shape of a gallows (67). The story is an example of radical subjectivity, a representation of the world as it appears to an individual man rather than the world as it really is. The truly frightening quality of Poe's stories lies in the suggestion that there may be no way of establishing a correspondence between subjective vision and objective reality. Just as the narrator of "The Black Cat" is trapped in his prison cell, so every man is trapped inside the chamber of his own senses and perceptions.

Through his delusional narrator, Poe subverts and warps the conventions of the first-person confessional poem or story. Though Romanticism is a highly varied movement of which Poe was a part, many Romantic poets such as Wordsworth, John Keats, and Percy Bysshe Shelley—and, in America, Walt Whitman—assumed that one man could speak directly to another, conveying the impression that some external sight or event produced in him. When Wordsworth describes a view from London Bridge, when Shelly describes Mont Blanc, when Keats describes the experience of reading Homer or *King Lear*, they do so in a mode that reproduces in the reader a vicarious echo of the emotion that the poet felt. The reader is not himself looking out from London Bridge, but he shares the poet's perspective and feels some measure of the poet's emotional response to what he has seen. Poe's narrator adopts Wordsworth's maxim that poetry is "emotion recollected in tranquility," musing from the tranquil confines of his prison cell on what he has seen and how he has felt. Yet the eye and the "I" of the poet have been pushed beyond the bounds of sanity. Subjectivity and individuality, in this story, have given way to madness. The narrator's insistence that his behavior can be rationally explained speaks to his radical subjectivity; because what he has done seems sensible to him, it must be sensible. His running argument with the reader amounts to a struggle to remain the subject rather than an object. As long as he can explain himself, the narrator reasons, he may not be objectified as a lunatic.

Yet the narrator ultimately fails to give a full accounting of his behavior, because he cannot close the distance between the "I" who writes calmly in a cell and the homicidal "me" who took an ax to his wife. The narrator simply cannot explain the rage that consumed him, and to blame it on drinking, as he does, feels like a dodge. His laconic descriptions of violence therefore work against him, as in "I suffered myself to use intemperate language to my wife. At length, I even offered her personal violence" (64). The measured, Latinate stateliness of this construction is at odds with the terrible actions that it denotes. The scene in which he murders his wife has a similar sangfroid: the narrator recalls that with "a rage more than demoniacal, I withdrew my arm from her grasp and buried the axe in her brain" (68). The narrator's coolness in describing his crime suggests that he has always felt at a remove from his own actions; his guilt is an abstraction rather than a lived reality. He writes out of a puzzlement over his own motivations, of his burgeoning awareness of what he terms "the spirit of PERVERSENESS" (65). This same perverseness causes him to rap on the false wall behind which he has hidden his wife, setting in motion the discovery that will lead to his eventual execution. He recognizes a self-destructive quality in himself, a "longing of the soul to vex itself," and the confession is a means by which he may explore this quality (65). Yet being puzzled by one's own subconscious motivations is very different from feeling guilty over how one's behavior has hurt another person. This narrator is too narcissistic truly to empathize with his wife or for his animals. He is, in sum, an utter sociopath, incapable of seeing the people around him as themselves subjects rather than objects. The narrator tries to pass off "The Black Cat" as a death-row confession, but the only victim for whom he feels genuine sympathy is himself.

The narrator of "The Tell-Tale Heart" could be brother to the narrator of "The Black Cat": he, too, has committed a terrible murder, immured his victim's body within his house, and then perversely given away the secret of its location. Like his earlier avatar, this narrator feels some measure of guilt. Convinced that he can hear the old man's heart still beating under the floorboards where he has concealed it, he surrenders to the police officers who have unsuccessfully searched the house. The story concludes with his frantic confession: "Villains! . . . dissemble no more! I admit the deed!—tear up the planks!—here, here!—it is the beating of his hideous heart!" (124). "The Tell-Tale Heart," published half a century before Sigmund Freud's *On the Interpretation of*

Dreams, anticipates the relationship between subconscious desires and conscious actions that would be central to Freud's model of psychology. While the text allows for the possibility of the supernatural, the reader suspects there is a different explanation at work. Had the narrator a better perspective on his own inner life, he might adopt a proto-Freudian interpretation of his self-destructive behavior, recognizing that the sound he heard emanating from below the floorboards was not real but rather a projection of his own subconscious desire to be apprehended and punished for his crimes. Because he cannot accept such a premise, he faces a stark dichotomy. Either his dismembered victim's heart continued to beat after death, or he himself has gone mad. The narrator insists that the former explanation is true, for he would rather the physical laws of the universe fail than his own sanity be called into question. In this respect, his reason for giving an account of his crime and his relationship to the reader are of a different order from that of the narrator of "The Black Cat." Where the former narrator dismisses at the outset the possibility that he is mad, the narrator of "The Tell-Tale Heart" imagines that the reader has challenged his sanity. The narrator tells his story not to unburden himself or seek forgiveness, but to make the case for his own sanity and in so doing to win the reader's confidence.

The narrator's initial use of direct address is disconcerting, for he speaks as if in response to an accusation that the reader or his narrative stand-in has made. The first line positions the reader as an adversary: "True!—nervous—very, very dreadfully nervous I had been and am; but why *will* you say that I am mad?" The fractured syntax of this opening line—with its words that are repeated, separated by long dashes, or set off as exclamations—reflects the narrator's fractured state of mind. Yet he takes great offense at the suggestion that his thoughts are as disordered as his speech. The tone of the question "why *will* you say that I am mad?" is one of exasperation; the italicized word *will* suggests ongoing action, as if the reader has been stubbornly and repeatedly insisting on the narrator's insanity. It is this sense of exasperation that prompts the narrator to tell his story, with the tacit assumption that when the reader is in full possession of the facts he will see that the narrator's account is "true" and that he is sane. "You fancy me mad," he argues. "Madmen know nothing. But you should have seen *me*. You should have seen how wisely I proceeded" (121). The relationship with the reader or audience is therefore an adversarial one, in that the narrator is defending himself against a charge the reader has leveled.

The double-voiced quality of the narrator's tale is such that his attempts to prove his sanity only call it further into question. His motive for committing the crime, for example, is incomprehensible to a sane audience. The narrator of "The Tell-Tale Heart" cannot say exactly why he killed the old man who was his patron and victim. He muses, "I loved the old man. He had never wronged me. He had never given me insult. For his gold I had no desire. I think it was his eye! yes, it was this!" (121). The old man's blue eye fills the narrator with fear and hatred; he says it "chilled the very marrow in my bones" (121). Though he is able to communicate his own disgust at the old man's eye, the narrator is incapable of describing the eye in such a way as to produce a comparable, vicarious disgust in the reader. For us, it is perhaps simply a staring blue eye, no more or less. Indeed, the reader can be as objective as an ophthalmologist, positing that the "hideous veil" over the eye may suggest the presence of cataracts or suggest some history of trauma. The old man may have had a stroke at some point in the recent past, for the eye's veiled and vacant stare is consistent with a temporary loss of oxygen to the brain. The reader can fully apprehend both the qualities of the old man's eye and the nature of the narrator's disgust, but he or she cannot really accept that the one produced the other. The motive for the crime therefore becomes a litmus test for measuring both the narrator's sanity and the reader's ability to sympathize with him.

By way of explanation, the narrator discloses the particulars of his crime:

> If you still think me mad, you will think so no longer when I describe the wise precautions I took for the concealment of the body. The night waned, and I worked hastily, but in silence. First of all I dismembered the corpse. I cut off the head and the arms and the legs. (123)

So fixated is the narrator on establishing his sanity, he fails to recognize the horror of what he has just described. Like the narrator of "The Black Cat," he can view his actions only through the lens of his own ego. He has no real sympathy for the old man he has murdered. In presuming that the reader will share his perspective, the narrator both signals his own overweening narcissism and creates for the reader a persona that is similarly invested in the killer rather his victim. The narrator of "The Tell-Tale Heart" operates under a series of assumptions about where the reader's sympathies will lie. At the outset of the story, he imagines that the reader thinks him insane and therefore assumes a combative, wheedling tone. As he reveals each successive detail of his crime, however, the narrator gradually transforms this imagined adversary into an advocate and accomplice.

Poe's short story "The Cask of Amontillado" further warps the dynamics of the confessional mode and refigures the relationship between narrator and reader. The narrator of "The Black Cat" confesses his crimes out of puzzlement over his own self-destructive perversity rather than out of grief for his victim. "The Tell-Tale Heart" is less a confession than a self-justifying argument mounted to convince the reader of the narrator's sanity. "The Cask of Amontillado" takes this progression to its logical extreme, for its narrator seems not to believe he has anything to confess. He admits to a monstrous and unjustified crime in full confidence that the reader will sympathize with what he has done. If the narrator is two-faced, his story is double-voiced, and he seems not to be aware that in recounting his tale of revenge he inadvertently damns himself.

The narrator Montresor relies on a mask of friendliness in order to lure his enemy Fortunato to his doom. As Montresor puts it, "neither by word or deed had I given Fortunato cause to doubt my good-will. I continued, as was my wont, to smile in his face, and he did not perceive that my smile now was at the thought of his immolation" (191). Having brought Fortunato down to his wine cellar with the promise of tasting a pipe of Amontillado wine, Montresor restrains his enemy and then entombs him behind a new-made wall. At the story's conclusion, the narrator hesitates for a moment before putting the last stone into position. He hears the bells on his enemy's carnival motley jingle, feels a pang of what could be remorse, then drives home the last stone and plasters it into place. In a sudden leap forward, the narrator reveals just how much distance he has on the story he tells, saying of the old bones that he lay before the new wall: "For the half of a century no mortal has disturbed them. *In pace requiescat!*" (196).

"The Cask of Amontillado" has become a classic revenge story, delivering in four or five pages some of the same impact that, say, Alexandre Dumas's *The Count of Monte Cristo* or *The Man in the Iron Mask* do in eight hundred. Yet one has only Montresor's word that this is, in fact, a revenge story and not a tale of motiveless malignancy. At the start of the story, Montresor confides, "The thousand injuries of Fortunato I had borne as I best could; but when he ventured upon insult, I vowed revenge" (191). What are these unspecified injuries? What is the unrepeatable insult? If we are to accept Fortunato's punishment as a just one—indeed, as a poetic one, in which a horrible crime meets with an appropriately horrible punishment—insult and injury must be great indeed. Perhaps Fortunato brought false charges against an innocent man or woman, causing that person to be locked away unjustly. This sets in motion the revenge plot of *The Count of Monte Cristo* and countless other stories. Perhaps he has killed a friend or relative of Montresor, yet escaped justice. Vigilantes of all stripes, from Orestes to Hamlet to Batman, have acted to avenge the murder of a parent or loved one. There are many other crimes that would prime the reader to accept as just and fair Montresor's punishment. We might even accept as a valid motive for revenge Montresor's having lost to Fortunato in love. Yet Montresor cites no single act or word that would justify the punishment; he simply assumes that we take him at his word and will require no further examination of the evidence against Fortunato.

Readers have a remarkable capacity for sympathizing with narrators, and we might do so here did we not witness Montresor's cordial exchanges with his enemy. He greets the motley-clad Fortunato as if they are old friends, saying, "My dear Fortunato, you are luckily met. How remarkably well you are looking to-day!" (192). This outward show of joy is, in fact, genuine, for Montresor admits, "I was so pleased to see him, that I thought I should never have done wringing his hand" (192). Montresor, we know, is two-faced, and has already admitted to presenting his enemy with a false show of friendship. His joy at seeing Fortunato stems from his "thought of his immolation" (191). What, however, would explain Fortunato's cordiality? Had he truly done something to anger and offend Montresor, he would approach the man with caution. Instead, he readily trusts him. It is Fortunato, at Montresor's prompting, who suggests a trip into the latter's vaults to taste the suspect bottle of Amontillado. Fortunato is motivated in equal parts by his own pride in his discriminating palate and by a sense of justice: he believes his friend has been sold a false bill of goods. "You have been imposed upon," he declares, and his insistence that he sample the pipe of Amontillado stems from a desire to verify this imposition. He is not proving Montresor wrong, but coming to his defense. Fortunato's lack of suspicion or guile, as evidenced by his readiness to follow his friend into the depths of the vaults, suggests that he has no reason to fear Montresor. Consequently, he fails to register several pointed remarks that Montresor directs his way, such as "You are happy, as once I was" and "The Montresors . . . were a great and numerous family" (193). Montresor, we imagine, sees these as cunning rebukes, reflections on his fallen state that should somehow make Fortunato blush with guilt. Fortunato reads nothing into these comments, of course, for he has done nothing at which a reasonable man might take offense. Unfortunately for Fortunato, Montresor is not a reasonable man.

"The Cask of Amontillado" therefore operates on two planes at once. The first consists of Montresor's version of events, in which a half-century ago he took righteous revenge on a bitterly hated and thoroughly despicable enemy. The reader is not only someone whom Montresor implicitly trusts but one whom he feels to be a shrewd judge of his own character and habits. In the story's second line, he addresses this listener directly, calling him, "You, who so well know the nature of my soul" (191). We do not know who the "you" is supposed to be: a specific person in whom the old man confides, a sympathetic reader, or some listening aspect of his own psyche. But whoever he may be, this listener is no confessor; Montresor, ultimately, sees himself as having nothing to confess. He tells his story to an auditor who he assumes will be an advocate, one whom he can trust with the details of his crime. In relaying his story, he therefore positions the reader as an accomplice after the fact. He tells us what he has done, but nothing in his words or tone suggests that he wishes to be judged or forgiven. Montresor might be surprised, therefore, to learn that his reader glimpses a second plane of reality underlying his story, a reordering of events in which Fortunato is a victim rather than a villain. "The Cask of Amontillado" gathers force and drama not only from the tension between Fortunato and Montresor but also from the tension between events as Montresor narrates them and the objective reality that his narration tries and fails to hide. Montresor's story and his wall are both cunningly constructed to hide the evidence of a crime. The effect is a paradoxical one: the more Montresor justifies his own behavior, the more we become convinced that his justification is a hollow one. By the same token, the artifice that Montresor relies on—a citing of grave but unspecified insults and injuries—leads the reader to reach beyond the narrator's version of events for some more truthful explanation of those events. Of course, all of the elements of Poe's story are the stuff of fiction: Montresor, Fortunato, the vaults, the cask, and the wall. Yet the deliberate fiction that Montresor creates to justify his murder of Fortunato creates the illusion that there is an objective reality somewhere beyond this fiction.

Some of the story's most interesting moments come when Montresor's narrative wall shows signs of crumbling. He recalls, toward the end of his account, pausing before putting in the last stone. Twice he calls to Fortunato, but receives no reply. Montresor says: "No answer still. I thrust a torch through the remaining aperture and let it fall within. There came forth only a jingling of bells. My heart grew sick; it was the dampness of the catacombs that made it so. I hastened to make an end of my labour" (196). Why does Montresor's heart grow sick? He himself is quick to ascribe the sensation to purely physiological origins, blaming the dampness of the vaults. He will not allow the sensation to occupy its own sentence, and the semicolon that punctuates the lines shows his eagerness to attach the feeling that he had to some physical cause that would explain it away. But something besides the damp is at work. The killer feels a twinge of guilt over his crime, and for a moment hesitates; only by acting quickly and decisively can he push through this crisis. Montresor has far more fortitude than the narrators of "The Black Cat" and "The Tell-Tale Heart," who could hide their crimes only for a few days or hours. Whatever guilt Montresor may be feeling, he restrains himself from self-incrimination. Even fifty years on, however, he remembers this moment in which he glimpsed his situation from the vantage point of his victim rather than of himself. For a moment, light shines through a chink in the wall and Montresor realizes that there are two sides to this situation. It is a fascinating passage that goes to the heart of why the narrator tells his story. The stone and plaster wall that Montresor constructed in the catacombs has stood undisturbed, but the wall he has put between himself and the enormity of his crime has fared less well. His final words are telling: "For the half of a century no mortal has disturbed them. *In pace requiescat!*" (196). To know that the bones have lain undisturbed, Montresor must have revisited them often; his return to the scene of the crime indicates how greatly these events still weigh on him. His final benediction, therefore, is unintentionally ironic. It is not just the bones on either side of the wall that must be told to rest in peace, but Montresor himself.

Had he more self-awareness, Montresor would recognize that he envies Fortunato's bones their undisturbed slumber.

At first glance, these three narrators seem to tell similar stories in similar ways: each admits to having killed someone and hidden his or her body in the bowels of his house. Yet there is a marked progression from one story to the next, as Poe redefines the relationship between an unreliable first-person narrator and the reader who he presumes will take his side. With this new narrative model, Poe—along with authors such as Hawthorne and Melville, Romantics who employed similar techniques—radically refigured the narratorial persona of other Romantic contemporaries such as Wordsworth, Shelley, Keats, and Whitman. In so doing, they cleared a way for Baudelaire and his generation. But Poe's significance extends beyond his influence on any single writer or school of writers; ultimately, his short stories did something to change the nature of reading itself.

Works Cited

Bakhtin, Mikhail Mikhailovich. *The Dialogic Imagination*. Ed. Michael Holquist. Austin: University of Texas Press, 1981.

Baudelaire, Charles. *Fleurs du Mal/Flowers of Evil*. Ed. Marthiel and Jackson Mathews. New York: New Directions, 1955.

Booth, Wayne. *The Rhetoric of Fiction*. Chicago: University of Chicago Press, 1967.

Poe, Edgar Allan. *Complete Stories and Poems*. New York: Doubleday, 1966.

Wu, Duncan. *Romanticism: An Anthology*. Oxford: Blackwell, 1994.

Edgar Allan Poe's Fantastic Short Stories_____

Santiago Rodríguez Guerrero-Strachan

Edgar Allan Poe wrote some forty short stories that have been variously categorized as horror, fantasy, mystery, science fiction, and Gothic tales. Richard M. Fletcher, in *The Stylistic Development of Edgar Allan Poe* (90), and J. R. Hammond, in *An Edgar Allan Poe Companion* (60), both describe Poe's work as belonging to these categories. But Charles May's *Edgar Allan Poe: A Study of the Short Fiction* and Scott Peeples's *Edgar Allan Poe Revisited* offer different categories that are as valuable and as sound as those previously mentioned. These are overlapping categories in some cases, particularly in fantastic stories that can be viewed as Gothic, horror, or mere fantasy, to say nothing of others that may have two or more conflicting interpretations, such as "The Fall of the House of Usher." The reason for this ambivalence lies, no doubt, in Poe's poetics. His writing never seems to stand on the firm ground of a single style; rather, it fluctuates between or combines two styles, one serious and the other humorous (Allen; Thompson, 1973). He always had the readers in mind, as he wrote to Thomas W. White: "[T]o be appreciated you must be read, and these things are sought with avidity" (*Letters*, 58). These things refer to the morbid, the bizarre and the satiric—a favorite of American readers at the time.

Despite the surface variety, there are two underlying principles that link all his stories—unity and reason—which may account for the sometimes conflicting categories attributed to his works. As May rightfully indicates, "the single unifying factor in all of Poe's works is the concept of unity itself" (11). Poe mentioned the principle of unity as fundamental to his fiction and poetry as he learned it from August Wilhelm Schlegel via Samuel Taylor Coleridge (Hoffmann 52-104). The lack of unity implies that the reader's mind cannot be focused on a single plot and will not perceive the resulting final effect. The overall structure of the tale works actively in conveying this effect. The other tenet is the ratiocinative nature of his stories. Because his stories are detailed and consciously crafted, there always remains the sense that all of Poe's stories are guided by a rational principle that is a consequence of Poe's interest in science and of his own literary use of contemporary science. This is easily discernible in the mystery and science fiction stories, and it is present in his horror, Gothic, and fantastic pieces as well.

I am going to expose Poe's poetics regarding his fantastic stories relative to the whole of his fictional prose writings. I am interested in pointing out the narrative strategies that he uses for the accomplishment of the fantastic as well as the importance of the unity of effect and the ratiocinative principle in the most important fantastic pieces, such as "The Fall of the House of Usher," "The Black Cat," "The Tell-Tale Heart," "Ligeia" and "Berenice."

There is more than horror and terror in Poe's fiction, but as Vincent Buranelli says, "these are, as far as his short stories are concerned, the characteristics that seem most prominent and have attracted most attention" (72). We must bear in mind that Poe took a genre that had already yielded its best works, namely the Gothic narrative, and transformed it into something new and suited to contemporary readers' tastes (and open to continuous renewal, demonstrated in Jorge Luis Borges's and Julio Cortázar's fantastic short stories). Scholars such as Clark Griffith and G. R. Thompson have suggested that Poe's tales are ironic twists of Gothic narratives.

What he masterfully achieves is the blending of the Gothic tale—regarded as a tale of "German terror"—and the tales of psychological derangement. He disregards the common idea that terror had a German origin; he believed it originated in the soul: "If in many of my productions terror has been the thesis, I maintain that terror is not of Germany, but of the soul" (*Collected Works*, 2: 473)—the soul, or in other words the mind, as Poe exemplifies in most, if not all, of his stories. As I will argue later, most of Poe's characters suffer a kind of mania that makes them see a distorted reality and is the cause of the fantastic.

Poe was not interested in the Romantic fantastic of Horace Walpole's *The Castle of Otranto* or William Beckford's *Vathek*, much less in Ann Radcliffe's Gothic novels. He realized that these were stages that had become outdated. If the fantastic was to be believable, it had to offer a new nature, a new narrator, and a new setting. It is true that, as Gerald Kennedy argues, "the supernatural paraphernalia of the Gothic, particularly phantasms of death and destruction, afforded a means of articulating this primal fear"; Kennedy refers to the "terror of the soul" (112).

Before Poe started writing, the fantastic was considered a preternatural event that took place in a setting that was estranged from everyday life. It is one of Poe's great achievements to have made the fantastic part of common life and to have stripped away its supernatural features. His is a psychological fantastic in most cases. Tzvetan Todorov argues that the fantastic takes place in the hesitation between the natural laws and the supernatural event (25). The reader cannot tell whether the events have a natural origin or they are supernatural. We can include Poe's fantastic here, provided we add that he favors a psychological explanation, as can be seen in three representative stories, "The Black Cat," "The Fall of the House of Usher" and "Ligeia." By psychological, I mean that real events are not as important as the manner in which the narrators perceive them. It is not really important that the main character in "The Black Cat" actually hears the cat's meow; what really matters is that he thinks he has heard it and confesses his deed. Similarly, in "Ligeia" the narrator sees Ligeia's eyes in Lady Rowena's face, and that is what really counts.

In "The Fall of the House of Usher," the mental derangement that the narrator experiences under Roderick's influence provokes the fantastic: "I felt creeping upon me, by slow yet certain degrees, the wild influences of his own fantastic yet impressive superstitions" (*Collected Works*, 2: 411). There is also another reason for the fantastic. Roderick thinks that the nature surrounding the house influences the building and exerts its influence upon its inhabitants:

This opinion . . . was the sentience of all vegetable things. But, in his disordered fancy, the idea had assumed a more daring character. . . . The belief was connected with the gray stones of the home of his forefathers . . . [The] influence which for centuries had moulded the destinies of his family. (*Collected Works*, 2: 408)

Both "Berenice" and "Ligeia" are included within the psychological fantastic. Berenice is presented as a creature, if not actually created, at least heavily determined by the narrator's mind:

I had seen her—not as the living and breathing Berenice, but as the Berenice of a dream—not as a being of the earth, earthy, but as the abstraction of such being—not as a thing to admire, but to analyze—not as an object of love, but as the theme of the most abstruse although desultory speculation. (*Collected Works*, 2: 214)

In the case of "Ligeia," the fantastic event, that is the appearance of Ligeia in the person of Lady Rowena, has a psychological reason as well, though in this case the opium administered to the narrator may also have distorted the perception of reality.

"The Black Cat" is one story in which the hesitation between the pure fantastic and the distorted perception of reality is most clearly present. The narrator does not fully explain if the cat's meow is heard by the policemen or whether he is the only person who hears and sees the animal. He simply says, "the corpse . . . stood erect before the eyes of the spectators" (*Collected Works*, 3: 859), obviously referring to his wife's corpse.

"The Tell-Tale Heart" presents a clear case of obsessive madness. The fantastic is purely psychological and is provoked by the narrator's obsession with the old man's eye and his assassination. When the policeman asks him about the old man's disappearance, he denies that he may have been involved in the murder, but he hears the old man's heartbeats: "It grew louder—louder—louder! And still the men chatted pleasantly and smiled. Was it possible they heard not?" (*Collected Works*, 3: 797).

All these events have a psychological origin. Poe is greatly interested in the clinical representation of mental excitement, especially, as Robert L. Carringer argues, "those forms of terror that are aroused by the prospect of death or derangement for his narrators" (18). Some critics, such as D. H. Lawrence or Marie Bonaparte, have linked Poe's obsession with the characters' state of mind to his own neurotic personality. It may be argued that Poe's obsessions are reflected in his narrative. But critics should not mistake Poe for his narrators for the sake of the analysis. Moreover, they should not dismiss the influence of eighteenth-century narrators. "The meaning of first-person narrative in stories by Poe becomes clearer in the context of his eighteenth-century precursors. [. . .] The fictional 'I' creates itself and, simultaneously, its frame" (Frieden 136). "First-person narratives, from Richardson to Poe, enact the unification of narrator and narrated, narration and event, creator and created" (147). To my view, the analysis of the narrator as a character and not as the author's mask is much more important, as I will explain later.

In most of Poe's stories, narrators suffer from a type of mania, either melancholy or madness, that distorts reality. Poe was acquainted with contemporary scientific theories and was attracted to phrenology, mesmerism, and psychology. He frequently mentioned hysteria, melancholy, madness, catalepsy, and other diseases of the mind that were prevalent in his age. His descriptions of melancholic and mad characters indicate that he was acquainted with Thomas Willis's *Two Discourses concerning the Soul of the Brutes, which is that of the Vital and Sensitive of Man* (1638), which was the first of a series of treatises analyzing madness and melancholy. Besides the medical description of both diseases, he indicated the features that they share. Among the books describing madness that Poe must have read are John Haslam's *Observations on Madness and Melancholy* (1809) and James Prichard's 1835 *Treatise on Insanity and Other Disorders Affecting the*

Mind (Zimmerman 2005: 350-351). The symptoms were instrumental in making the fantastic believable and in providing an explanation that might insert it into everyday life, while at the same time connecting it with the poetics of sensibility prevalent in Poe's time (Zimmerman 2007: 47-56).

Not only did Poe use modern theories of psychology or David Hartley's theories about mental association; he was widely read in mesmerism and used it for his own literary purposes. Bruce Mills argues that Poe realized that mesmerism could be used to build "his short-story aesthetic on the foundation of human psychology" (55). I would add that he built the poetics of the short story as well as that of the fantastic (which implies that both genre and mode went hand in hand in Poe's poetics). As Mills points out later, "the mesmeric turn of the era, then, followed the larger paradigmatic reorientation toward inward states" (63). The orientation toward these states of the mind allowed mesmerism and psychology to play an important role in the creation of the fantastic. Since that time, the fantastic could be created in the narrator's mind and, to explain this, the writer would have a set of scientific explanations that were understood by the readers.

Important as the rational explanation may be, there is still a more important reason for the psychological origin of the fantastic. As May points out, Poe creates a type of narrator who controls the narrative tightly by consciously narrowing the point of view and focus. As May says, Poe employs "a teller so obsessed with the subject of his narration that the obsession creates the tightly controlled unit" (8). This obsessed narrator, who focuses on his nightmarish reality exclusively, tells his experience not as it has been but as he has experienced it, meaning he narrates it as he thinks it has happened. The move from reality toward perception can be masterfully achieved, provided the narrator has a sound cause that explains the shift. Indeed, narrators in Poe's stories can be divided into two groups, those who continually reject their madness and those who admit that they suffer from melancholy or a disease of the senses—called attentive in some stories. For example, in "Berenice," Egaeus says, "This monomania, if I must so term it, consisted in a morbid irritability of those properties of the mind in metaphysical science termed the *attentive*" (*Collected Works*, 2: 211). Interestingly enough, there is an exception to these characters of great imagination. The narrator in "Ms. Found in a Bottle" admits that he lacks imagination: "a deficiency of imagination has been imputed to me as a crime" (*Collected Works*, 2: 135). This may be seen as a necessary feature for the fantastic in this story, a fantastic that is not caused by the imagination.

Readers should see the difference between the narrator and Poe as the real author. But this has not always been the case. A large number of critics have equated the two, and it was not until James W. Gargano's article "The Question of Poe's Narrators" that they were taken into account seriously as independent from Poe the real person. "Poe's narrators possess a character and consciousness distinct from those of their creator. These protagonists, I am convinced, speak their own thoughts and are the dupes of their own passions" (164). More important still is Gargano's assertion that Poe "often so designs his tales as to show his narrators' limited comprehension of their own problems and states of mind" (165). Since Gargano's article, other readers have focused on the importance of narrators in Poe's fiction (basically the fantastic). Gregory S. Jay argues that "the ordeals of Poe's narrators tell us much about the fallacy of equating 'self' and 'self-consciousness'" (93). As Zimmerman says, there is "an aesthetic detachment from his protagonists" (2005: 15), and Donald Barlow Stauffer, when analyzing "Ligeia," points out that "the predominantly emotional quality of its style may be defended by its appropriateness to both the agitated mental state of the narrator and the supernatural event he relates" (323).

The narrator of "Berenice," asserts Scott Peeples, "lives mainly through his intellect, born in a library, where he spends seemingly all his time" (Peeples 50). "Yet differently we grew—I ill of health and buried in gloom [. . .] mine the studies of the cloister—I living within mine own heart, and addicted body and soul to the most intense and painful meditation" (*Collected Works*, 2: 210), and "my passions always were of the mind" (*Collected Works*, 2: 214). This means that Berenice is a character partly real and partly created by the narrator's imagination. In fact, as Peeples has pointed out, they (Berenice, Ligeia, and other female characters) are in fact seeking their own identity, whereas the male characters project their subconscious desires or obsessions (51).

In "Ligeia," the narrator falls into a state of sadness caused by the loss of a beloved person. This leads him to seek a replacement in the person of Lady Rowena. He refuses to accept that he has lost Ligeia. Moreover, he confesses that he cannot remember her family's name or the details about their first meeting (*Collected Works*, 2: 310). He is forced to accept that reality cannot be avoided indefinitely. His obsession with Ligeia's eyes can be equated with the cousin's obsession with Berenice's teeth. In both cases, the narrators focus their attention on a part of the beloved's body as a substitute for their losses.

In "The Fall of the House of Usher," the narrator presents the reader with a landscape view that provokes in him a feeling of gloom (*Collected Works*, 2: 397). The narrator describes the shades of the evening, the melancholy they produce, the gloom that he feels, and the lack of sublimity in the scene. It is the whole atmosphere, gloomy and nightmarish, that creates the fantastic element in "Usher." This has to be seen in psychological terms, that is to say, subjective terms and not in terms of ambiguity or ambivalence, as Todorov argues (29). By creating a propitious state of mind in the characters, the fantastic may justifiably materialize. All this poses the problem of the narrator's reliability, discussed by Patrick F. Quinn (1981a: 303-312; 1981b: 341-353) and Thompson (1981: 313-340). Some critics have seen Roderick and Madeline as the narrator's projections of the mind (Wilbur 255-277; Hoffmann 295-316; Thompson, 1973: 87-98). However, I would say that rather than projections he is influenced by the ambience that surrounds him, in which, we must not forget, Roderick and Madeline are the central characters.

There is also another problem, and this is the narrator's attitude. As Jay says, "the madness of the narrator would be his rationality in reading, his refusal to recognize the other inhabiting the text" (107). This may be said of all the narrators. There is not a single narrator who accepts that he is mad. In fact, their failure to understand what is happening or has happened is greatly caused by their reading of reality. The narrators of "The Black Cat" and "The Tell-Tale Heart" are prime examples of this.

In "The Black Cat" and "The Tell-Tale Heart," the narrators are obsessed with their supposed madness, which they insistently deny. The narrator of "The Tell-Tale Heart" says, "True!—nervous—very, very dreadfully nervous I had been and am; but why *will* you say that I am mad?" (*Collected Works*, 3: 792), and in "The Black Cat," "mad indeed would I be to expect it, in a case where my very senses reject their own evidence. Yet, mad am I not" (*Collected Works*, 3: 849). It is this obsession, along with the extremely narrow point of view of their narratives, that makes the fantastic appear.

In the first stage of his career, Poe favored those settings might be similar to those of British Gothic stories: that is, abbeys, castles, or ancient houses located in Europe. Examples include the locations in "The Oval Portrait," "The Fall of the House of Usher," "William Wilson," "Metzengerstein," "Berenice," and "Ligeia." He would place fantastic stories in a remote country that was at the same time familiar so readers could identify them as Gothic or fantastic. He would also use a remote time to make it believable, not only because readers were accustomed to a sort of medieval age but also because the supposedly fantastic event could not be ascertained or denied. Gradually, Poe seemed to realize that settings need not be distanced from the readers' ordinary locations. Instead, the modern city could be a suitable scenario for the psychological fantastic. This was not a source external to the narrator, nor was it preternatural; consequently, the setting could be and should be as realistic as possible for contemporary readers. Otherwise there would not be a congruent relationship between the nature of the fantastic and the setting.

"The Black Cat" and "The Tell-Tale Heart" are two good examples of this argument. They are not located in a distant somewhere or in a remote period, although there is the necessary ambiguity in both setting and time so that a too realistic description of either would not make the story unbelievable. We must keep in mind that Poe was writing in the Romantic period and that Realism would not come until the end of the century, despite the fact that he and other authors, Melville for example, took the first steps toward writing more realistic stories. As Carringer has stated, "the Poe protagonist is conspicuously within something [. . .] the principal activity takes place within a single room, and within a series of rooms in two others [. . .] Most key moments of action in Poe conspicuously involve severely restrictive enclosures" (19-20). There is no doubt that Poe is largely indebted to Gothic fiction, as J. Gerald Kennedy reminds us (115).

Among Poe's locations, the house stands as the most important. It is not merely the place people inhabit. There is a clear relationship between the house and the narrators' minds. This has been explained in terms of Freudian and Jungian theories (Bonaparte, Wilbur, and Knapp). The house is a symbol of the mind. As such, it may be understandable that the rooms may symbolize the brain's different areas and functions. Within the house, the library has particular importance. The library, so critical in Poe's fantastic fiction, represents the imaginative function of the human mind. In "Berenice," a story pervaded by the dreamy atmosphere of unreality and imagination, the narrator spends a large part of his life in the library, as he admits. Roderick Usher, the protagonist in "The Fall of the House of Usher," owns a library with a large number of books of fiction. He has not been in the open air for a long time, implying that his life experience is almost exclusively fed by such a room. These two are basically melancholic characters. Others, such as those in "The Black Cat" and "The Tell-Tale Heart," do not mention the library. Instead of an imagination stimulated by a room full of books, their madness is provoked by a cat and an old man's eye. In these two cases, the fantastic does not come from fancy as it was understood during the Romantic period. This poses the question of the power of imagination regarding fantastic fiction. Poe seems to be theorizing and practicing the limits of imagination. His insistence on some rational cause to explain the fantastic seems to indicate that he no longer believes in supernatural theories of the fantastic. At the same time his use of enclosed locations as the appropriate setting for the fantastic seems to point toward a psychological explanation, which is reinforced by the manic character of his narratives.

There are other stories, such as "Ms. Found in a Bottle" and "A Descent into the Maelstrom," located aboard ships at sea. Curiously enough, these stories do not have a psychological explanation for the fantastic. Instead, they are models of mastery in the creation of fantastic short fiction through skilled writing. However, they are distanced from Poe's other stories, since they do not propose a psychological cause to the fantastic. This is quite interesting, as "Ms. Found in a Bottle" was written in a very early stage of his career, probably when he was still hesitant to write about the fantastic. Poe did not, however, leave the psychological totally aside in the story; the narrator mentions opium: "We had also on board coir, jaggeree, ghee, cocoa-nuts, and a few cases of opium" (*CW*, 2: 136). "A Descent into the Maelstrom" is another example of Poe's interest in science as the source of the fantastic. It was also written at an early stage in his career. In the story, there is no hint of a psychological cause. It is in fact a sort of scientific riddle that makes the fantastic function.

The new fantastic, that is the fantastic as practiced by Poe, needed a narrator whose focus was tightly centered on a single event or character. The tight focus was thought of as a means to achieve the unity of effect that is characteristic of the modern short story. Poe examined the ratiocinative method in mystery and science fiction, which simply parallels the psychological aspects of fantastic stories since they all come from the same poetics of the story. Naturally, this implies that Poe had in mind the same ideas for his stories, no matter how they fell into one category or another.

Works Cited

Allen, Michael. *Poe and the British Magazine Tradition.* New York: Oxford University Press, 1969.

Bonaparte, Marie. *The Life and Works of Edgar Allan Poe: A Psychoanalytical Interpretation.* London: Imago, 1949.

Buranelli, Vincent. *Edgar Allan Poe.* Boston: Twayne Publishers, 1977.

Carringer, Robert L. "Circumscription of Space and the Form of Poe's Arthur Gordon Pym." *The Tales of Poe.* Ed. Harold Bloom. New York: Chelsea House Publishers, 1985. 17-24.

Fletcher, Richard M. *The Stylistic Development of Edgar Allan Poe.* The Hague: Mouton, 1973.

Frieden, Ken. "Poe's Narrative Monologues." *The Tales of Poe.* Ed. Harold Bloom. New York: Chelsea House Publishers, 1985. 135-147.

Gargano, James W. "The Question of Poe's Narrators." *Poe: A Collection of Critical Essays.* Ed. Robert Regan. Englewood Cliffs, NJ: Prentice-Hall, 1967. 164-171.

Griffith, Clark. "Poe's 'Ligeia' and the English Romantics." *The Naiad Voice: Essays on Poe's Satiric Hoaxing.* Ed. Dennis W. Eddings. Port Washington, NY: Associated Faculty, 1983. 1-17.

Hammond, J. R. *An Edgar Allan Poe Companion.* Totowa, NJ: Barnes and Noble Books, 1981.

Hoffmann, Gerhard. "Edgar Allan Poe and German Literature." *American-German Literary Interrelations in the Nineteenth Century.* Ed. Christoph Wecker. Munich: Wilhelm Fink Verlag, 1983. 52-104.

Jay, Gregory S. "Poe: Writing and the Unconscious." *The Tales of Poe.* Ed. Harold Bloom. New York: Chelsea House Publishers, 1985. 83-110.

Kennedy, J. Gerald. "Phantasms of Death in Poe's Fiction." *The Tales of Poe.* Ed. Harold Bloom. New York: Chelsea House Publishers, 1985. 111-133.

Knapp, Bettina, L. *Edgar Allan Poe.* New York: Continuum, 1986.

Lawrence, D. H. *Studies in Classic American Literature.* London: Penguin, 1977.

May, Charles. *Edgar Allan Poe: A Study of the Short Fiction.* Boston: Twayne, 1991.

Mills, Bruce. *Poe, Fuller, and the Mesmeric Arts. Transition States in the American Renaissance.* Columbia: University of Missouri Press, 2006.

Peeples, Scott. *Edgar Allan Poe Revisited.* New York: Twayne, 1998.

Poe, Edgar A. *Collected Works.* 3 vols. Ed. Thomas O. Mabbott. Cambridge: Harvard University Press, 1969.

_____. *The Letters of Edgar Allan Poe.* Ed. John Ward Ostrom. New York: Gordian Press, 1966.

_____. *Tales and Sketches.* 2 vols. Ed. Thomas O. Mabbott. Cambridge: The Belknap Press of Harvard University Press, 1978.

Quinn, Patrick F. "A Misreading of Poe's 'The Fall of the House of Usher.'" *Ruined Eden of the Present: Hawthorne, Melville and Poe.* Ed. G. R. Thompson and Virgil Lokke. West Lafayette, IN: Purdue University Press, 1981a. 303-312.

_____. "'Usher' Again: Trust the Teller!" *Ruined Eden of the Present: Hawthorne, Melville and Poe*. Ed. G. R. Thompson and Virgil Lokke. West Lafayette, IN: Purdue University Press, 1981b. 341-353.

Stauffer, Donald Barlow. "Style and Meaning in 'Ligeia' and 'William Wilson.'" *Studies in Short Fiction* 2 (1965): 316-330.

Thompson, G. R. "Poe and the Paradox of Terror: Structures of Heightened Consciousness in 'The Fall of the House of Usher.'" *Ruined Eden of the Present: Hawthorne, Melville and Poe*. Ed. G. R. Thompson and Virgil Lokke. West Lafayette, IN: Purdue University Press, 1981. 313-340.

_____. *Poe's Fiction: Romantic Irony in the Gothic Tales*. Madison: University of Wisconsin Press, 1973.

Todorov, Tzvetan. *The Fantastic: A Structural Approach to a Literary Genre*. Trans. Richard Howard. Ithaca, NY: Cornell University Press, 1975.

Wilbur, Richard. "The House of Poe." *Poe: A Collection of Critical Essays*. Englewood Cliffs, NJ: Prentice-Hall, 1967. 98-120.

Zimmerman, Brett. *Edgar Allan Poe: Rhetoric and Style*. Montreal and Kingston: McGill-Queen's University Press, 2005.

_____. "Sensibility, Phrenology and 'The Fall of the House of Usher.'" *The Edgar Allan Poe Review* 8, no. 1 (2007): 47-56.

CRITICAL
READINGS

Irresistible Impulses:
Edgar Allan Poe and the Insanity Defense_____

John Cleman

Poe's fascination with stories of crime, sometimes gleaned from contemporary newspaper accounts, is obvious enough from such examples as "The Oblong Box" (1844), "The Mystery of Marie Rogêt" (1842-43), and "The Murders in the Rue Morgue" (1841). In these and similar tales Poe's interest centers on the processes of detection, leaving the moral issues of the crimes either largely unaddressed or curiously deflected. "The Murders in the Rue Morgue" presents a rather stark version of this formulation. The crime solved turns out to be no crime at all: the fiend who brutally kills and mutilates an innocent mother and daughter is an orangutan, and neither the beast nor its owner can be held morally responsible. Furthermore, this stripping of moral content seems a purposeful irony or tantalization. The processes of social and legal justice, apparently set in motion by the detective work of both the police and Auguste Dupin, lead to a blank or dissolution where the presumptions of human agency are blurred into an image of instinctive brutality.

Such a treatment can be seen as part of an apparent lack of interest in moral themes throughout Poe's work. As Stuart Levine observes, "It is fair to say that in most of his stories which raise moral issues, Poe's concern is focused elsewhere."[1] To some degree, this seeming indifference to moral issues can be explained by Poe's aesthetic in which the "Moral Sense," "Conscience," and "Duty" have, at best, "only collateral relations" with the primary concerns: for poetry "*The Rhythmical Creation of Beauty*,"[2] and for prose fiction "the unity of effect or impression."[3] Apart from the aesthetic, Poe's emphasis is usually read to center in the psychological or in the exercise of an individual will acting as a microcosm of the Universal Will. Edward Davidson, for example, observes that "Poe removed all moral and religious considerations as far as possible from any social code or body of religious warrants."

Operating in a universe in which there is "no other god but the self as god,"[4] each of the characters "in Poe's moral inquiries is his own moral arbiter, lodged in a total moral anarchy. Society has invented law and justice, but these are mere illusion and exact no true penalty."[5] Similarly, Vincent Buranelli insists, "Poe does not touch morality. Although his aesthetic theory admits that goodness may be a by-product of art, he himself does not look for it. Sin and crime are absent from this part of the universe; and the terrible deeds that abound there are matters of psychology, not of ethics."[6]

Davidson's and Buranelli's readings, characteristic of the general tendency to view Poe's fiction as largely divorced from the social and historical context in which he wrote, pose a particular problem for stories of crime such as "The Murders in the Rue Morgue," especially when the stories center in the mind of the criminal. "Matters of psychology" are inescapably relevant to the formulation of the *mens rea* and, therefore, are crucial to the definition of acts as crimes. Thus, to deflect the significance of a crime from the social and moral to the psychological has a specific social and legal meaning, most apparent in the instance of an insanity defense. Such deflections, in fact, were a significant part of a controversy over the use of the insanity defense in the first half of the nineteenth century, particularly in the early 1840s. Three stories from this period—"The Tell-Tale Heart" (1843), "The Black Cat" (1843), and "The Imp of the Perverse" (1845)—especially invite a reading in the context of the insanity-defense controversy because each of the three tales includes a self-defensive, insane murderer whose story is told within the processes of legal justice.[7] The stories suggest that Poe's narrowed focus on the aberrant psychology of the accused criminal, for whatever it owes to his aesthetic theory, general "otherworldliness," and private demons, also has a locus in specific jurisprudential issues of his day.

In England, the controversy over the increased use of the insanity defense in the first half of the nineteenth century was stimulated by a number of factors.[8] The political nature of the most celebrated cases, especially that of Daniel McNaughton in 1843, argued to many that the defense was undermining civil order.[9] In addition, asylum reform and the increased popularity of what was known as "moral treatment" of the insane certainly contributed to the public perception that to be acquitted on the basis of insanity was to avoid punishment. Through most of the two centuries prior to Pinel's celebrated unchaining of several mentally ill patients at Bicêtre in 1793, the insane were treated very much like criminals, often locked up together in the same prisons, subjected to similar restraints and corporal punishments short of execution.[10] With the reforms, the insane were housed apart from criminals and, to some degree, treated with the compassion and care afforded the physically ill.[11] Finally, there was an increased use of medical testimony in court to determine insanity, corresponding to a broader movement to establish the study of the mind on a scientific basis. This testimony not only presented a strongly deterministic view of human nature; it also described as insane, and therefore not culpable, individuals who gave every appearance of rationality.

Poe's familiarity with the scientific/medical accounts of insanity of his day has been well established,[12] and his awareness of the issues of the insanity-defense controversy can be linked to two specific cases in which the defense was employed, both occurring in the environs of Philadelphia where Poe resided between 1838 and 1844, and both featuring the same attorney, Peter A. Browne, who "had distinguished himself . . . for his great subtilty and deep metaphysical research in the matter of *insanity*."[13] In the first of these, James Wood was acquitted on the grounds of insanity of the deliberate murder of his daughter. Lengthy accounts of the trial appeared daily in the Philadelphia *Public Ledger* from 24 to 30 March 1840, and a comment at its conclusion appearing in the 1 April 1840 issue of *Alexander's Weekly Messenger* has been attributed to Poe.[14]

The second case, the trial of Singleton Mercer, while less directly linked to Poe, signals more clearly the terms of the insanity-defense controversy. Mercer was charged with murdering his sister's seducer in February 1843. Both Mercer and his victim were well-known "men about town"[15] in Philadelphia, and the Philadelphia and New York newspapers carried daily accounts of the court's proceedings, loaded with sensational details of sex, violence, and public corruption.[16] Poe's friend and lifelong supporter George Lippard made direct use of the case in his best-selling novel *Quaker City, or The Monks of Monk Hall* (1844). The fact that a later stage version was banned in Philadelphia out of fear that the attendance of Mercer and his supporters would cause a riot suggests that the case had a long, prominent life in the consciousness of Philadelphians.[17] In short, the Mercer trial was a major part of Philadelphia public life from 1843 to 1845, and it is nearly impossible to imagine Poe not being aware of it.

The importance of the Mercer case for Poe's fiction, however, may be less its notoriety and lurid details than the fact that insanity was made the primary grounds of defense.[18] A complete transcript of Browne's opening remarks on the defense was printed on the front page of the 31 March 1843 issue of the Philadelphia *Public Ledger*. In light of the likelihood that Poe read them, Browne's arguments are interesting and significant because they include a fairly thorough synopsis of the main legal, medical, and philosophical issues underlying the insanity defense. They also reflect the terms of the controversy surrounding its increased use. Thus, at the very least, Browne's remarks provide a window on the public consciousness of the insanity defense—for both Poe and his readers—during the time in which "The Tell-Tale Heart," "The Black Cat," and "The Imp of the Perverse" were written and published.[19]

Several features of Browne's insanity-defense argument have particular significance as a backdrop to the three stories we are considering. In the first place, he begins by directly acknowledging the controversy over the use of the defense. He admits that the defense "has of late become an object of ridicule," in part because it "has been abused, by relying upon it where none [no insanity] existed." He also acknowledges that some may find the ideas supporting his arguments to be either "'new-fangled doctrines'" or, even worse, a "*modern French* notion." His first task, therefore, is to establish the legitimacy of the defense itself, and to do so he will need not only to cite legal principle and precedent but also to undermine the popular suspicion that the concept of the defense is a foreign and speciously sophisticated intrusion into the American world of common sense and plain Christian morality.

More significant, Browne focuses on partial insanity or monomania as the central issue inviting controversy. With regard to the general use of the insanity defense it is enough for him simply to assert, "In all civilized countries, ancient and modern, insanity has been regarded as exempting from punishment." The problem was that up to the end of the eighteenth century the most common test of exculpatory insanity rooted in Christian morality was "the knowledge of good and evil."[20] The equation between reason and the moral sense was nearly absolute, and therefore any sign of rationality—such as appearing calm and reasonable in court, premeditating or planning the crime, or seeking to hide or avoid punishment—demonstrated the presence of an indivisible conscience and concomitant moral responsibility. Thus, to qualify for legal exemption, the mentally defective individual needed to be, in the well-known opinion of one eighteenth-century judge, "a man that is totally deprived of his understanding and memory, and doth not know what he is doing, no more than an infant, than a brute, or a wild beast."[21] Few qualified under this "wild beast" test, and those that did met commonsense, obvious-perception standards of madness. However, as the courts in the nineteenth century began increasingly to accept arguments for an exculpatory *partial* insanity, more qualified for the defense, its use increased, and the accused frequently no longer fit the obvious, commonsense image of insanity. Hence, in large part, the controversy.

Browne cites numerous legal and medical authorities, mostly from the late eighteenth century on, to demonstrate that the equation between rationality and moral responsibility is not absolute. An individual may display considerable powers of intellect on a wide range of subjects, including the planning and execution of his crime, and still not be responsible for his actions. Even the knowledge of good and evil, he insists, is an inadequate test of insanity, for it does not answer the crucial question, whether or not the accused was "incapable of exercising free will." For Browne, the only test of exculpable lunacy is fairly clean-cut: "A lunatic is one 'WHO HAS LOST THE USE OF HIS REASON,'" not totally lost or "deprived of his reason" but "one 'who hath lost the USE of his reason,' which includes those who still having intellect cannot use it, because either their affections or their will are deranged."[22]

A third point suggesting links to Poe is Browne's use of Dr. Isaac Ray, America's leading nineteenth-century authority on medical jurisprudence, cited in the McNaughton trial and best known, perhaps, for developing the theory of "irresistible impulse," a form of "moral insanity." What is interesting here is that his central concept of the human mind—hence the basis of his medical jurisprudence—was grounded in the phrenological theories of Gall and Spurzheim. Ray argued that the moral (affective) and rational (intellectual) functions of the brain were physically separate, located in different mental organs and each independently susceptible to disease and deformation. Thus, an individual suffering a disease of the moral organs could become a victim of "moral insanity" in which "no *delusion* is present to disturb the mental vision" and yet he "finds himself urged, perhaps, to the commission of every outrage, and though perfectly conscious of what he is doing, unable to offer the slightest resistance to the overwhelming power that impels him."[23] To illustrate this, Ray recounts the cases of a number of homicidal maniacs and then concludes that "they all possess one feature in common, the *irresistible, motiveless impulse to destroy life.*"[24]

By the time of Ray's *Treatise*, however, phrenology had become a disreputable science, not only because of the quackery of many of its bump-reading practitioners but also because it had long been recognized as irreligious. Furthermore, when phrenology was employed in insanity-defense cases, conservative legal authorities objected that it provided an argument for excusing all criminal behavior as the result of diseased mental organs. Thus, to one of Ray's leading opponents in the 1850s and 1860s the phrenologically based concept of moral insanity was merely "another name for depravity," a sign of chaotic nature.[25] In writing his *Treatise* Ray consciously sought to play down and hide overt references to phrenology, but the work offered, nevertheless, an essentially deterministic view of the human mind.[26]

Thus, the insanity-defense arguments of the mid-nineteenth century—those such as Browne's which helped provoke the controversy—posited a view of human nature ruled not by reasoned choice but by chance and ultimately mysterious physical forces. Not only was the boundary between the rational and irrational blurred, often wearing the same mask, the grounds for moral responsibility shifted as well. As Browne observed, courts and the public were asked to change their opinion "as to [the] *real nature of actions*, which are either *atrocious crimes*, or the *dreadful effects of disease*."[27] The signalling feature to effect this shift from condemnation to pity was an inexplicable compulsion, an impelling force potential in everyone.

Of the three tales we are considering, "The Tell-Tale Heart" presents the most apparent evidence of Poe's use of the issues of the insanity defense. The characteristic form of all three tales is not confession but self-defense, an attempt to provide a rational account of apparently irrational events and behavior. In "The Tell-Tale Heart" there is a good deal of dramatic immediacy to this defense. The narrator addresses a specific but unnamed "you" sometime after his arrest but obviously before his execution (if there is to be one). His aim is to refute "you"'s claim that he is insane, a charge that has apparently been both specific and formal enough for the narrator to feel the necessity of responding in earnest and in detail. From the abrupt opening ("True!—nervous—very, very dreadfully nervous I had been and am: but why *will* you say that I am mad?") to the final dramatic breakdown ("and now—again!—hark! louder! louder! louder! *louder!*") the narration seems more spoken than written, something like a courtroom outburst or final statement of the accused.[28]

The point of suggesting such a context for the tale's telling is to underscore a particular significance of the narrator's insistence on his own sanity. The argument he offers reflects the issues of the insanity-defense controversy, both in the way he measures his own state of mind and in the type of madman he reveals himself to be. His argument echoes the terms by which an eighteenth-century prosecutor, employing the "wild beast" test of insanity, might have differentiated the accused (himself) from the recognizably nonculpable madman. Such madmen, according to the narrator, are mentally defective ("Madmen know nothing"), physically impaired ("senses . . . destroyed . . . dulled"), incapable of wisdom or "sagacity" (pp. 792-93) in planning, at the mercy of impulse and passion. He, on the other hand, exhibited unmistakable signs of rational behavior in the way he carried out his crime: note, he repeatedly insists, "how wisely I proceeded—with what caution—with what foresight." He also asks the auditor to "observe how healthily—how calmly" he "can tell you the whole story." Thus, insofar as the narrator is manifestly not a "wild beast," the "prosecutor's argument" succeeds: the narrator is capable of reason and is, therefore, morally and legally responsible for his acts.

Of course, in telling his tale, particularly if imagined as a statement in court, the narrator is also offering clear evidence that he is by contemporary standards partially insane. Like the many monomaniacs Browne describes, the narrator has a highly developed intellect, is capable of planning and remembering his actions in great detail, but his intellect and energies are fixed unreasonably on a single goal or "one dominant idea" (the old man's "vulture eye") "that rides roughshod over his brain—that haunts him day and night until it is granted."[29] Elizabeth Phillips has demonstrated that the narrator resembles the homicidal maniacs described by Ray and Rush in several respects, including his singular lack of rational motive, his unusual cruelty, his remaining at the scene of the crime, his symptoms of delusions and hallucinations, and his acuteness of the senses, headaches, and ringing in the ears.[30] However, the most convincing proof of his insanity seems to be the very mask of sanity he purports to wear. Ray argued that "madness is not indicated so much by any particular extravagance of thought or feeling, as by a well-marked change of character or departure from the ordinary habits of thinking, feeling and acting, without any adequate external cause."[31] Thus, the narrator's calmness, deliberateness, and rationality signal insanity insofar as they are at variance with his "normal" state ("very, very dreadfully nervous I had been and am"), particularly as that is revealed in the frenetic last few paragraphs. Even the narrator's insistent denial of the charge of insanity fits the pattern of symptoms of the homicidal maniac, so that the act of the tale's telling and its self-defensive posture constitute evidence in a determination of partial insanity.[32]

The irony of ostensible sanity signalling insanity could not have been lost on Poe, for this parallels his point in "The Trial of James Wood." Poe does not question Wood's acquittal but believes that the defense "omitted . . . an argument which, with many minds, would have had more weight in bringing about a conviction of the prisoner's insanity than any urged in his behalf." Poe reasons that Wood's calm, rational deliberation when he purchased the pistols used to kill his daughter, the signs that, "upon a cursory view . . . do certainly make against the accused, and imply a premeditated and cold-blooded assassination," are the clear signs of insanity "to the metaphysician, or the skilful medical man." Following Ray, the specific basis for this claim is that Wood's "remarkable calmness" was at variance with "his usual nervous habit" and the "cause for agitation which he is known to have had." More generally, Poe extols "the cunning of the maniac—a cunning which baffles that of the wisest man of sound mind—the amazing self-possession with which at times, he assumes the demeanor, and preserves the appearance, of perfect sanity."[33]

Brigham and Mabbott may be right in suggesting that Poe drew on the James Wood trial in writing "The Tell-Tale Heart," but if so, the important points are Poe's fascination with rational behavior as evidence "bringing about a conviction of . . . insanity"[34] and his awareness of the consequences of that determination. Poe points out that Wood's acquittal "on the ground of insanity" meant his "legal confinement as a madman until such time as the Court satisfy themselves of his return to sound mind," a time Poe believes and hopes will never come: "His monomania is essentially periodical; and a perfect sanity for months, or even years, would scarcely be a sufficient guaranty for his subsequent conduct. A time would still come when there would be laid to his charge another—although hardly a more horrible—deed of sudden violence and bloodshed."[35] In light of this concern, Poe's interest in the "cunning of the maniac" in simulating "perfect sanity" has more than clinical or literary significance: properly recognized it may convict the accused of insanity, but it thereby acquits him of murder and offers the possibility of his ultimate release to murder again.

In "The Tell-Tale Heart" the outcome is less certain, but the same concerns seem to apply. If the narrator demonstrates his own insanity paralleling the homicidal mania evidenced by Wood, then the telling of the tale would seem to lead to acquittal and to an uneasily indeterminate incarceration. In this light, the death wish many critics have described as the essence of the narrator's compulsions to crime and confession would seem to be thwarted or deflected.[36] But, if the evidence of the narrator's insanity seems clear, it is difficult to read the story with the sense that he is exonerated because of it: the recognition of his madness does not convert his condemnable "*atrocious crimes*" to pitiable "*effects of disease.*" This may be due in part to the pride and arrogance of the narrator's intellect. It is due even more to the way the elements of the madness figure in the acts themselves. If, as Browne insists, the key test of exculpable insanity is the loss of the "USE" of reason, the most mysterious, unreasoned, and irresistible act in the story is the act of confession. In this way, Poe inverts or re-deflects the central argument of the insanity defense so that compulsion accounts not for the crime but for the exposure of the crime and its perpetrator.

The pattern of the narrator seeking to defend his rationality but revealing instead his partial insanity is replicated in "The Black Cat." In this case, the issue of a charge of insanity is more oblique and subtle. It is suggested initially by the "indeed" in his opening observation: "For the most wild, yet most homely narrative which I am about to pen, I neither expect nor solicit belief. Mad indeed would I be to expect it." The implication of this seems to be that some have thought him mad, either for his acts or, perhaps, for his babblings about a persecuting demon cat. Or, at least, by laying his account of events before the bar of reason he is inviting the charge of insanity. Like the narrator of "The Tell-Tale Heart," he is self-conscious of the imputation that something either in the nature of the events he recounts or in the manner of his relating them will signal mental imbalance. Thus, he describes his narrative as "mere household events" (p. 849) that have "presented little but Horror" to him but "to many . . . will seem less terrible than *baroques*" (p. 850). "Hereafter," he hopes, "some intellect may be found which will reduce my phantasm to the commonplace—some intellect more calm, logical, and far less excitable than my own, which will perceive, in the circumstances I detail with awe, nothing more than an ordinary succession of very natural causes and effects."

In "The Black Cat" this attempt at rational explanation also reveals a pattern of madness that in certain respects parallels the monomania in "The Tell-Tale Heart." In the narrator's perception of the images of a cat on the wall of the burnt house and of a gallows on the breast of Pluto's successor, both of which he interprets as signs of a demonic persecution, we may recognize elements of delusion. His increasingly obsessive fear and hatred of the cats is also, like "The Tell-Tale Heart" narrator's excess of rational planning, a motiveless distortion and perversion of what might seem an otherwise healthy human impulse, his special fondness for animals. It is important to recognize the terms of this distortion, for while the narrator's criminal behavior may be blamed on "the Fiend Intemperance," a case of *mania a potu*,[37] the primary agents of his criminal fate were part of his nature, an excess of his distinguishing virtues: as he asserts, "From my infancy I was noted for the docility and humanity of my disposition. My tenderness of heart was even so conspicuous as to make me the jest of my companions." Whether or not because of this teasing, he indicates that he became "especially fond of animals," devoted most of his time to his pets, and "never was so happy as when feeding and caressing them." What is clearly a preference for animal over human companionship, he says, "grew with my growth, and, in my manhood, I derived from it one of my principal sources of pleasure." That this preference is in some degree *anti*-human can be recognized in his assertion, "There is something in the unselfish self-sacrificing love of a brute, which goes directly to the heart of him who has had frequent occasion to test the paltry friendship and gossamer fidelity of mere *Man*" (p. 850).

Clearly there is an imbalance in the narrator's makeup. His exceptional sweetness can find a reciprocating perfection of fidelity and kindness only in the mindless devotion of animals. Although no "wild beast" himself, the narrator ironically exhibits his monomania in attributing the values of both good and evil to the bestial. It is in this regard that the play of issues recognizable in the insanity-defense controversy becomes particularly interesting. The narrator, by his own account, is driven to his crimes by an irrational compulsion which he calls "the spirit of PERVERSENESS." This spirit, "one of the primitive impulses of the human heart—one of the indivisible primary faculties, or sentiments, which give direction to the character of Man," is defined as a principle of negation, the "unfathomable longing of the soul *to vex itself*—to offer violence to its own nature—to do wrong for the wrong's sake only." That this "irresistible impulse" has nullified his will against the dictates of a still viable conscience is manifest when he hangs Pluto, as he says, "*because* I knew that it had loved me, and *because* I felt it had given me no reason of offence;—hung it *because* I knew that in so doing I was committing a sin—a deadly sin that would so jeopardize my immortal soul as to place it—if such a thing were possible—even beyond the infinite mercy of the Most Merciful and Most Terrible God" (p. 852).

On these grounds we might recognize an exculpatory partial insanity, but as in the case of "The Tell-Tale Heart," the effect is other. Just as the narrator locates his early inordinate kindness in the love of animals, his explanation of perverseness locates an aspect of moral behavior in the irrational innocence of compulsion. It should be remembered that the concept of mind underlying the shift from a "wild beast" test of insanity to a test recognizing an exculpable partial insanity widened the domain of the bestial by widening the range of innocence. As if to expose this expansion, Poe develops the play of good and evil, of reason and madness, all centering on the animal, the cat: object, agent, and emblem. It is killing the cat that torments the narrator's conscience, that makes him believe he is beyond God's mercy. By contrast, when he kills his wife he shows almost no signs of remorse. He sets forth "with entire deliberation" to hide her body, and when he believes that concealment safely accomplished and the cat has fled the premises, he admits, "The guilt of my dark deed disturbed me but little" (p. 858). It is the first cat's innocence that drives him perversely to murder the beast, and with its unconscious markings it is the second cat that prefigures his fate and goads him to meet it. As agent of the narrator's fate and chief emblem of his monomania, the cat is to him "the hideous beast, whose craft had seduced me into murder, and whose informing voice had consigned me to the hangman" (p. 859).

Thus, in "The Black Cat" Poe would seem again to undermine the insanity-defense argument in several ways. Paralleling the pattern in "The Tell-Tale Heart," the moral insanity of the narrator, the derangement of the affections that leads him to murder his wife out of a deflected rage against a cat, becomes in the figure of that cat the means to his exposure and punishment, the agent not of exculpation but of a kind of poetic justice. Furthermore, the arguments that locate all the terms of good and evil in the *brute beast* (p. 856) are the self-serving rationalizations of a madman. This is even more interestingly the case with the concept of "perverseness," which, like the arguments of Ray and other medical authorities, is presented as a logical, "philosophical" explanation that voids overtly immoral acts of their moral implications.

The sense in which perverseness ironically echoes the moral terms of the insanity-defense arguments and achieves a form of justice is presented more clearly, albeit more intricately, in "The Imp of the Perverse." The structure of the narrative resembles the patterns of the other two stories in that the narrator's overt aim is to make the apparently unreasonable reasonable, to ground the irrational in reason and logic. As in "The Tell-Tale Heart," the narrator addresses a "you," an unnamed second-person auditor/reader. He hopes to "assign to you something that shall have at least the faint aspect of a cause for" his "wearing these fetters, and . . . tenanting this cell of the condemned," so that "you" will not misunderstand him or "with the rabble" (pp. 1223-24) fancy him mad. The "cause" he refers to is perverseness, and the theory of mind that he uses to account for it is phrenology. One significance of the narrator's use of phrenology is that the allusion to the scientific/ medical underpinnings for the insanity defense, perhaps implicit in "The Black Cat,"[38] is made fairly specific in "The Imp of the Perverse." This allusion seems underscored by the narrator's distinction between perverseness and a "modification of that which ordinarily springs from the *combativeness* of phrenology" (p. 1221), for it was precisely accounts of such modifications, caused by childhood diseases or head injuries, that phrenologists used to explain how criminal actions were the result of mental illness. Pointedly and ironically, in "The Imp of the Perverse" the narrator's phrenological analysis argues for a healthy, "normal" organ of perverseness rather than a damaged organ of some other kind to account for destructive behavior. Also, as in "The Tell-Tale Heart" and "The Black Cat," the narrator aims less to account for his criminal actions than to make rational his irrational compulsion to expose them: phrenology becomes the science of inexplicable confessions.

The irony of this shifting of the "scientific" arguments of the insanity defense is even more significantly felt in the way it mirrors the radical alteration of moral perceptions Browne sought to effect for Singleton Mercer, that is, to convert his condemnable "*atrocious crimes*" to pitiable "*effects of disease.*" Such an alteration involves an excision of the moral content of ostensibly evil acts, a deflection of focus from the apparent value and meaning of the accused's actions—particularly their horrific aspect—to the physiological-psychological mechanisms that impelled them. Perhaps more than in either "The Tell-Tale Heart" or "The Black Cat," in "The Imp of the Perverse" the narrator is strikingly indifferent to the moral content or even the details of his crime. He does take some pride in his "deliberation" over "the means of the murder," but he trivializes the killing itself by devoting little space to it, describing the details as "impertinent" (p. 1224) and only hinting casually at a perfectly rational and culpable motive—greed. As in the insanity defense, what has redirected focus away from the killing and all but effaced its moral content has been a preoccupation with "the *prima mobilia* of the human soul" (p. 1219). Put in terms of Poe's narrative strategy, a tale of greed and murder is reformed as an article on a quasi-scientific subject, the vitalizing human actions and motives approached so indirectly, the interest so redirected, as nearly to obliterate them altogether.

A final ironic turn on the insanity defense can be seen in the way Poe plays on the argument made by some critics of the defense that phrenology could be used to explain all criminal acts as the result of brain disease or injury. In the narrator's phrenology, perverseness is identified or proven not "*a priori*" by assumptions of God's mind or purposes, but "*a posteriori*" from an examination of "what man usually or occasionally did, and was always occasionally doing" (pp. 1219-20). Such an argument, of course, can be seen as a madman's fashioning universals out of his own insane proclivities. Nevertheless, the important point is that for Poe, as for the narrator, perverseness is clearly a propensity with a moral aspect or role. On the one hand, a "*mobile* without motive, a motive not *motivirt*," perverseness is a value-neutral "paradoxical something" that arises as the dialectically opposed concomitant of another principle or impulse. On the other hand, it is characterized as "an innate and primitive principle" to do ill or harm, the "overwhelming tendency to do wrong for the wrong's sake." He suggests that "we might, indeed, deem this perverseness a direct instigation of the archfiend, were it not occasionally known to operate in furtherance of good" (p. 1223). In this regard, one effect of the narrator's argument is to extend the range of phrenology to account for all acts, including all crimes, in terms of determined behavior.

But Poe's perverseness differs in operation from the theories of his narrators. That is, as set up or explained by the narrators in both "The Imp of the Perverse" and "The Black Cat," perverseness appears to be malign and destructive, but the stories' action demonstrates it to be ultimately beneficent and restorative. The effect seems comparable to the kind of justice achieved in such stories as "The Cask of Amontillado" (1846) and "Hop-Frog" (1849), not a personal vendetta but a vengeance inherent in the Universe, "*graven . . . within the hills, and . . . upon the dust within the rock.*"[39] Considered as *"prima mobilia"* of the human soul—a constitutive feature of existence—perverseness seems to reflect the apocalyptic vision of Poe's *Eureka* in which the something-thingness of existence predicates a prior nothingness, differentiation predicates a prior unity, and "*all* phaenomena [of existence] are referable to" the twinned principles of "'*attraction'* and '*repulsion.*'"[40] Such a vision, like the arguments underlying the concept of moral insanity, posits a universe that seems both deterministic and without clear moral order, one in which such stable categories as right and wrong, reason and unreason, are obliterated or, at least, blurred. But, for Poe, such a vision is at every point, in each side of every dialectic, a projection of God's will and ultimate purpose to return to the "normal" state of original Unity.[41] This indeed seems the case with perverseness, a principle of balancing negation inherent in the nature of existence, overriding will and antithetical to reason, a primary, indivisible determinant of human behavior whose effect is to address without motive or exterior purpose the horror of the trivialized murder, to secure, in other words, a form of justice through retribution.

At least in the three stories we have considered, Poe's centering of interest in "matters of psychology" can be understood not as indifference to moral issues but as a play on the treatment of those issues in the context of the insanity-defense controversy of his day. Whereas the insanity defense sought to alter radically the moral content of brutal acts, Poe's perverseness and the parallel confession compulsions in "The Tell-Tale Heart" and "The Black Cat" effect a radical restoration of their moral consequences. Both utilize a concept of obliterated will and "loss of the use of reason"—an aberration of normality in the insanity defense, a normality of aberration in Poe's perverseness. But, as if responding to the unsettling resolution of successful insanity defenses, the apparently incongruous disjunction between brutal acts and a response of pity or sympathy, Poe's deterministic forces lead the guilty to the hangman.

From *American Literature* 63, no. 4 (December 1991): 623-640. Copyright © 1991 by Duke University Press. Reprinted by permission of Duke University Press.

Notes

1. *Edgar Poe: Seer and Craftsman* (DeLand, Fla.: Everett/Edwards, 1972), p. 181.

2. "The Poetic Principle," *Edgar Allan Poe: Essays and Reviews*, ed. G. R. Thompson (New York: Library of America, 1984), p. 78.

3. Rev. of *Twice-Told Tales* by Nathaniel Hawthorne, Thompson, p. 576.

4. *Poe: A Critical Study* (Cambridge: Harvard Univ. Press, 1957), pp. 190, 194.

5. Davidson, p. 194.

6. *Edgar Allan Poe* (New Haven: College and University Press, 1961), p. 72.

7. Citations for "The Tell-Tale Heart," "The Black Cat," and "The Imp of the Perverse" will be to *Tales and Sketches, 1843-1849*, ed. Thomas Ollive Mabbott, Vol. 3 of *Collected Works of Edgar Allan Poe* (Cambridge: Harvard Univ. Press, 1978) and will be included within the text.

8. See Roger Smith, "The Boundary Between Insanity and Criminal Responsibility in Nineteenth-Century England," in *Madhouses, Mad-Doctors and Madmen: The Social History of Psychiatry in the Victorian Era*, ed. Andrew Scull (Philadelphia: Univ. of Pennsylvania Press, 1981), p. 365.

9. See Thomas Maeder, *Crime and Madness: The Origins and Evolution of the Insanity Defense* (New York: Harper & Row, 1985). The trials referred to are those of James Hadfield (1800), John Bellingham (1812), and Edward Oxford (1840). In the

McNaughton case, the accused had bungled an attempt to assassinate the Prime Minister, Robert Peel, shooting instead Peel's private secretary. The event occurred during the period of the Chartist uprisings and was thought by some to be part of a political conspiracy. McNaughton's acquittal so outraged the British public that the House of Lords was directed to devise guidelines in determining culpable insanity in order to prevent such acquittals in the future. These guidelines are known and still cited as the "McNaughton Rules."

10. Michel Foucault, *Madness and Civilization: A History of Insanity in the Age of Reason*, trans. Richard Howard (1961; New York: Vintage-Random, 1988). See especially chap. 2, "The Great Confinement," pp. 38-64.

11. Poe satirizes these reforms in "The System of Doctor Tarr and Professor Fether."

12. See Levine; Elizabeth Phillips, "Mere Household Events: The Metaphysics of Mania," *Edgar Allan Poe: An American Imagination* (Port Washington, N.Y.: Kennikat, 1979), pp. 97-137; and Allan Smith, "The Psychological Context of Three Tales by Poe," *Journal of American Studies*, 7 (1973), 279-92.

13. "By the Southern Mail: The Trial of Singleton Mercer for the Murder of Hutchinson Heberton," *New York Herald*, 29 March 1843, p. 2.

14. Charles S. Brigham in his edition of *Edgar Allan Poe's Contributions to "Alexander's Weekly Messenger"* (Worcester, Mass.: American Antiquarian Soc., 1943) describes this report of Wood's trial as "distinctly by Poe" (p. 64). See also Mabbott, p. 798.

15. Joseph Jackson, "George Lippard: Misunderstood Man of Letters," *Pennsylvania Magazine of History and Biography*, 59 (1935) 383.

16. A special "Double Number" supplement of the Philadelphia *Dollar Newspaper* devoted entirely to the Mercer trial was issued on 4 April 1843, the day before the regular edition of the same weekly announced the short-story prize-contest to which Poe submitted "The Gold Bug."

17. See David S. Reynolds, *George Lippard* (Boston: Twayne, 1982), pp. 10-11.

18. Justifiable homicide was actually the first point of defense, insanity the second, but the judge's instructions to the jury virtually negated the argument that the murder was justified ("Trial of Singleton Mercer," *Public Ledger*, 7 April 1843, p. 2).

19. In America, the Mercer case caused more of a sensation than did the McNaughton trial, but the two were frequently linked as symptomatic of a decline in law and order. For example, in the view of one contributor to the *New York Herald*, "The trials and acquittals of McNaughton, Mercer, and [Alexander] McKenzie, are all pregnant illustrations of the same general fact—the growing and alarming laxity in the administration of criminal justice" ("Administration of Criminal justice," 19 April 1843, p. 2). See also "Licentiousness and Crime," *New-York Daily Tribune*, 13 April 1843, p. 2; "Criminal Justice" by An Old-Fashioned Fellow, Letter, *New York Herald*, 15 April 1843, p. 2; and "Murder Made Honorable," *Public Ledger*, 18 May 1843, p. 2.

20. Maeder, p. 7.

21. Browne quotes Justice Tracy from the trial of Edward ("Mad Ned") Arnold in 1724. See Maeder, pp. 10-11.

22. "Trial of Singleton Mercer," *Public Ledger*, 31 March 1843, p. 2.

23. *A Treatise on The Medical Jurisprudence of Insanity*, ed. Winfred Overholser (Cambridge: Harvard Univ. Press, 1962), p. 43.

24. Ray, p. 169.

25. S. P. Fullinwider, "Insanity as the Loss of Self: The Moral Insanity Controversy Revisited," *Bulletin of the Institute of the History of Medicine*, 49 (Spring 1975), 94.

26. John Starett Hughes, *In the Law's Darkness: Isaac Ray and the Medical Jurisprudence of Insanity in Nineteenth-Century America* (New York: Oceana, 1986), pp. 18-19.

27. "Trial of Singleton Mercer," *Public Ledger*, 31 March 1843, p. 1.

28. Reports of the trial of Benjamin White in January 1843—shortly after the first publication of "The Tell-Tale Heart"—offer striking parallels to Poe's tale. In court White admitted killing his father, rejected the argument of insanity that had been the basis of his lawyer's defense, and insisted on the rationality of his motives and actions, but he became clearly agitated and irrational while recounting his feelings about the victim. ("A Willful Murder of a Father by his own Son—the Effects of Infidelity and Irreligion," *New York Herald*, 4 April 1843, p. 1).

29. "Trial of Singleton Mercer," *Public Ledger*, 31 March 1843, p. 1.

30. Phillips, pp. 128-30.

31. Ray, p. 110.

32. Ray, p. 170.

33. Brigham, pp. 63, 64.

34. Brigham, p. 63.

35. Brigham, p. 64. Poe's language here closely parallels that of the summation of the trial in the *Public Ledger* ("The Case of Wood," 30 March 1840, p. 2).

36. J. Gerald Kennedy, *Poe, Death and the Life of Writing* (New Haven: Yale Univ. Press, 1987), pp. 134-35.

37. Phillips, pp. 131-36.

38. In the discussion of perverseness after the sentence, "Of this spirit philosophy takes no account," the earliest published version of "The Black Cat" includes the line, "Phrenology finds no place for it among its organs" (Mabbott, p. 852).

39. *The Narrative of Arthur Gordon Pym*, in *Edgar Allan Poe: Poetry and Tales*, ed. Patrick F. Quinn (New York: Library of America, 1984), p. 1182.

40. "*Eureka*: A Prose Poem," Thompson, p. 1282.

41. Joseph Moldenhauer argues similarly in linking Poe's moral and aesthetic visions with the cosmology of *Eureka* ("Murder as a Fine Art: Basic Connections between Poe's Aesthetics, Psychology, and Moral Vision," *PMLA*, 83 [1968], 284-97).

The Limits of Reason:
Poe's Deluded Detectives_____

J. Gerald Kennedy

In a canon of fiction preponderantly devoted to terror, madness, disease, death, and revivification, Poe's tales of ratiocination provide a revealing counterpoint in their idealization of reason and sanity. During the productive years 1841-44, Poe explored the theme of rational analysis in various ways: the three adventures of C. Auguste Dupin—"The Murders in the Rue Morgue" (1841), "The Mystery of Marie Rogêt" (1842-43), and "The Purloined Letter" (1844)—established the prototype of the modern detective story by focusing on the investigative methods of a master sleuth. Ratiocination led William Legrand to buried treasure in "The Gold Bug" (1843) and enabled the narrator of "'Thou Art the Man'" (1844) to solve a backwoods murder; analytical operations figured less prominently in "A Descent into the Maelstrom" (1841) and "A Tale of the Ragged Mountains" (1844). But publication of "The Purloined Letter" marked the last of Poe's investigative fiction; none of the tales after 1844 returned to the subject of ratiocination. Two basic questions to be considered here, then, are why Poe initially became interested in the detective story, and why, after the technical achievement of "The Purloined Letter," he abandoned the genre, reverting to the familiar materials of horror and the grotesque.

The significance of Poe's ratiocinative phase can perhaps be best understood in the context of his broader thematic concerns. The search for the figure in Poe's fictional carpet has produced myriad interpretations: Patrick F. Quinn has termed the Doppelgänger motif the "most characteristic and persistent" of Poe's fantasies, while Edward H. Davidson states that the "central bifurcation" in Poe lies between "two sides of the self, between emotion and intellect, feeling and the mind." Harry Levin sees the essential Poe hero as an "underground man" embodying "reason in madness," while more recently, Daniel Hoffman has identified "duplicity" or "the doubleness of experience" as Poe's chief theme.[1] Behind the evident diversity of opinion about Poe's fundamental fictional concerns looms a point of focus: the author's preoccupation with the relationship between the mind, or rational consciousness, and the sensational influence of the world beyond the self. Constantly in Poe's fiction irrational forces and inexplicable phenomena threaten "the monarch Thought's dominion." In an important sense, his serious tales return continually to the process of reason—the way in which the mind orders and interprets its perceptions. Poe's narrators repeatedly seek a clarification of experience, only to discover, in the tales of terror, that rational explanation is not possible.

The condition of terror and uncertainty does not obtain, however, in the tales of ratiocination. Joseph Wood Krutch once lapsed into the assertion that "Poe invented the detective story in order that he might not go mad."[2] The biographical fallacy aside, however, it is true that the ratiocinative tales posit a vision of reason and order not elsewhere evident in Poe's fiction. His detective hero, engaged in "that moral activity which *disentangles*,"[3] not only restores law and order to the world of mundane human affairs; he also explains the seemingly inexplicable, thereby demonstrating the ultimate comprehensibility of the world beyond the self. While the Gothic protagonist typically succumbs to a paroxysm of fear, uncertainty, or madness, the ratiocinator discerns the causes behind effects, proving that nature's laws are accessible to the man of reason. The emergence of this man of reason and his eventual disappearance from Poe's fiction can be observed in "The Man of the Crowd" (1840) and "The Oblong Box" (1844), tales which respectively signal the beginning and end of Poe's ratiocinative cycle.

I

Though it is impossible to determine the origin of Poe's ratiocinative interests (his 1835 essay on "Maelzel's Chess-Player" reveals an early analytical bent), the appearance of nine "Unpublished Passages from the Life of Vidocq, the French Minister of Police" in *Burton's*

Gentleman's Magazine (Sept., 1838-May, 1839) likely helped to stimulate his curiosity about the investigation of crime. According to Valentine Williams, Vidocq was Poe's "fount of inspiration"[4]; and if Poe had not already read Vidocq's *Mémoires* in the 1828 translation of George Borrow, he surely saw the installments in the *Gentleman's Magazine* (of which he became editor in June, 1839). Poe's onerous duties with the magazine apparently hindered his fictional efforts, for after the splendid narratives of the late thirties—"Ligeia," "The Fall of the House of Usher," and "William Wilson"—the first tales of the new decade showed little imagination.[5] However "The Man of the Crowd," the first tale published after Poe's break with Burton, gave evidence of both renewed intensity and a developing fascination with what Poe later called "the principles of investigation."[6]

Long one of Poe's most perplexing tales, "The Man of the Crowd" presents, outwardly at least, another version of the Doppelgänger motif employed in "William Wilson." Yet the theme of the double is inverted significantly: rather than flee his malevolent counterpart, the narrator of "The Man of the Crowd" actively pursues his double, seeking knowledge of the man's inner nature through a detective-like scrutiny of his outward appearance and behavior. Critical interpretation of the tale has dealt primarily with the symbolic importance of the aged peripatetic: Quinn terms the stranger a "prophetic image" of the narrator's "future self," while Davidson argues that he represents "man's abandonment of the moral prescription within which he is supposed to live." Herbert Rauter in turn links the old man to the idea of disintegration, identifying him as one of Poe's *"ruhelosen Wanderern zwischen Leben und Tod."*[7] But critical emphasis on the significance of the stranger has perhaps obscured the real conflict in the tale: the psychological tension between the narrator's detached, analytical view of human experience and his mounting subjective fascination with the "man of the crowd."

As the tale immediately preceding "The Murders in the Rue Morgue," "The Man of the Crowd" stands as a transitional work between the haunting Gothic tales of the late thirties and the ratiocinative fiction of the early forties, possessing obvious qualities of both. The opening paragraphs portray a narrator suffering, like many of Poe's characters, from an indefinable mental excitation. Recovering from an unspecified illness, he derives a febrile pleasure "even from many of the legitimate sources of pain" (IV, 135), and though his mind is literally working at a fever pitch, he compares his heightened awareness to "the vivid yet candid reason of Leibnitz," the German philosopher whose vision of a rationally designed universe of cause and effect was satirized (as Poe punningly reminds us) in Voltaire's *Candide*. The narrator appropriately identifies himself with the Enlightenment tradition, for he too seeks a rational, scientific clarification of experience. Analyzing pedestrians passing before the window of a London coffeehouse, he remarks, "At first my observations took an abstract and generalizing turn. I looked at the passengers in masses, and thought of them in their aggregate relations. Soon, however, I descended to details, and regarded with minute interest the innumerable varieties of figure, dress, air, gait, visage, and expression of countenance" (IV, 135). Much like Sherlock Holmes, Poe's narrator infers from precise observation the occupations of passersby; for example, the "upper clerks of staunch firms" are known "by their coats and pantaloons of black or brown, made to sit comfortably, with white cravats and waistcoats, broad solid-looking shoes, and thick hose or gaiters.—They had all slightly bald heads, from which the right ears, long used to pen-holding, had an odd habit of standing off on end. . . . They always removed or settled their hats with both hands, and wore watches, with short gold chains of a substantial and ancient pattern" (IV, 136-37).

Belief in his perceptiveness tempts the narrator to a more dramatic claim: "In my then peculiar mental state, I could frequently read, even in that brief interval of a glance, the history of long years" (IV, 139)— anticipating Dupin's boast in "The Murders in the Rue Morgue" that "most men, in respect to himself, wore windows in their bosoms" (IV, 152). But the narrator of "The Man of the Crowd" is no Dupin. The narrative in fact disproves his claim that he can "read" men's lives, a circumstance foreshadowed in the opening lines: "It was well said of a certain German book that 'es lässt sich nicht lesen'—it does not permit itself to be read. There are some secrets which do not permit themselves to be told" (IV, 134). In a key essay, James W. Gargano notes that Poe "often so designs his tales as to show his narrators' limited comprehension of their own problems and states of mind."[8] The ironic structure Gargano finds in tales like "Ligeia" and "The Tell-Tale Heart" also appears to inform "The Man of the Crowd," where the narrator, a would-be detective, essentially demonstrates his failure to grasp the "principles of investigation" later used by Dupin.

This failure occurs primarily because the narrator cannot maintain a critical detachment; he confesses, "As the night deepened, so deepened to me the interest of the scene" (IV, 139). The transformation of the crowd, whose "gentler features" give way to "harsher ones," corresponds to a subtle shift in the narrator's attitude from dispassionate objectivity to subjective fascination. By his own admission, the "wild effects" of the gas lamps have "enchained" him to "an examination of individual faces." Gradually fancy subverts abstract reason. Like many of Poe's Gothic protagonists, he falls under the influence of vague sensations; the rational mode of cognition is steadily undermined by irrational impulses. In such a state he glimpses the face of the old man, significantly regarding it in imaginative rather than analytical terms: "I well remember that my first thought, upon beholding it, was that Retzsch, had he viewed it, would have greatly preferred it to his own pictural incarnations of the fiend" (IV, 140). Wishing to remain ratiocinative, the narrator struggles "to form some analysis" of the haunting visage but receives only conflicting impressions of "vast mental power, of caution, of penuriousness, of avarice, of coolness, of malice, of blood-thirstiness, of triumph, of merriment, of excessive terror, of intense—of supreme despair." Overwhelmed by a "craving desire" to keep the stranger in sight, he quits his observation post—the coffeehouse window—to plunge into the chaos of the streets, symbolically abandoning a detached, analytical perspective for a more visceral involvement in the world of human striving.

While the narrator's account of his nocturnal adventure draws attention to the stranger's peculiar and seemingly perverse actions, it simultaneously reveals, on another level of understanding, the egotism and self-deception of the narrator. Much like the narrator of "The Tell-Tale Heart," whose "sagacity" betrays his madness, the aspiring sleuth exposes his foolishness even as he celebrates his investigative prowess. One of the many delusions plaguing the narrator is his intuition that the stranger (an incarnation of "the fiend") conceals a terrible secret: "How wild a history," the narrator assumes, "is written within that bosom!" Predictably, his perceptions begin to "confirm" his suspicions; close examination of the man leads him to remark, "My vision deceived me, or, through a rent in a closely-buttoned and evidently second-handed *roquelaire* which enveloped him, I caught a glimpse both of a diamond and of a dagger" (IV, 140-41). The tantalizing ambivalence of his statement, like the description of the ruby-colored drops in "Ligeia," reveals more about the narrator's state of mind than about the physical reality of the situation. Entering a realm of fantasy and hallucination (objectified in the nightmarish cityscape), the narrator believes he has seen, by the "fitful and garish lustre" of gas lamps, emblems of the old man's sinister nature. Unlike Dupin, who calmly withholds judgment until the evidence has been weighed, he begins his investigation already convinced, by the illogic of the subconscious, that the old man is somehow evil.[9]

The narrator's second major delusion arises from his method of surveillance. Throughout the latter portions of the tale, he refers frequently to his own stealth, as if to reassure both the reader and himself. He speaks of following the man "closely, yet cautiously, so as not to attract his attention" (IV, 140) and says again, "Never once turning his head to look back, he did not observe me" (IV, 141). He later remarks, "It required much caution on my part to keep him within reach without attracting his observation" (IV, 142). A fourth insistence on his discretion—"At no moment did he see that I watched him" (IV, 142)—produces ironic reverberations of the sort heard in "The Tell-Tale Heart." The narrator's "stealth" is moreover called into question by his constant proximity to the stranger: he follows closely enough to study the texture of the man's clothing; he walks "close at his elbow" for half an hour; he pursues him through "many crooked and peopleless lanes." At length he even adopts the plural pronoun: "A blaze of light burst upon our sight, and we stood before one of the huge suburban temples of Intemperance" (IV, 144). That the narrator has actually escaped detection seems unlikely, particularly in light of numerous references to the stranger's visage—to the eyes that "rolled wildly from under his knit brows," to his "wild and vacant stare," to the "intense agony of his countenance"—which indicate that the narrator has been virtually face to face with his counterpart.

Significantly, just after the half-hour at the "elbow" of the stranger, the narrator notes a change in behavior: the wanderer crosses and recrosses streets "without apparent aim," retraces his path around a square several times, and then wheels about "with a sudden movement." An obvious explanation for the man's singular conduct (and his affinity for crowds) is his awareness of the narrator's presence. Indeed, the narrator has already marked himself as a threatening figure, for in wrapping a handkerchief about his mouth (IV, 1140), he has unconsciously (or perversely) assumed the mask of a felon. If the man of the crowd were aware of his pursuer, as the details of the narrative tend to suggest, then the tale hinges on the theme of mutual suspicion. Such a reading must, however, remain speculative, since Poe never permits us to share the thoughts of his enigmatic old man. And this is as it should be; the story is after all concerned with the limits of knowledge and the ambiguities which frustrate our efforts to penetrate the veil of appearances. Regardless of what we may infer from his actions, the man of the crowd retains the ultimate inscrutability of Melville's white whale, symbolizing (if anything) man's inability to ascertain, by means of reason, any absolute knowledge of the world beyond the self.

The ironic form of "The Man of the Crowd" seems finally a manifestation of Poe's own ambivalence toward his art, for the tale is poised between rationality and irrationality, between understanding and terror. Read as the account of a reliable observer who correctly recognizes aberrant behavior, the story leads plausibly to the diagnosis, "This old man . . . is the type and the genius of deep crime. He refuses to be alone" (IV, 145). Yet the headnote to the tale (*"Ce grand malheur, de ne pouvoir être seul."*) applies as well to the narrator, a meddlesome detective guilty of what Dupin, in "The Mystery of Marie Rogêt," called "romantic busy-bodyism" (V, 34). Through the ironic design of "The Man of the Crowd" Poe expresses his own unfulfilled rage for order and clarity; even as the narrator seeks enlightenment about the old man, he sinks into the darkness of subconscious fantasies. The "mad energy" of the stranger only mirrors the narrator's compulsive behavior—his monomaniacal attempt to become the man of reason, to read the book that will not permit itself to be read.

II

In "The Murders in the Rue Morgue," Dupin says of Vidocq, the French minister of police: "He erred continually by the very intensity of his investigations. He impaired his vision by holding the object too close" (IV, 166). His remark succinctly defines the shortcoming of the bedeviled detective in "The Man of the Crowd." Poe describes precisely the opposite difficulty, though, in "The Oblong Box," a parody of the ratiocinative tale.[10] Here the analytical narrator attempts to solve from a distance the mystery of an oblong box brought aboard a ship bound for New York. With comic pertinacity, he constructs an utterly wrongheaded interpretation, reached through an abstract contemplation of events. Considerably less complex than "The Man of the Crowd," "The Oblong Box" nevertheless employs the motif of self-deception, as Poe again pokes fun at "romantic busy-bodyism" and the inclination to play detective.[11]

At the outset, the narrator offers another version of the heightened-consciousness syndrome: "I was, just at that epoch, in one of those moody frames of mind which make a man abnormally inquisitive about trifles" (V, 275). A puzzling circumstance arouses his curiosity: Cornelius Wyatt, an artist-friend, has reserved three staterooms for a party which apparently includes only Wyatt, his new bride, and his two sisters. The intrigued narrator confides: "I busied myself in a variety of ill-bred and preposterous conjectures about this matter of the supernumerary stateroom. It was no business of mine, to be sure; but with none the less pertinacity did I occupy myself in attempts to resolve the enigma" (V, 275). In busying himself with the affairs of Wyatt, the narrator identifies himself as a Poesque Paul Pry, a detached spectator regarding human experience primarily as a subject for analysis.

Further developments compound the mystery of the extra stateroom. On the eve of the ship's scheduled departure, the narrator learns that Mrs. Wyatt will not board the ship until the hour of sailing, thus postponing his introduction to the artist's bride. Unexplained "circumstances" then delay the departure nearly a week, and when Wyatt finally comes aboard with a heavily-veiled woman, he fails to introduce her to the narrator. A greater source of bafflement, though, is the oblong box placed in Wyatt's stateroom rather than the ship's hold. Disregarding the coffin-like dimensions of the box—which, as we discover later, actually contains the corpse of Mrs. Wyatt—the narrator concocts a theory rife with grotesque irony:

> The box in question was, as I say, oblong. It was about six feet in length by two and a half in breadth;—I observed it attentively, and like to be precise. Now this shape was *peculiar*; and no sooner had I seen it, than I took credit to myself for the accuracy of my guessing. I had reached the conclusion, it will be remembered, that the extra baggage of my friend, the artist, would prove to be pictures, or at least a picture; for I knew he had been for several weeks in conference with Nicolino:—and now here was a box which, from its shape, *could* possibly contain nothing in the world but a copy of Leo-

nardo's "Last Supper"; and a copy of this very "Last Supper," done by Rubini the younger, at Florence, I had known, for some time, to be in the possession of Nicolino. This point, therefore, I considered as sufficiently settled. I chuckled excessively when I thought of my acumen. (V, 277-278)

With all his "precision," the narrator manages to overlook the most obvious interpretation of the oblong box; the smug reference to his "acumen" in effect announces the satirical point of the tale.

Like the narrator of "The Man of the Crowd," the aspiring detective in "The Oblong Box" is both intrigued and deceived by minute details. He suspects, for example, that the "peculiarly disgusting odor" emanating from the box derives from the paint used to letter an address on its side; he attributes Wyatt's melancholy appearance to an unhappy marriage. The disparity between the narrator's assumptions and the actual situation reveals itself best, however, in his effort to elicit the secret of the box from the mournful artist:

> I determined to commence a series of covert insinuations, or innuendoes, about the oblong box—just to let him perceive, gradually, that I was *not* altogether the butt, or victim, of his little bit of pleasant mystification. My first observation was by way of opening a masked battery. I said something about the "peculiar shape of *that* box"; and, as I spoke the words, I smiled knowingly, winked, and touched him gently with my fore-finger in the ribs. (V, 281)

What the narrator believes to be cleverness is of course monumental indelicacy; the encounter throws Wyatt into a swoon and the narrator into further confusion.

Other misapprehensions beset the stupefied sleuth. Twice observing the supposed Mrs. Wyatt stealing into the extra stateroom, he concludes that Wyatt and his wife are on the verge of a divorce. Not until the end of the tale does he learn that the woman was Mrs. Wyatt's former maid masquerading as the wife of the artist to conceal from superstitious passengers the fact that the ship was transporting a corpse. More perverse than the divorce theory is his comment upon hearing Wyatt pry open his oblong box: "Mr. Wyatt, no doubt, according to custom, was merely giving the rein to one of his hobbies—indulging in one of his fits of artistic enthusiasm. He had opened his oblong box, in order to feast his eyes on the pictorial treasure within" (V, 283). The reference to the "pictorial treasure" could scarcely be more ironic, for textual evidence indicates that Mrs. Wyatt has been dead at least ten days.

Though not a major work in the Poe canon, "The Oblong Box" delivers, through the narrator's grotesque misinterpretations, a clever satiric version of the detective hero. The headnote to "The Purloined Letter" furnishes a penetrating comment on the narrator's self-deception: "Nil sapientiae odiosius acumine nimio" (There is nothing more inimical to wisdom than too much acumen, VI, 28). His failure provides another instance of the ratiocinative process run amuck. "Truth is not always in a well," Dupin remarks in "The Murders in the Rue Morgue" (IV, 166); neither is it found in abstract analysis divorced from that world of human realities which it proposes to explain.

III

Nearly delimiting the period of Poe's interest in ratiocination by their dates of publication, "The Man of the Crowd" and "The Oblong Box" help to clarify, by the negative example of "failed" detectives, Poe's view of the nature and scope of the ratiocinative process. Both narrators resemble the comically ineffectual Prefect of Police in the Dupin stories, being "somewhat too cunning to be profound" (IV, 192). Like him, they overlook the obvious and find a way "*de nier ce qui est, et d'expliquer ce qui n'est pas.*" Yet the differences between the two tales are even more significant. Initiating the ratiocinative cycle, "The Man of the Crowd" dramatizes the effort to escape the conditions of terror and hypersensitivity through a rigidly analytical system of thought.

But because the narrator has not yet been delivered from the nightside experience, because the principles of ratiocination have not yet been mastered, he falls prey to the same sensational influences which distort the perceptions of Roderick Usher, William Wilson, and the narrator of "Ligeia." However, "The Oblong Box" presents the opposite extreme—a narrator so detached from the subject of his investigation, so deluded by his own intellectual pretensions, that his ratiocination achieves no resemblance to actuality. The tale portrays the *reductio ad absurdum* of rational analysis: reason dissociated from reality.

Between these two poles of experience, C. Auguste Dupin balances imaginative involvement with analytical detachment. Like his adversary in "The Purloined Letter," Dupin is both poet and mathematician. As a mathematician he understands the "Calculus of Probabilities" which ordinarily governs natural phenomena. As a poet, though, he recognizes the surprising paradoxes of human experience which make an "ordinary" case sometimes more difficult to solve than one "excessively outré." According to Poe's epistemology, the two modes of cognition are inextricably related; "the *truly* imaginative [are] never otherwise than analytic," he writes in "The Murders in the Rue Morgue" (IV, 150). But both methods of knowing are ancillary to the kind of pure reasoning to which Dupin alludes in his remark about the letter thief: "As poet *and* mathematician, he would reason well; as mere mathematician, he could not have reasoned at all" (VI, 43). The detective's ability to combine imagination and analysis causes the narrator of "The Murders in the Rue Morgue" to recall "the old philosophy of the Bi-Part Soul" and imagine a "double Dupin—the creative and the resolvent" (IV, 152). In the same tale Poe reminds us that "intuition" has nothing to do with the analyst's solutions, which are obtained "by the very soul and essence of method" (IV, 146).[12] Dupin's method typically involves both a meticulous examination of physical evidence (involvement in the world of men) and a dispassionate consideration of the case as a whole (withdrawal to the realm of abstract thought). Out of this dialectical tension between involvement and detachment, poetry and mathematics, emerges the Truth which is the detective's goal.

Significant though Dupin's conquest of the unknown may seem in the context of Poe's artistic quest for a rational vision of experience, the fact remains that the author discarded his detective hero after "The Purloined Letter." A partial explanation comes from Poe himself, who wrote to Philip Pendleton Cooke in 1846: "These tales of ratiocination owe most of their popularity to being something in a new key. I do not mean to say that they are not ingenious—but people think them more ingenious than they are—on account of their method and *air* of method. In the 'Murders in the Rue Morgue,' for instance, where is the ingenuity of unravelling a web which you yourself (the author) have woven for the express purpose of unravelling?"[13] That Poe came to see the detective story as a rather superficial and mechanical exercise in mystification seems evident from his comment to Cooke. That realization also appears to inform "The Oblong Box," where the narrator's failure illustrates the speciousness of an intellectual system out of touch with the problems of human fallibility and mortality. Poe's fundamental vision of the human condition, the vision which even through ratiocination he could not at last escape, saw man as the predestined victim of the Conqueror Worm. In abandoning the detective story, Poe finally acknowledged that ratiocination answers no questions of genuine importance, clarifies nothing about the hopes and fears of humankind. For a brief period in Poe's career, ratiocination perhaps offered a distraction from the recurring nightmare of death and disintegration. But he could never fully recover, through his fictional man of reason, the reassuring eighteenth-century myth of a rationally designed universe; the inescapable terrors of the imagination made that task impossible.

From *American Literature* 47, no. 2 (May 1975): 184-196. Copyright © 1975 by Duke University Press. Reprinted by permission of Duke University Press.

Notes

1. Quinn, *The French Face of Edgar Poe* (Carbondale, Ill., 1957), p. 197; Davidson, *Poe: A Critical Study* (Cambridge, Mass., 1957), p. 259; Levin, *The Power of Blackness* (New York, 1958), p. 164; Hoffman, *Poe Poe Poe Poe Poe Poe Poe* (Garden City, N. Y., 1972), p. 210.

2. *Edgar Allan Poe: A Study in Genius* (New York, 1926), p. 118.

3. "The Murders in the Rue Morgue," *The Complete Works of Edgar Allan Poe*, ed. James A. Harrison (New York, 1902), IV, 146. All subsequent page references to Poe's tales are to the Harrison edition.

4. "The Detective in Fiction," *Fortnightly Review*, CXXXIV (Sept. 1, 1930), 384.

5. "Why the Little Frenchman Wears His Hand in a Sling" and "The Business Man" at best represent witty hack work. "The Journal of Julius Rodman," published serially from January to June in the *Gentleman's Magazine*, exploits the vogue for travel writing by lifting material from earlier narratives. See Stuart Levine, "Poe's Julius Rodman: Judaism, Plagiarism, and the Wild West," *Midwest Quarterly*, 1 (Spring, 1959), 245-259. John J. Teunissen and Evelyn J. Hinz argue that the work has redeeming parodic elements in "Poe's *Journal of Julius Rodman* as Parody," *Nineteenth-Century Fiction*, XXVII (December, 1972), 317-338.

6. Letter to Joseph Evans Snodgrass, June 4, 1842, *The Letters of Edgar Allan Poe*, ed. John Ward Ostrom (Cambridge, Mass., 1948), I, 202.

7. *The French Face of Edgar Poe*, p. 230; *Poe: A Critical Study*, pp. 190-191; "Edgar Allan Poe's 'The Man of the Crowd,'" *Neueren Sprachcn*, N. S. XI (Nov., 1962), 504.

8. "The Question of Poe's Narrators," in *The Recognition of Edgar Allan Poe*, ed. Eric W. Carlson (Ann Arbor, Mich., 1966), p. 309.

9. Davidson hints that the narrator may be "so terrified of admitting who or what he is that he projects himself into this desperate and wholly imagined fugitive." See *Poe: A Critical Study*, p. 191. G. R. Thompson suggests that the tale may be read as the "deluded romanticizing of the tipsy narrator, who perversely attributes a Romantic significance to an old drunk." See *Poe's Fiction: Romantic Irony in the Gothic Tales* (Madison, Wisc., 1973), p. 170. Neither critic explores the implications of the narrator's unreliability, however.

10. "The Oblong Box" was published in the September, 1844, number of *Godey's Lady's Book*, at about the same time "The Purloined Letter" appeared in *The Gift* for 1845 (issued in the fall of 1844). See John Cook Wyllie, "A List of the Texts of Poe's Tales," in *Humanistic Studies in Honor of John Calvin Metcalf* (Charlottesville, Va., 1941), I, 333-334.

11. A detective story of sorts lies behind the only articles heretofore published on "The Oblong Box." C. V. Carley's "A Source for Poe's 'Oblong Box,'" *American Literature*, XXIX (Nov., 1957) 310-312, closely parallels Clifford Carley Vierra's "Poe's 'Oblong Box': Factual Origins," *Modern Language Notes*, LXXIV (Dec., 1959), 693-695. The extraordinary resemblance between the articles (the same source and details appear in both) indicates plagiarism, but the similarity of the authors' names suggests a Poesque hoax perpetrated on the scholarly community.

12. The narrator of "The Mystery of Marie Rogêt" also comments on Dupin's seemingly spontaneous awareness of first causes. "The Chevalier's analytical abilities acquired for him the credit of intuition," he says, because the "simple character" of his "inductions" was never publicly explained. But the narrator adds that "his [Dupin's] frankness would have led him to disabuse every inquirer of such prejudice" (V, 3-4).

13. August 9, 1846, *The Letters of Edgar Allan Poe*, II, 328.

What Happens in "The Fall of the House of Usher"?

J. O. Bailey

What happens in "The Fall of the House of Usher"? This story contains many suggestions of psychic and supernatural influences upon the feelings of the narrator and the nerves of Roderick Usher. But the influences are not defined. No ghosts appear. Surely, Poe as craftsman intended the story to do what it does, to arouse a sense of unearthly terror that springs from a vague source, hinted and mysterious. Poe stated that his aim in tales of terror was to create "terror . . . not of Germany but of the soul,"[1] or not of the charnel but of the mind. He wrote to Thomas W. White, owner of *The Southern Literary Messenger,* that tales of terror are made into excellent stories by "the singular heightened into the strange and mystical."[2] The influences that seem to drive Roderick Usher to madness, to kill him and Madeline, and even to destroy the House are certainly strange and mysterious. They seem rooted in some postulate of the supernatural, but the postulate is concealed. This paper will examine the story and offer about its phenomena a surmise that may explain them.

I

Perhaps we first need to examine Poe's method of concealing the basis of terror. I suggest that Poe's chief device for concealment was to tell the story in the first person of a narrator who was a rationalist and a skeptic regarding the supernatural—a man who habitually dismissed any explanation not in accord with commonplace fact. We have more than these limitations to suggest that the narrator does not speak for Poe. If Poe put himself into the story, he must be chiefly in the character of Roderick Usher. Roderick's features present "the most perfect pen-portrait of Poe himself which is known."[3] Roderick reads to the narrator a poem he had written, "The Haunted Palace." This is Poe's poem, published in the *Baltimore Museum* for April, 1839, five months before "Usher" was published.[4] Perhaps we should look to Roderick for explanation of what happens.

Let us first observe how the narrator rejects evidence of the supernatural. At his first glimpse of the House, he feels "a sense of insufferable gloom."[5] He ponders various "shadowy fancies" and concludes rationally that "there *are* combinations of very simple natural objects which have the power of thus affecting us," but that "analysis of this power lies among considerations beyond our depth." He is predisposed to regard Roderick as mad and therefore to reject any explanation Roderick suggests. Mentioning Roderick's letter, he speaks of "nervous agitation . . . mental disorder" and "much more" that he perhaps finds incredible. When he gazes into the tarn, his "first singular impression" is deepened, but his "consciousness" dismisses the "superstition—for why should I not so term it?" The House reminds him of "old woodwork . . . rotted . . . in some neglected vault." His impressions form in his mind some nightmarish pattern, but he shakes from his spirit "what *must* have been a dream."

When the narrator observes Roderick Usher, he thinks of a "lost drunkard" or "irreclaimable eater of opium." This rational explanation is wrong; nothing else in the story speaks of alcohol or opium.[6] When Roderick suggests an evil influence from the House, the narrator thinks of "superstitious impressions" and dismisses it as a "supposititious force . . . too shadowy here to be re-stated."

When Madeline passes "through a remote portion of the apartment," she arouses in the narrator "utter astonishment not unmingled with dread," but he finds "it impossible to account for such feelings." He supposes he is admitted "unreservedly into the recesses of [Roderick's] spirit," but he is unable to "convey an idea of the exact character" of Roderick's interests. At Roderick's strange music and paintings, the narrator "shuddered knowing not why," but calls Roderick a "hypochondriac" and his conceptions "phantasmagoric." Regarding Roderick's theory of the sentience of the House, the narrator is stubbornly rationalistic. Speaking of it only because Roderick "maintained it" with "pertinacity" and "earnest *abandon*," he judges it the product of "disordered fancy" and says, "Such opinions need no comment, and I will make none."

When Roderick explains why he wishes to place the corpse of Madeline in a vault for a fortnight, the narrator accepts Roderick's "worldly reason," though this phrase and "so he told me" suggest that he has an inkling of some deeper reason. He observes in Madeline's corpse evidences of life, but concludes only that these marks are "usual in all maladies of a strictly cataleptical character." He attributes Roderick's increased agitation after Madeline's entombment to "the mere inexplicable vagaries of madness," even though he himself feels the "wild influences" of Roderick's "fantastic yet impressive superstitions." When Roderick forces him to observe the unnatural features of the storm, the narrator sees that Roderick thinks the storm supernatural, but he himself calls it "merely electrical phenomena not uncommon—or it may be that they have their ghastly origin in the rank miasma of the tarn." His own observation of this origin suggests nothing to his mind.

Throughout the story, the narrator speaks of Roderick as a madman. But when Madeline stands outside the door, it is Roderick who calls the narrator: "Madman! . . . *Madman*!" From our point of view as readers, the narrator is indeed obtuse; he explains away as nonexistent, as illusion, or as superstition every phenomenon that he considers unnatural or does not understand. He seems wilfully blind to facts that Roderick perceives, understands, and tries repeatedly to point out. Logically, to Roderick the narrator is the madman.

Therefore, to see what happens in "Usher" we must look beyond the narrator to the events he reports, and to understand what happens we must observe Roderick and his theories. In the following examination of these items, I use a method of questions and answers. The questions are intended to show the difficulty in making sense of the story in terms of the narrator's explanations. The answers are surmises that, right or wrong, do explain the phenomena.

II

Roderick seems engaged in a struggle against a power that he feels to be supernatural. Apparently, as in the strange books he reads, he seeks knowledge of this power and how to combat it. He has found some explanations in a quasi-scientific theory about the sentience of vegetable matter.[7] He seeks the help of objective reason by calling upon the narrator, to whom he repeatedly attempts to explain the nature of his invisible foe. But the narrator refuses to believe that the threatening power exists outside Roderick's imagination.[8]

What is this supernatural power? Poe's apparent use of materials from vampire lore in "Berenice," "Morella," "Ligeia," and "The Oval Portrait" suggests that he used this lore as a basis for the phenomena of "Usher."[9] A sizable body of Gothic poetry, fiction, and drama of the early nineteenth century—for instance, Lord Byron's "The Giaour" (1813), John William Polidori's *The Vampyre* (1819), and J. R. Planché's *The Vampyre* (1820)—found a crude basis for terror in vampire legends.[10] To use this crude material without dealing in gore, Poe had only to apply his own stated formula, to heighten the "terror . . . of Germany" into "the strange and mystical." The process requires that anything disgusting be refined and concealed. We have observed how Poe concealed. To observe how and what he refined, I propose that we examine whether the phenomena of "Usher" are explained by items common in the lore and literature of vampires.

A basic definition of *vampire* is found in Rees's *Cyclopaedia*, which Poe is known to have consulted at various times. It reads: "VAMPYRE, in *Mythology*, a name given to an imaginary demon, which, it is pretended, sucks the blood of persons during the night, and thereby destroys them. These vampyres were supposed to animate the bodies of dead persons, which when dug up were found fresh, florid, and full of blood. Those who were killed by vampyres were said to become vampyres themselves; the way to destroy them was to drive a stake through them, at which time they would give a horrid groan."[11] I think it a safe guess that Poe also read Polidori's *The Vampyre*, which has a six-page introduction to define a vampire and discuss various legends.[12] These definitions state only the central features of lore related, in legends and literary developments, to a complex "kith and kin" of demonic possession and witchcraft. I think it impossible to discover exactly what Poe read, but logical to compare his story with typical features of vampire lore.

Hints that may suggest a vampire appear in the first view of the House. The vegetation around the House is dead; though water is usually a symbol of life, the "black and lurid tarn" seems dead. It amplifies the House, reflecting it in "remodelled and inverted images." The narrator feels "an iciness" and "a sickening of the heart." He sees "about the whole mansion . . . a pestilent and mystic vapor, dull, sluggish, faintly discernible and leaden-hued."[13] On entering the House, the narrator meets the family physician, whose countenance wears "a mingled expression of low cunning and perplexity." The physician accosts him "with trepidation."[14]

Certain details about Roderick Usher seem significant. As a boy in school he displayed a hereditary "peculiar sensibility of temperament." This sensibility would make Roderick an easy prey to psychic or supernatural influence. His present illness has developed since he has lived in the House, "whence, for many years, he had never ventured forth." Thus, some influence in the House is suggested. It may be vampiric. Montague Summers's study of vampire lore states that when a person psychically sensitive even "visits a house which is powerfully haunted by malefic influences . . . a vampirish entity may . . . utilize his vitality," causing "debility and enervation" in the victim.[15]

The narrator offers the apparently irrelevant information that recently, "of late," the Ushers have done "repeated deeds of munificent yet unobtrusive charity." Why have the solitary Ushers, living withdrawn from the world, begun to bestow alms? A possible answer is penance. The "evil things" of Roderick's poem "The Haunted Palace," the donjon where Madeline is laid away, and Roderick's "favorite volume . . . the 'Directorium Inquisitorium'" suggest that the

Ushers sought to counteract a curse placed upon the family in days long past.[16]

The narrator describes Roderick in a perfect pen-portrait of Poe, with one striking difference. Roderick's "hair of a more than web-like softness and tenuity . . . silken . . . suffered to grow all unheeded," so that "in its wild gossamer texture, it floated rather than fell about the face," is not Edgar Poe's hair. There is something unnatural about it: the narrator "could not, even with effort, connect its Arabesque expression with any idea of simple humanity." Why does the portrait emphasize this strange difference? We may surmise why, when we examine the fungi on the House.

Roderick speaks of his malady as "a constitutional and a family evil and one for which he despaired to find a remedy," though he adds that it "would undoubtedly soon pass off." How will a constitutional illness for which there is no remedy soon pass off? In the story, the illness ends with the death of the Ushers and the fall of the House. Perhaps Roderick knew something that would make this end inevitable and spoke in bitter irony.

Let us turn to the events of the story to discover what he possibly knew. As the narrator approaches the House, he observes that the windows are "eye-like." Roderick's poem later gives the palace the features of a human head. These suggestions seem to mean that the House itself has some evil, destructive life, manifest in a spirit faintly visible as a vapor. Can it be regarded as a kind of vampire? In vampire lore, places or houses may be possessed: "Even to-day there are places and there are properties in England which owing to deeds of blood and violence . . . entail some dire misfortune upon all who seek to enjoy . . . them."[17]

But, in contrast with the dead vegetation *around* the House, parasitic vegetation that forms a part of the House, grows from it, and seems to knit its crumbling stones together, is in luxuriant growth. Minute fungi hang "in a fine tangled web-work from the eaves."[18] This "web-work" above the "eye-like windows" suggests an affinity with Roderick's "unheeded . . . wild" hair "of a more than web-like softness and tenuity." Is this correspondence a random coincidence? If the House has a kind of parasitic life, this affinity may have meaning. Though most vampires feed upon blood, "there is a vampire who can . . . support his life and re-energize his frame by drawing upon the vitality of others. He may be called a spiritual vampire or as he has been dubbed a 'psychic sponge.' Such types are by no means uncommon."[19] We may surmise that the House as a psychic sponge drains Roderick's vitality through his hair and lives on it.[20] How? Poe's motto for the story,[21] taken from Béranger, indicates Roderick's sensitivity; it is consistent with the idea of a psychic current flowing from Roderick's hair to the fungi as the House makes demands upon him. Perhaps it was not beyond Poe's imagination to see in "*Sitôt qu'on le touche il rèsonne*" the suggestion: "As soon as he is tuned in, he responds."

The windows are "altogether inaccessible from within," in a sense imprisoning Roderick from the outside world. They let into his apartment only an "encrimsoned light." Everything inside the House seems entombed under its "vaulted" ceiling. The "Many books and musical instruments . . . scattered about" fail "to give any vitality to the scene." Then Madeline also is a prisoner-victim. In the narrator's brief first glimpse of her, she looks and behaves like the typical walking undead of vampire lore, though presumably she is at this time alive. Her disease "had long baffled the skill of her physicians. A settled apathy, a gradual wasting away of the person, and frequent although transient affections of a partially cataleptical character, were the unusual diagnosis." In the *usual* diagnosis of vampire lore, these symptoms describe the victim of a vampire. Typically, the still-living victim is "attacked by a great languor and weariness, he loses all appetite, he visibly wastes and grows thin."[22] The "partially cataleptical character" of her disease is associated with vampirism. Madeline's trances may mark periods of severe draining of her vitality.[23]

Roderick exhibits similar symptoms, with his "cadaverousness of complexion" and "lips . . . very pallid"—a "wan being." He seems incoherent, speaking in a "series of feeble and futile struggles. . . . His voice varied rapidly from a tremulous indecision (when the animal spirits seemed utterly in abeyance) to . . . that abrupt, weighty, unhurried, and hollow-sounding enunciation—that leaden, self-balanced, and perfectly modulated gutteral utterance" Poe elsewhere attributes to a dead man, M. Valdemar.

Roderick's symptoms include "a morbid acuteness of the senses; the most insipid food was alone endurable; he could wear only garments of certain texture; the odors of all flowers were oppressive; his eyes were tortured by even a faint light; and there were but peculiar sounds, and these from stringed instruments, which did not inspire him, with horror." These are specific symptoms of vampiric attack. Vampires, if not always their polluted victims, seldom touch ordinary food. Though some vampires, for instance Ruthven in Polidori's *The Vampyre*, wear ordinary clothing, most vampires appear in the garments of the grave.[24] If Poe had vampire lore in mind, why did he say "the odors of all flowers"? We may look first at odors. Disgusting odors are associated with vampires. A vampire's breath is "unbearably fetid and rank with corruption, the stench of the charnel."[25] This is the very material Poe rejected. The House draws vitality instead of blood; flowers seem a similar substitute for heightening the gory into the strange and mysterious. Poe's "all flowers" had to be left vague. If Poe had mentioned garlic and its whitish flower, universally accepted specifics against vampirism, he would have given away the secret he sought to suggest, but conceal.[26] It seems significant that Poe mentions flowers at all. No garden can grow near the House; no flowers would be ordered from a tenant or a market if Roderick finds them oppressive. The mention seems Poe's tauntingly deliberate effort to be faithful to the lore he was using, without defining it.[27] Perhaps the odors of flowers were "oppressive," rather than welcome to ward off attack, because Roderick was already polluted to the extent that he shared the aversions of the vampire.[28] Most vampires cannot endure daylight; they must return to the tomb at the first hint of dawn.[29] Roderick's horror of all sounds except those of stringed instruments seems natural for anyone who senses the presence of a demon. Poe often associates stringed instruments with angelic forces.

After detailing his symptoms, Roderick cries out: "I *must* perish in this deplorable folly." What folly? for none is mentioned. Perhaps his folly is that, through living as a recluse in the House and through curious reading, Roderick had laid himself open to attack. A "Vampire was often a person who during his life had read deeply in poetic lore and practised black magic."[30] Roderick says, "I dread the events of the future, not in themselves, but in their results." Perhaps he does not dread death, but fears becoming a vampire if killed by a vampire.

At this point Roderick states—specifies—that the attack upon his vitality comes from the House. The narrator, reporting with scorn, says: "He was enchained by certain superstitious impressions in regard to the dwelling which he tenanted . . . , in regard to an influence . . . which some peculiarities in the mere form and substance of his family mansion had . . . obtained over his spirit—an effect which the *physique* of the gray walls and turrets, and of the dim tarn into which they looked down, had . . . brought about upon the *morale* of his existence."

Madeline seems a victim of the same attack, and she dies. When? On the evening of the first day Roderick tells the narrator "with inexpressible agitation" that Madeline had "succumbed . . . to the prostrating power of the destroyer." But she is not declared dead, that she "was no more" and is ready for burial, until several days later. Perhaps in the interval she is undead, "living" as a vampire. All definitions say that a person killed by a vampire becomes a vampire with a craving to pass on the pollution.

During these days, wherever or whatever Madeline is, Roderick turns to music and art. Among his "phantasmagoric" pictures, he paints a vault, illuminated by "a flood of intense rays," deep beneath the surface of the earth. It cannot be a preview of Madeline's vault, for Madeline is later entombed by "half smothered" torchlight that "gave us little opportunity for investigation" in a vault "entirely without means of admission for light." What can Roderick's painted vault mean, lighted with what the narrator calls "ghastly and inappropriate splendor"? Vampire lore suggests that anything saintly is, to some extent, a charm against vampires. Legends include "cases of irradiation when the . . . rooms of great saints and mystics become luminous, emitting rays of light."[31] Roderick's painting may be a charm against the actual dark vault, which he hoped to purge with saintly light before laying Madeline's body there.

Then Roderick composes and sings "The Haunted Palace." For what purpose? Poe had published this poem several months before "Usher"; to some extent, the story seems developed from the symbolism of the poem. But in the story the poem seems one of Roderick's efforts to make the narrator see that the House has the demonic life of a vampire. The "luminous windows" of the palace that become "red litten" are like the "eye-like windows" of the House that shed an "encrimsoned light" on its interior. The color suggests the red eyes typical of the vampire.[32] The narrator fails to see the point, but he says that "suggestions arising from this ballad led us into a train of thought wherein there became manifest an opinion of Usher's"—Roderick's theory of "the sentience of all vegetable things," and, "under certain conditions," of inorganic matter.[33] The House fulfils these conditions in "the method of collocation of these stones—in the order of their arrangement, as well as in that of the many *fungi* which overspread them . . . above all, in the long undisturbed endurance of this arrangement, and in its reduplication in the still waters of the tarn. Its evidence" is found in "the gradual yet certain condensation of an atmosphere of their own about the waters and the walls. The result was . . . that silent, yet importunate and terrible influence which for centuries had moulded the destinies of his family, and which made *him* what . . . he was." Though Roderick does not use the word *vampire*, his statement is clear as a quasi-scientific explanation of how the House has a parasitic vitality evidenced in a miasma, and how it in some way has long lived upon the vitality of the Usher family. Roderick's theory is consistent with vampire lore. Summers says, "Vampirism . . . may be said to leave its trace throughout almost all nature. Just as we have the parasitic men and women, so have we the parasitic plants."[34] The purpose of a vampire is to "vitalize . . . his own dead body by draining the blood from the veins of his victims," for "the spirit or the soul in some mysterious way lies in the blood."[35] Taken together, these items seem to define Roderick's theory: through the arrangement of its stones and the fungus growths that penetrate them, the House acquired the miasmatic spirit that the narrator, we recall, observed as a faintly discernible vapor. This spirit, it appears, lives upon the souls of the Ushers by sucking vitality through its fungi tuned into their hair.

Failing to enlighten the narrator with this forthright explanation, Roderick leads him to books over which they "pored together." These are real books in extravagant, mystic, spiritualistic, and terror literature, treating voyages between worlds and into the center of a hollow earth, magic, medieval torture, and death watches. As all the books "concern in one way or another the idea that spirit is extended throughout all matter,"[36] this reading seems a part of Roderick's effort to explain his theory and his foe—an oblique effort to let the narrator discover for himself in "authorities."

Among these books, Roderick's "chief delight . . . was found in the perusal of an exceedingly rare and curious book in quarto Gothic— the manual of a forgotten church—the *Vigiliæ Mortuorum secundum Chorum Ecclesiæ Maguntinæ*." The narrator calls the content of this book a "wild ritual."[37] At this point we have a puzzle. It is a real book, described in bibliographies in just the terms Poe used. It is, as the story says, exceedingly rare—a fact stated in the bibliographies.[38] I located a copy in the library of Cambridge University, England, and with the help of Professor Siegfried Wenzel examined a photograph of it. It contains precisely the modern Roman Office for the Dead, with a few exceptions that do not basically alter its structure or substance. Why did Poe emphasize it and call its ritual wild?

I doubt that he ever saw the book, for I was not able to locate a copy in the United States. Perhaps he found only the title and physical description in a list of rare books. For a story to be published in an American magazine, he could imply that the book contained anything he pleased, on the assumption that no one could check on his accuracy. Perhaps he cited this Office for the Dead of a medieval church in Mainz, Germany, and called its ritual wild to mystify his readers, as in his treatment of the narrator, though Poe himself may have conceived Roderick as seeking a formula to exorcise a vampire from Madeline's body.

Perhaps Roderick is partly sincere in his "worldly reason" for preserving Madeline's body in a vault before burial: her malady was a subject of "eager inquiries on the part of her medical men" and the burial ground was "exposed." What is the hinted, unworldly reason he did not state? If Roderick believes that Madeline's body is possessed by a vampiric spirit, we may surmise any one (or all) of four reasons: 1) the body of a vampire may escape its tomb by acquiring "subtility," dematerializing, passing through crevices, and rematerializing.[39] Roderick may suppose it possible to seal the tomb so tight that Madeline cannot escape as a mist and then rematerialize as a vampire. 2) The moon at this time is approaching the "full . . . blood-red" phase it reaches the night of the storm. A body from which a vampire has been driven must not be laid in the rays of the moon, "especially if the moon be at her full, for in this case he will revive with redoubled vigour and malevolence." Even a vampire that has been "shot and killed, with a silver bullet that has been blessed by a priest" has power to revive under a full moon.[40] If buried out of doors, whether or not exhumed by her physicians, Madeline might be vitalized by the moon, as she might not in a vault deep underground, "entirely without means of admission for light." 3) Roderick may wish to keep her body within the House so that he may employ the ritual of the *Vigiliæ* to exorcise the evil spirit that had killed Madeline and that now possesses her body and may use it to attack him. Roderick performs no religious service in the presence of the narrator: no priest appears, no "Ave" is spoken. But possibly, in

what the narrator calls his "objectless" wanderings, "tremulous qua-
ver" of utterance, and "gazing upon vacancy for long hours," Roderick
may be struggling to invoke the powers of the *Vigiliæ*.[41] And 4)
Madeline's vault seems to be a place of evil, where, perhaps, a curse
had been pronounced upon the Usher family. The vault had been used
"in remote feudal times, for the worst purposes of a donjon-keep." In
Roderick's reading, "One favorite volume was . . . the 'Directorium
Inquisitorium,' by the Dominican Eymeric de Gironne."[42] These items
suggest Roderick's effort to understand the power and operation of a
curse uttered by a martyr. Vampire lore speaks of "the fearful power of
a curse . . . which . . . works out its vengeance through the whole stock
of kith and kin, involving in misfortune and destruction, innocent and
guilty alike."[43] Perhaps Roderick, already having tried to purge the
dark vault with his painting of a brilliantly lighted vault, would now attack the House at the source of its life, the vault where the curse was uttered, with Madeline's undead body as bait to localize its otherwise
pervasive force.

During the entombment, the narrator notices a "striking similitude
between the brother and sister." Roderick explains that he and
Madeline "had been twins" and that "sympathies of a scarcely intelligible nature had always existed between them."[44] What were these sympathies? T. O. Mabbott has stated, I think rightly, that "Poe's twins
share their family soul with the HOUSE, and Roderick knew it."[45] If
Madeline was destroyed by the House, she is now a vampire; a vampire
attacks first its closest blood-kin. A French writer on vampire lore,
Augustin Calmet, says: "Cette persécution ne s'arrête pas à une seule
personne; elle s'étend jusqu'à la dernière personne de la famille."[46]
This feature of vampirism is presented in Lord Byron's "The Giaour."
A curse dooms an Infidel to become a vampire and to

> . . . suck the blood of all thy race;
> There from thy daughter, sister, wife
> At midnight drain the stream of life.[47]

Thus, just because he is a twin, Roderick has reason to be terrified of Madeline.

Perhaps she died the night after the narrator saw her pass through the apartment. If so, that no dissolution is evident when she is entombed several days later is to be expected if a vampire possessed her body. Perhaps Roderick postponed entombment to be sure what had taken place. She has the traits of a vampire when she is placed in the vault. The "mockery of a faint blush upon the bosom and the face" and a "suspiciously lingering smile upon the lip" are characteristic of the undead.[48] Roderick now feels his danger to be extreme. If the evil spirit of the House possesses Madeline's corpse, it has added to its power as psychic sponge the control of a human body able to attack the jugular vein. In vampire lore, "The vampire is . . . generally believed to embrace his victim . . . and after greedily kissing the throat suddenly to bite deep into the jugular vein."[49] Madeline's attack would not merely kill Roderick: it would doom him to becoming himself a vampire. Roderick's increased pallor, his "ghastly hue," and his dead eye, its "luminousness . . . utterly gone out," a few days after the entombment, suggest an increased sapping of his vitality, even though Madeline has not yet reappeared.

The assumption that this lonely man fights a vampire with all he has, chiefly in recitals of his ritual, is supported by the events of the night when Madeline reappears. These events suggest that Roderick's struggle for her soul and for his own life and soul makes enough headway to rouse the House to a similarly desperate struggle, the exertion of a full power that even the narrator feels as "an incubus of utterly causeless alarm."[50] The storm seems evidence of this struggle, for vampires cause storms.[51] It is centered in the House, the focal point of a whirlwind; clouds press upon the turrets; an "unnatural light of a faintly luminous and distinctly visible gaseous exhalation . . . enshrouded the mansion." The phenomena seem to "have their ghastly origin in the rank miasma of the torn," or, we may imagine, in Madeline's vault, presumably below the tarn. Roderick understands what the storm means. His repeated "And you have not seen it?" cannot mean that the narrator is unaware of a storm. Roderick throws open a casement to force the narrator to observe the bizarre peculiarities of *this* storm.

Then, while the "wild light" of a "full . . . blood-red moon" bathes the storm-enshrouded House, redoubling its "vigor and malevolence,"[52] and to the accompaniment of Canning's "Mad Trist,"[53] Madeline reappears. As she approaches, Roderick speaks in a "gibbering murmur" of which the narrator, understanding only fragments, "drank in the hideous import." The narrator thinks Roderick says, *"We have put her living in the tomb!"* Can this be true? Readers have generally supposed that Roderick buried his sister alive.[54] Aware of her struggles, Roderick *"dared not speak!"* He lacks the courage to rescue her, though what courage it would require if she still lives is not clear.[55] Frankly, to suppose her alive seems to me less reasonable than to suppose that Madeline was placed in the vault dead (or undead in the vampire sense), and returns as a ravening vampire. Presumably, Madeline's physician had pronounced her dead, though Roderick's "worldly reason" for not burying her suggests the physician's perception of something odd about the corpse. If alive, she was already weakened to the brink of death. The lid of her coffin was "screwed down," presumably till air tight. The vault was so nearly air tight that "our torches" were "half smothered in its oppressive atmosphere." Madeline lay in her coffin until "late in the night of the seventh or eighth day" after being placed there. Even if she had been only in a trance and had not required air for a week, she would have needed air for the superhuman strength[56] to break out of her coffin and open the door of "massive iron" and "immense weight" that closed this vault. Roderick and the narrator had "secured the door of iron" when they left this room formerly used "for the worst purposes of a donjon-keep." The phrasing suggests a prison for victims of torture.

If Madeline were an ordinary vampire buried in a cemetery, she could dematerialize, escape through crevices, and rematerialize. But how could she escape from a sealed coffin in an airtight vault closed and secured by an iron door? I suggest that Poe established these seemingly impossible conditions because he had in mind a supernatural agency in Madeline's escape. If she is now a vampire killed by the House and therefore the agent of the House, the House might help set her free. To do so, it seems, required the total vitality of the House, with added draughts from Roderick's life, all redoubled in power by the full moon, and engaged in the violent effort manifested in the storm. How could the House help set her free? Let us observe below how it opened heavy doors for her to reach Roderick.

Roderick hears her approach and asks, "Is she not hurrying to upbraid me for my haste?" He may mean his haste in sealing her in the vault before his own death. Perhaps Roderick knows that when he dies—if he can die before Madeline sucks his blood—the House and Madeline must also die in "final death-agonies."

As Madeline approaches with a "heavy and horrible beating of her heart," typical of the vampire,[57] Roderick speaks in his "gibbering murmur, as if unconscious of [the narrator's] presence." What is he saying? Perhaps part of his monologue is an incantation from the *Vigiliæ*.[58] When Madeline reaches the "huge antique panels" of the chamber, she simply stands there waiting. The doors open. The narrator says, "It was the work of the rushing gust." How can this be? These doors face the interior of the House, not the storm outside. The casement has been closed. This gust may be the spirit of the vampire House, rooted in Madeline's vault, and manifest in the forces of the storm. When the doors of the chamber throw "slowly back . . . their ponderous and ebony jaws," between these jaws stands the "lofty and enshrouded figure of the lady Madeline of Usher," with "blood upon her white robes." Are these images a symbolist painting: between the jaws of the vampire House stands its white and blood-stained tooth poised to plunge into Roderick's life-stream?[59]

For a moment, Madeline "remained trembling and reeling to and fro upon the threshold." Perhaps she wavered between remnants of human compassion aided by Roderick's incantations, and the evil power driving her onward. But she "then, with a low moaning cry, fell heavily inward upon the person of her brother, and in her violent and now final death-agonies, bore him to the floor a corpse, and a victim to the terrors he had anticipated." Was Roderick's death heart failure? The narrator does not stop to observe: he "fled aghast." But the somewhat erotic embrace of its victim, the prone position for the kill, and the moan of pleasure are commonplaces of vampire lore.[60] In terms of this lore, Madeline reached the jugular vein. But as Roderick dies, Madeline and the House die, for their source of vitality is cut off. Does Roderick continue undead, a vampire by pollution, as "he had anticipated"? When a vampire is destroyed, it squeals or screams horribly.[61] As the fragments of the House sink into the tarn, there is a "shouting sound like the voice of a thousand waters." Perhaps, as both Madeline and the House die in the instant of Roderick's death, the curse is fulfilled, and Roderick's soul is, after all, saved by the finally innocuous water.[62] The narrator observes no more except the "full, setting, and blood-red moon."

III

In conclusion, to assume that Poe made use of vampire lore, skilfully concealed and refined from the usual gore to the strange and mystical, seems to answer the questions that arise if we try to make sense of the story in terms of the narrator's explanations. We need not suppose that in using this material to plot a piece of fiction Poe believed in vampires.

To the extent that the present reading is valid, it has, I think, some biographical significance. Roderick Usher is often called a self-portrait of Poe, illustrating his split personality. But in the present reading, Roderick's fears are justified, and there is little split in his personality. Yet the "barely perceptible fissure" in the face of the House seems to symbolize something, perhaps a split between the two sides of Poe's nature represented by Roderick and the narrator. On the Usher side is the Poe who as a boy would wake to "feel an ice-cold hand laid upon his face in a pitch dark room . . . or . . . see an evil face gazing close into his own,"[63] and who as a man dreamed into life his Arabesque tales of terror. On the other side is Poe the critic, proud of his "ratiocination," a challenger to solve cryptographic puzzles, and the creator of M. Dupin. "The Haunted Palace," in which perhaps the story began, doubtless did express Poe's fear that the ghost-seeing side of his nature was destroying his sanity. The poem treats this side of his nature as an inherited evil, a degenerative strain. But in the story, Roderick, psychic and intuitive, sees truth that the narrator cannot see; he calls the representative of Reason a madman. And yet the narrator, if he represents Reason, is saved when he "fled aghast." The stories that seem to represent Poe as M. Dupin perhaps try to solve the puzzle by combining reason with intuition and exalting the combination. At any rate, we may agree, I think, with A. H. Quinn that "The Fall of the House of Usher" represents, among other things, Poe's search for "identity."[64]

Further biographical implications of the fact that the story seems built upon vampire lore and seems a symbolic or allegorical story lie beyond the scope of this essay.

From *American Literature* 35, no. 4 (1964): 445-466. Copyright © 1964 by Duke University Press. Reprinted by permission of Duke University Press.

Notes

1. Arthur Hobson Quinn, *Edgar Allan Poe: A Critical Biography* (New York and London, 1941), p. 289.

2. Dated Baltimore, April 30, 1835, in John Ward Ostrom, ed., *The Letters of Edgar Allan Poe* (Cambridge, Mass., 1948), p. 58.

3. Hervey Allen, *Israfel: The Life and Times of Edgar Allan Poe* (New York, 1934), p. 357.

4. Quinn, p. 271.

5. The text of "Usher" used in this article is that edited by Arthur Hobson Quinn and Edward H. O'Neill, *The Complete Poems and Stories of Edgar Allan Poe* (New York, 1946), I, 262-277.

6. Except the narrator's use of the word *opium* to describe his feeling on first seeing the House.

7. Poe footnoted the theory with references to three scientists and "'Chemical Essays,' vol. V."

8. Poe here inverts a technique of Gothic fiction. He apparently was familiar with Mrs. Radcliffe's romances, for he mentions her in the first sentence of "The Oval Portrait." Mrs. Radcliffe's apparently supernatural phenomena turn out to be natural; what Poe's narrator seeks to interpret as natural can be explained only as supernatural. Later footnotes point out other, similar inversions.

9. Materials that seem drawn from vampire lore appear in "Berenice" (1835) as the erotic attraction to strangely developed teeth extracted from an undead corpse; in "Morella" (1835) as the transfer of the "dead" Morella's vitality to her child; in "Ligeia" (1838) as drops of bloodlike liquid forming from the atmosphere, and Ligeia's gradual possession of Rowena's body; and in "The Oval Portrait" (originally "Life in Death," 1842) as the absorption of the bride's vitality into her portrait. Mario Praz, *The Romantic Agony* (London, 1933) cites D. H. Lawrence's analysis of "Ligeia," in which the "husband's consciousness" is called a spiritual vampire. See similar suggestions in Darrel Abel, "Coleridge's 'Life-in-Death' and Poe's 'Death-in-Life,'" *Notes and Queries*, N. S. II, 218 (1955). Vampirism in "Usher" is briefly suggested in Allen Tate, "Our Cousin, Mr. Poe," *The Forlorn Demon* (Chicago, 1953), pp. 79-95; Tate thinks Madeline may be a vampire. It is treated more fully in Lyle H. Kendall, Jr., "The Vampire Motif in 'The Fall of the House of Usher,'" *College English*, XXIV, 450-453 (March, 1963). The present paper was sent to *American Literature* before I had seen or heard of this article, which identifies Madeline as a vampire, but does not suspect the House. In revision, I have footnoted significant differences between Kendall's article and my own.

10. Kendall, p. 450, lists nine well-known poems or stories of vampires Poe may have read and suggests that many more were available to him. Besides these titles, Praz (pp. 76-77) discusses vampire materials in Goethe's *Braut von Korinth* (1797), Maturin's *Melmoth the Wanderer* (1820), and Nodier's *Smarra* (1821). Other Gothic "Themes like that of the Bleeding Nun, who comes at night to torment her victim . . . approach in certain respects the vampire-theme" (Eino Railo, *The Haunted Castle*, London and New York, 1927, p. 380, n. 270). After Planché's drama was produced at the Lyceum in London, so many plays about vampires appeared that certain trapdoors came to be called "vampire traps" (Allardyce Nicoll, *A History of Early Nineteenth Century Drama, 1800-1850*, Cambridge, 1930, I, 37). A brief list of vampire plays is given in Dorothy Scarborough, *The Supernatural in Modern English Fiction* (New York and London, 1917), pp. 159-160. Many English plays were, of course, produced on American stages. Poe's parents acted in Gothic dramas while they were associated with Mr. and Mrs. Usher of Boston. Probably Poe drew chiefly from poetry, fiction, and drama, but no doubt also from his apparently extensive reading in mythology.

11. Abraham Rees, *The Cyclopaedia; or, Universal Dictionary of Arts, Science, and Literature*, First American Edition (Philadelphia, undated), Vol. XXXVIII, unpaged.

12. Originally published in the *New Monthly Magazine*, April 1, 1819, as "by Lord Byron," but later published anonymously, *The Vampyre; a Tale* (London, 1819). The tale is gory and dull, but perhaps just the thing Poe might "heighten."

13. These are typical features of vampire stories. It is peculiar only that the tarn reflects the House, for commonly a vampire casts no shadow and is not reflected in water or a mirror. Purely for illustrative purposes, I am citing from Bram Stoker's *Dracula* (New York, 1947) certain items that parallel "Usher," because *Dracula*, the modern "classic" treatment of the subject and "orthodox" in its use of vampire lore, may help define this lore in "Usher." In *Dracula* the Count is not reflected in a mirror, and the female vampires cast no shadow. I suggest that Poe deliberately inverted this feature of the legends. The "iciness" parallels the touch of Dracula's hand, "cold as ice—more like the hand of a dead than a living man" (p. 16). The "mystic vapor . . . faintly discernible" suggests a demonic entity. In *Paradise Lost*, IX, 179-190, Satan enters Eden and then the serpent's mouth in the form of a mist. In *Dracula*, the Count dissolves himself into a "faint vapour" (p. 203); he "can come in mist which he creates" (p. 256). See also pp. 299 and 302. Three female vampires lie in their coffins through the clay, but emerge in the moonlight as particles of mist, and then materialize (p. 48). When faced with a crucifix, Dracula was able to disappear as a "faint vapour" that "trailed under the [closed] door" (p. 303).

14. Kendall says that the physician's "low cunning" denotes knowledge of a curse upon the Ushers (p. 451), but "perplexity" suggests that his medical knowledge is baffled.

15. *The Vampire: His Kith and Kin* (New Hyde Park, N. Y., 1960), p. 197. Hereinafter, I refer to this book as Summers.

16. Poe may have inverted a suggestion found in Polidori's *The Vampyre*. The vampire himself, Lord Ruthven, is extravagantly liberal, especially to vicious characters, though whether in penance, fellowship, or mockery is not stated (p. 33).

17. Summers, p. 160. Beginning with the ruined Abbey of Glastonbury, Summers lists eight such places and discusses the legends associated with them. The list does not include Melrose Abbey, but Scarborough mentions it, for "a vampire was burned there" (p. 159). Poe could have found in various places the suggestion that a ruined castle or ancient house may be possessed by demons. Robert Burton in *The Anatomy of Melancholy* presents instances when the Devil haunts "many men's houses after their deaths" and takes "possession of their habitations, as it were, of their palaces." He mentions "forms of exorcism" useful in "houses possessed with devils." Clearly Poe drew details for his House from the haunted castles of Gothic romances: the tarn, the mouldering walls, high windows of stained glass, massive doors, subterranean vaults, the storm, and the moon. See Railo, *passim*. Whether or not thinking of Poe's House as a vampire, twentieth-century stories have developed the haunted house as itself possessed by a demon, for instance, William Hope Hodgson's "The Whistling Room" in *Carnachi, The Ghost Finder* (Sauk City, Wis., 1947).

18. The typical Gothic castle is hung with moss or ivy; Poe's fungus seems a unique and more deadly parasite, invented for a purpose to be examined.

19. Summers, p. 133-134. The "spiritual vampire" was dubbed a "psychic vampire, stealing the vital powers of others, a human sponge, absorbing the strength, the ideas, the soul, of others" in Scarborough's discussion of such a vampire in Algernon Blackwood's "The Transfer" (p. 164).

20. The biblical story of Samson reflects the ancient belief that the strength or the

soul resides in the hair. Sir James George Frazer in *The Golden Bough* presents numerous instances of this belief.

21. Added in the 1845 edition; see Quinn, p. 466.

22. Summers, p. 199. The introduction to Polidori's story (p. xx) states that victims of vampires "became emaciated, lost their strength, and speedily died of consumption." In *Dracula*, "'Jonathan is in a stupor such as we know the Vampire can produce'" (p. 304).

23. Summers says that "cases of catalepsy . . . which resulted in premature burial . . . reinforce the tradition of the vampire and the phenomenon of vampirism" (p. 34). Kendall says that Madeline's trances reflect "the common ability of witches to enter at will upon a trance-like, death-like state of suspended animation. Her 'settled apathy' and 'gradual wasting away of the person' are to be accounted for by the corresponding condition in her victim" (p. 451). As I see it, this explanation is only partly right; Roderick is not yet her victim; both she and Roderick are victims of the House.

24. Kendall says that his symptoms show Roderick's illness to be pernicious anemia (p. 450). But in *Dracula* it is emphasized that the Count is never seen to eat, even when he serves breakfast to his guest, and his victim Lucy, after being attacked, loses appetite. Poe's garments of "certain texture" may exclude silk, as horrible to one polluted by a vampire and therefore sharing its aversions; or may include silk, if he seeks to ward off attack. In *Dracula* a silk handkerchief about the throat is a charm against a vampire (p. 157).

25. Summers, p. 179.

26. Though I have not found these items in particular stories written before "Usher," the vampires of later stories dread also the mountain ash, the wild rose, the dog rose, the mayflower, and the whitethorn. These specifics appear in *Dracula, passim.*

27. The same effort is suggested in Poe's omission of other, obvious wards against vampires: the crucifix, a sacred wafer, anything blessed by a priest, and a blessed circle drawn around a potential victim. These items sear the flesh of any vampire that touches them.

28. *Dracula* presents a parallel. Mina, only partly polluted and struggling against pollution, has her forehead seared when a holy wafer is placed on it.

29. Summers, p. 199. Polidori's Ruthven appears in daylight and so does Stoker's Dracula, but they cannot exercise demonic powers by day. When Polidori's Aubrey has to ride through a wood said to be the haunt of vampires, he is urged to return "ere night allowed the power of these beings to be put in action" (p. 45).

30. Summers, p. 195.

31. Summers, p. 121. If the actual vault was cursed, it was no fit place for a burial; Madeline's soul could find no rest there until the vault was somehow blessed. The idea that the painting was intended to sanctify the vault is paralleled in *Dracula*, where holy wafers are placed in vampires' tombs to keep the vampires from returning.

32. After Monk Lewis, at least, "the attention of the school of romantic horrors was especially directed to the power inherent in the human eye" (Railo, p. 175). The peculiarity of vampire eyes is redness; vampires have "eyes glaring red like fire" (Summers, p. 164). A vampire is "generally described" with "eyes wherein are glinting the red fire of perdition" (p. 179). "Generally," but not always; in Polidori's story, the vam-

pire Ruthven has a "dead grey eye, which . . . fell upon the cheek with a leaden ray" (pp. 28-29). But *Dracula* emphasizes the vampire's red eyes: the Count's "eyes were positively blazing. The red light in them was lurid, as if the flames of hell-fire blazed behind them" (p. 41); see also pp. 53, 97, 100, 225, 226, 300, 303, 308, 330, and 407. Among the "facial" features of the palace in happy days are teeth of "pearl." Nothing is said of its teeth in evil days. A vampire's canine teeth developed into sharp points. Perhaps when Poe wrote the poem he did not think of it in relation to the vampirism developed in the story. To alter the poem by mentioning sharp teeth perhaps would define more than Poe wished to make clear. The sharp teeth may be symbolized in the "pointed" windows of the House. Another item in Poe's palace, the "ruler of the realm . . . in the olden / Time long ago," is paralleled in *Dracula*: "The Draculas were . . . a great and noble race, though now and again were scions who were held by their coevals to have had dealings with the Evil One" (p. 258).

33. Perhaps Roderick thought the narrator would accept animism as a first step toward the "more daring" idea that a House may have a soul.

34. Summers, p. 135.

35. Summers, pp. 14-15.

36. Thomas O. Mabbott, "Poe's Vaults," *Notes and Queries*, CXCVIII, 543 (1953). One of the books, Swedenborg's *Heaven and Hell*, deals with correspondences between the physical and the spiritual worlds.

37. Kendall says that the *Vigiliæ* "is, of course, the 'Black Mass'" (p. 452). Perhaps Poe intended his readers to think so, but it is not.

38. See, for instance, Jean George Theodore Graesse, *Trésor de Livres Rare et Précieux* (Leipzig and Paris, 1900), *Supplement*, VIII, 490.

39. Summers, p. 196. See also n.13, above.

40. Summers, p. 209. In Polidori's *The Vampyre*, when Ruthven has been shot and is dying, he asks that his corpse be laid in the moonlight. It is carried "to the pinnacle of a neighbouring mount," where it is "exposed to the first cold ray of the moon that rose after his death." When Aubrey goes to look for the body, it is not there, but Ruthven later turns up "alive" in London (pp. 55-56). Influences other than the moon might help revive Madeline. Poe begins the action of the story "in the autumn of the year," which may be early October. Perhaps Madeline is entombed in the dark of the moon about eight days before the full moon on Halloween, when, according to numerous legends, the souls of the dead are given special powers.

41. In *Dracula* the vampire that possesses Lucy is destroyed to the accompaniment of a prayer for the dead read from a book (not named), "that so all may be well with the dead that we love and that the Un-Dead pass away" (p. 230).

42. Kendall says that the *Directorium Inquisitorium* treats exorcising witches and ferreting out heretics (p. 452).

43. Summers, p. 158. The introduction to Polidori's tale notes that one may become a vampire as punishment "for some heinous crime" (p. xxii), Lord Byron's "The Giaour" curses an infidel to become a vampire.

44. In Polidori's tale, Aubrey "was an orphan left with an only sister . . . by parents who died while he was yet in childhood" (p. 29). The vampire Ruthven attacks first Aubrey but is driven off; then, while Aubrey goes into a decline approaching madness,

"Aubrey's sister . . . glutted the thirst of a VAMPYRE!" (p. 72). That Madeline and Roderick were twins seems to indicate Poe's effort to heighten a similar action.

45. P. 542. Kendall regards Roderick's speaking of his "tenderly beloved" sister as ironic, as he speaks with a "bitterness which [the narrator] can never forget" (p. 451). I suggest that the bitterness lies in Roderick's knowledge that Madeline is a victim of the House.

46. *Traité sur les Apparitions* (1751), quoted in Summers, p. 212, n.47. I have not found Calmet's work easily available; the date suggests that Poe may have read it.

47. Ll. 758-760. The curse occupies ll. 747-786.

48. Not all corpses of those killed by vampires seem flushed. In Polidori's book, Ianthe has "a stillness about her face that seemed almost as attaching as the life that once dwelt there," but the corpse shows "no colour upon her cheek, not even upon her lips" (p. 48). Poe seems to "improve" Polidori by inversion. But in *Dracula*, when Lucy has been killed by a vampire, her pallid "brow and cheeks had recovered some of their flowing lines; even the lips had lost their deadly pallor" (pp. 172 and 179). Lying in her tomb, Lucy's "lips were red, nay redder than before; and on the cheeks was a delicate bloom" (p. 213). Poe's "mockery" of a blush and "suspiciously lingering smile" resemble the mocking smiles on the faces of Dracula and the female vampires when seen in their coffins (p. 55).

49. Summers, p. 184.

50. The word *incubus*, twice used in the story, literally means a male demon said to have intercourse with women by night. The narrator feels the presence of a demonic spirit, but does not know what it is.

51. J. A. MacCulloch, "Vampire," in Hastings's *Encyclopaedia of Religion and Ethics*. Spirits of many kinds may control the weather, as in Frazer, *passim*, and, for example, Ariel in Shakespeare's *The Tempest*, I, ii. A storm is a nearly universal feature of Gothic romances, usually to signal demonic attack. In Polidori's tale, Ruthven's attacks upon Aubrey and Ianthe take place in a raging storm—though it is not *said* to be caused by the vampire. Also in view of the widespread belief that twin children possess magical powers over nature, especially over rain and the weather, perhaps Madeline helped the House create the storm of "Usher." In Stoker's novel, Dracula "can, within his range, direct the elements; the storm, the fog, the thunder" (p. 253).

52. Quoted above from Summers. Perhaps Roderick's painting and the *Vigiliæ* held Madeline in her tomb until the full moon gave the House new "life."

53. This book seems used for theatrical effect. K. A. Spaulding, in "Poe's *The Fall of the House of Usher*," *Explicator*, X, Item 52 (1952), suggests that the "Mad Trist" "reveals symbolically the relationship between brother and sister. For Ethelred . . . is Madeline's counterpart." He discusses "Madeline's mindless instinctive urge toward unity." The urge seems to me vampiric hunger.

54. See, for instance, Leo Spitzer, "A Reinterpretation of 'The Fall of the House of Usher,'" *Comparative Literature*, IV, 351-363 (1952); Mabbott, *op. cit.*; and Maurice Beebe, "The Universe of Roderick Usher," *Personalist*, XXXVII, 147-160 (1956).

55. But it would require courage to save her if he knows she is a vampire; he would have to cut off her head and drive a stake through her heart. The introduction to Polidori's book describes how a vampire is killed. Arnold Paul, buried for "twenty or

thirty days," has returned as a vampire; his body is exhumed, and "A stake was driven entirely through the heart and body . . . at which he is reported to have cried out dreadfully, as he had been alive. This done, they cut off his head, burned his body, and threw the ashes into his grave" (p. xxi). In *Dracula*, Lucy's soul is saved when a stake is driven through her heart and her head is cut off.

56. In Polidori's tale, when the vampire attacks, Aubrey "felt himself grappled by one whose strength seemed superhuman . . . he was lifted from his feet and hurled with enormous force against the ground" (p. 47). In *Dracula*, the Count has the strength of twenty men. He amazes London draymen by lifting coffins filled with earth.

57. Kendall points out that the "slow and heavy pulse is traditionally characteristic of preternatural creatures" (p. 452).

58. If so, why does the ritual not stop Madeline? It may not be enough on a night of the full moon, perhaps also Halloween. Summers says, "But cases happen in which the priest is not a sufficiently powerful exorcist thus easily [by reading a ritual] to stop the nocturnal rambles and misdeeds of the undying one" (*The Vampire in Europe*, London, 1929, p. 221).

59. That doors fly open "untouched by human hands" is a Gothic commonplace since Clara Reeve's romances (Railo, p. 58). Blood stains upon the revenant's clothing is a convention of Gothic fiction, at least after "Monk" Lewis's description of the Bleeding Nun. In *Dracula*, when Lucy has become a vampire, blood "stained the purity of her lawn death-robe" (p. 225). If Poe thought of Madeline as a vampire, what is the meaning of Roderick's "I heard her first feeble movement in the hollow coffin"? If the "rushing gust" broke open her coffin and opened the donjon door, what explains the blood upon her robes? These characteristic features of Gothic romance seem intended to lead the reader, as they led the narrator, away from suspicion that Madeline is a vampire. Perhaps Madeline tried to escape her coffin, but found it too tightly sealed even for "mist." Perhaps she struggled in vain until the night of the full moon, when she and the House had power to create the storm. Perhaps she struggled with superhuman strength, helping other forces to open the Alcatraz, so to speak, that Poe describes. In any event, it is typical of the revenant that she should appear flecked with blood.

60. The vampire craving is violently erotic; see, for instance, Summers, *The Vampire in Europe*, p. 38. Can Madeline's attack upon her twin be called incestuous? Incest was a constant theme in Gothicism; see Railo, chap. viii, "Incest and Romantic Eroticism." Criticisms of "Usher" have suggested some kind of incest. Allen Tate, in "Our Cousin, Mr. Poe," speaks of "pure" (non-physical) incest in the story; D. H. Lawrence called "Usher" a "rather overdone, vulgar fantasy," telling a story of incest (Matlaw and Lief, eds., *Story and Critic*, New York, 1963, pp. 97-100). Praz, agreeing with Lawrence, speaks of Poe's tales as "always a symbolical, mythological translation of the same thirst for unrealizable love . . . and of the desire for that complete fusion with the beloved being which ends in vampirism" (p. 145). But as I see it, vampiric attack does not imply incest in the usual sense.

61. MacCulloch, XII, 591, and Summers, *passim*.

62. Would the House send Madeline to suck Roderick's blood, knowing that when he died, it would die? A vampire is driven by irresistible craving. The House had to fulfil the curse that created its life. A parallel appears in *Dracula*: Mina, though polluted

by a vampire, may be saved if the vampire may be killed before she dies. She is told, "Until the other, who has fouled your sweet life, is true [*sic*] dead you must not die; for if he is still with the quick Un-Dead, your death would make you even as he is" (p. 373). When Dracula is killed, Mina's marks of pollution disappear.

63. Allen, p. 98.

64. Quinn, pp. 284-285. To the extent that Roderick represents Poe, who is Madeline? In general, scholars have supposed that Madeline was drawn from Poe's wife, Virginia: for example, see Allen, pp. 312 and 358. In some particulars, Madeline may suggest Virginia. But in the identification of Roderick with the side of Poe's nature that inherited a degenerative strain, it seems to me possible to identify Madeline with Poe's sister, Rosalie. Rosalie, one year younger than Edgar, "failed to develop mentally after she was about twelve years of age" (Quinn, p. 93). In his mental distresses, Poe was reminded "through Rosalie's lack of mental growth, of the heritage that was his" (Quinn, p. 226). The fact that Madeline dies during the story, though Rosalie lived until 1874, is essential in dramatizing the story; moreover, it may reflect Poe's understandable thought of her as if she were dead—and the fear that his reason would die under attack of the same inherited strain. Virginia also lived more than seven years after "Usher" was published. Perhaps, since other "heroines" in Poe's stories do seem based on Virginia and since Virginia, too, as a blood relative, may have shared Poe's inheritance of mental instability, Madeline is based upon a composite of the two.

Poe and the Powers of the Mind_____

Robert Shulman

In his best fiction Poe achieves acute insights into the mysteries, processes, and terrors of the human personality without draining our shared inner life of its basic mystery. After all the attacks and denigration, after all the emphasis on his dubious metaphysics or even more unfortunate personal pathology, we can still go to Poe's fiction for illumination that writers of a more psychologically sophisticated era are oddly handicapped from providing. In Poe criticism that usually implies bad news—more necrophilia and incest, more maternal deprivation and twisted sex. But by stressing Poe's concern with the powers of the mind and the situation of the poet, I want to recall attention to some of the other psychological and intellectual matters that make Poe a living force.

The most interesting Poe criticism of the last decade has established that Poe's aesthetics and cosmology are central to an understanding of his fiction and poetry. I propose to reverse the usual recent emphasis and, while taking Poe's theory seriously into account, to emphasize the psychological revelations of the fiction. Whereas the usual psychological study of Poe treats the fiction as an unconscious manifestation of the author's problems or as an unconscious confirmation of orthodox Freudian categories, it seems to me that in his best stories Poe has a genuine understanding of unconscious processes and imaginative powers.[1] In the psychological criticism, Poe often emerges as a rather bedraggled victim of tendencies he failed to understand. My view, however, is that in much of his fiction Poe had unusual insight into often obscure mental processes and that, although he may not have grasped consciously all the implications—what human being ever does?—for purposes of his art he had remarkable understanding and control. Before trying to develop this view, however, since Poe has a consciously formulated theory of the mind, we must first consider the bearing of that theory on his imaginative understanding of our complex inner life.

In his Longfellow review (1842) and "The Poetic Principle" (1846 ff.)—the more revealing fiction will come later—Poe divides the mind into the three faculties of Intellect, Taste, and the Moral Sense.[2] Taste, we recall, is the most important faculty, since it does not deal with Truth or moral values but with Beauty and finally with that ideal, supernal Beauty, Unity, and Perfection that, on Poe's view, man and the universe originated in and have since fallen away from into the multiplicity, disintegration, and "state of progressive collapse" we now know.[3] Eventually the universe will disintegrate, Poe argues in *Eureka*, personal identity will be lost, but, more than compensating for this "inevitable annihilation" (XVI, 186), the original, Divine Beauty, Life, and Unity will prevail. In the meantime, under the guidance of Taste, by rearranging earthly forms and through suggestive imagery and music, poetry can begin to satisfy our inborn thirst for this eternal Beauty and Divine Perfection. By exciting our souls, Taste and the poem can elevate us and give us the insight we crave, the vision of eternity, the vision of an eternal realm of Beauty and Unity superior to anything we can know on earth.

Poe's landscape essays are allegories on this view of the mind and universe; or rather, on those phases, emphasizing poetic beauty, not annihilation and collapse. It is no wonder, then, that "The Domain of Arnheim" and the others have found few readers, just as it is fortunate if symptomatic that there is such a split between the emphasis on Beauty and Perfection in Poe's theory, particularly his critical theory, and the emphasis on darker qualities in his best fiction.[4] For Poe, through the soul-exciting elevation of Taste and the poem—or what unpredictably amounts to the same thing, through the terrifying catastrophe of death and annihilation—for Poe the highest aim of the self and the universe is to lose individuality and multiplicity, to go beyond the nature and life we know, and to become one with the Divine Unity and Beauty. That Poe has intensely mixed feelings about this process is suggested by the discrepancy between the dominant tone and revelations of most of his fiction and the dominant tone and emphasis of his theoretical pieces.

One example out of many is that, although Poe frequently mentions the elevated soul striving for Loveliness, his explicit critical theory does not take account of his major contribution to fiction, his imaginative understanding of the self, creating and suffering under the pressure of obsession, hatred, and dread. Poe's cosmological theory, to select another example, stresses disintegration as a prelude to Unity with Divine Beauty, but, although obsession and madness are types of disintegration, the more general and philosophical terms conceal much of what is actually going on in stories like "The Tell-Tale Heart" or "The Masque of the Red Death." Poe's vocabulary and concepts disguise much of his actual accomplishment. To be even more specific, and to return to our starting point, Poe's model of the mind in his critical essays allows no place at all for a depth dimension, no provision for what the tare, the abyss, and the dark, hidden chambers in his fiction suggest—that realm associated, not with supernal Beauty but with conflict, chaos, hostility, and fear, the depths his power comes from, much as Poe would like it otherwise and prettier.[5]

A case in point is "The Masque of the Red Death," often admired for its suggestive atmosphere and formal unity or as evidence that Poe was impelled to imagine ultimate annihilation, even that of an entire community, or as evidence that death is merely a prelude to a not undesirable union with Divine process and perfection.[6] The story is more immediately an allegory on Poe's scheme of the mind—he published "The Red Death" a month after his Longfellow review—and from the start it suggests Poe's dissatisfaction with that faculty of Taste his theory would lead us to expect him to present sympathetically. Prince Prospero, as his name indicates, represents one style of artist and imaginative man, the embodiment of one style of Taste, apparently frolic but actually terrified of impending madness. His magnificent palace, a variant on "The Haunted Palace" of the mind and the House itself in "The Fall of the House of Usher," is "the creation of the prince's own eccentric yet august taste" (IV, 250). It is absolutely isolated from the rest of the world and from the other faculties of the mind; in this secluded palace, "it was folly to grieve, or to think" (IV, 251), which are for the Moral Sense and Intellect.

Poe has real insight into that basically irrational strategy by which the mind attempts to preserve itself from its own forces of madness, disease, and disintegration by rigidly isolating itself and by assuming that the threat is external when in fact it is internal. This poetic mind, ostensibly given over to pleasure and Beauty, is actually given over to what it fears most, to those "sudden impulses of despair or of frenzy from within" (IV, 251) which, because of the unbreakably bolted doors, can neither escape nor originate in the outside world.

The dark labyrinth of the mind, excluded from Poe's formal theory, is richly (and perhaps overrichly) represented in the story by those irregular chambers of the mind, lighted not by the natural sun but by flickering torches filtered through dark Gothic windows and emblematic of the prince's strange imagination—some "thought him mad" (IV, 253). The prince's "own guiding taste" had decorated the bizarre interior of the palace and had also "given character to the masqueraders" who "stalked, in fact, a multitude of dreams" (IV, 254), through these lurid chambers. The protagonist is understandably threatened by the black clock of mortality and impending decay. In the inmost recess of his palace, the prince finally confronts the one fear he had refused to admit—Poe often takes a phrase or figure of speech literally—and Poe brings to a climax his suggestive allegory on the decay, madness, and disintegration of a mind exclusively given over to Taste; increasingly terrified of insanity, decay, and death; and altogether shut up in its own concerns and processes. Where Hawthorne might deal with the morality of isolation, Poe achieves remarkable insights into the irrational defenses of the mind, and into irrationality itself. In his imaginative work, even when he is deliberately using his formal model of the mind, Poe does not confine himself within the limits of that theory but suggests processes that, though they may originate in his personal preoccupations, have a disturbing and revealing general relevance.

"The Masque of the Red Death" suggests that we might stay alert to

Poe's tendency to be ambivalent about, to disguise, and to vary his treatment not only of the concerns he stresses in his theory but also in his fiction. We should not be surprised that a writer with Poe's imaginative understanding of the ordinarily concealed recesses and powers of the mind and universe should in his fiction emphasize ordinarily suppressed emotions, processes, and terrors or that he should to some extent conceal what he was revealing, as he does in "The Masque of the Red Death" (originally published as "The Mask of the Red Death"), or that he should seek to imagine more satisfying alternatives, as he does in the critical and landscape essays, some of the poems, and parts of *Eureka*. The problem for criticism is to understand and evaluate the results.

One major tendency in recent Poe criticism is to reconcile the serious differences in emphasis within and between Poe's theory and fiction by assigning priority to his aesthetic and religious values and by stressing them in interpreting the imaginative work.[7] The comic and satiric pieces aside, however, Poe's fiction succeeds to the extent that he can suggestively, precisely, and intensely illuminate the interior of the self, the powers and processes of the mind—and frequently the destructive and irrational powers. The stories can have profound implications for the universe, as in "The Fall of the House of Usher" and "A Descent into the Maelstrom," but they are less successful when the emphasis is almost exclusively cosmological, as in "The Conversation of Charmion and Eiros," or when Poe relies almost exclusively on melodramatic atmosphere, as in "The Assignation," so that his ability to probe inner states is not also called into play. The melodramatic trappings designed to suggest depth, mystery, and obscurity are not a major distraction when, instead of being a substitute for profundity, the depths are in fact explored, as in "The Masque of the Red Death."

Poe often seeks to find metaphoric equivalents for his explicit theoretical concerns—with identity and oneness in unexpected guises, with the importance of analogy, with the life and death power of writing and art to stimulate supernatural and finally fatal visions, with the terror and awe of moving from life to death to a strange afterlife or of swoon-ing and awakening to strange perceptions, novel sensations, and "to the verge of some stupendous psychical discoveries."[8] In a typical story, through the swooning or dizziness of the protagonist and through sym-bolic setting—a journey to the interior of foggy, secluded ravines or the dark, inner chamber of a castle or the hold of a ship—Poe organizes a series of episodes to suggest his main theoretical concerns and to es-tablish unconventional states of mind in which ordinary reason and common-sense are superseded and strange mergings, suggestions, and discoveries can occur. "The setting of a Poe story," as a recent critic says, "is not an external world at all, but the world of imagination made substantial for the purpose of coming to know it better."[9]

But in contrast to "A Descent into the Maelstrom," "The Tell-Tale Heart," or "The Cask of Amontillado," in his lesser works—"A Tale of the Ragged Mountains," "The Premature Burial," or "Morella," for example—Poe's revelations about the interior of the self and the pow-ers of the mind are relatively generalized and tame, relatively less pre-cise, less profound, and less intense than in his major fiction. One ra-vine is very much like another, ten swoons are not necessarily more suggestive than one, and Poe, as he is always tempted to do, relies heavily on mechanical conceits, strained effects, and overinsistent rhythms and rhymes. Although they illuminate facets of Poe's aes-thetic and cosmological theory, stories like "A Tale of the Ragged Mountains" and "Morella" do not pass beyond the possibility or "verge of some stupendous psychical discoveries." In his more successful work, however, the "discoveries" are precisely and suggestively ex-plored, often through Poe's strategy of sustaining tension between an ordered prose and an irrational subject matter or of dealing in a meticu-lously organized story with the powers of chaos and disintegration, or through Poe's ability to imagine and bring to fictional life his major symbols—the abyss, the darkened chambers, the teeth and eyes that animate much of his best work.

Perhaps the most significant pattern in Poe's career is that he developed the ability and technical control during the late 1830's and early 1840's to probe sharply those inner states and powers he had earlier suggested only quite generally and "philosophically." The contrast between "MS Found in a Bottle" (1833) and "A Descent into the Maelstrom" (1841) is an example of this tendency. When, as in many of the stories of 1844, Poe reverts to more generalized fiction related in theme and tone to his theoretical views, the quality declines, as the contrast between "The Tell-Tale Heart" (Jan., 1843) and "Mesmeric Revelation" (Aug., 1844) illustrates. Since the development of Poe's fiction is often overlooked, these changes in approach and quality are worth stressing to counter the impression that for all practical purposes the stories were written at the same time and that they can be best appreciated from the perspective of Poe's consciously articulated theory.

We must now turn to some major stories to suggest how, in ways his theory disguises or overlooks, Poe does in practice sustain precise, revealing insights into the powers of the mind and universe. He has, for example, a well-known ability to dramatize our latent powers of hostility and the destructive, cruelly punitive impulses which animate the recesses of the mind and which find their proper symbolic setting and enactment in "the inmost recesses of the catacombs" (VI, 171) in "The Cask of Amontillado." Less well-known but equally revealing are the insights into the destructive powers of hostility, drinking, and thwarted creativity Poe dramatizes in "Hop-Frog."

In one of modern literature's most moving versions of the tortured, alienated artist, Hop-Frog, jester to the King, is presented as a deformed dwarf and cripple, a stranger in the midst of other men, marked off from them by his foreign origins, his suffering, his talent, and his deformities. Hop-Frog's crippled movements, excessive sensitivity to wine, and rebellious subservience to his public further constitute an early portrait of the literary man as a drunk and an unwilling toady—hop, frog—those two guises for the artist that in the century to follow will be repeated again and again both sympathetically and hostilely. Hop-Frog, at the mercy of his employer, suffers indignities, watches his lady friend being callously abused, and, despite his protests, is forced first to drink the two glasses of wine he cannot stand and then to satisfy his employer's demand for "invention," for "characters," for "something novel—out of the way" (VI, 219). In thus suggesting a relation between drinking and writing, Poe places the blame for the drinking outside, on the cruel demands of the public, so that from Poe's point of view the account is self-excusing and partly true (the damage his own drinking did his wife is reflected and deflected by having the King throw the wine in the companion's face). More profound and fully dramatized is Poe's insight into the dynamics of destructive hostility and thwarted creativity, into the impulses the wine releases and allows Hop-Frog to express.

Poe shows that Hop-Frog's powerless subservience to his public is combined with thwarted creative power, represented partly by the powerful teeth, arms, and chest above the crippled legs. The image of the parrot's beak grating remorselessly against its cage, the harsh noise dominating the entire chamber, is one major symbol of the resulting hatred, frustration, and threatening, aggressive contempt the caged artist turns against those who have degraded him into a parrot, no nightingale or raven. The cruel noise dominates the final scene of awful revenge and turns out to be the grating of Hop-Frog's fang-like teeth, so that beak and teeth, in other contexts perhaps suggestive of masculine creative power, here further our insight into creative energies thwarted and turned to destructive uses.

"Inspired" by the wine, Hop-Frog turns to new uses an old story by Froissart and, with their own consent, by tarring and feathering King and court, chaining them, and dressing them as apes, he makes a monkey of his public as he feels they have made a parrot of him. In another of Poe's Gothically darkened chambers of the mind, Hop-Frog, "with the rapidity of thought" (VI, 216), then illuminates the mind's destructive powers in his terrifying final action. At the climax, the chamber's one source of light, the lamp, traditional symbol of imaginative creativity, becomes an implement of vicious torture and the abused, caged victim has been goaded into inhuman, all-too-human victimizer. For those who cannot separate the story from their knowledge of Poe's life and death, perhaps the most painful turn is the sense that, whatever the origins in Poe's drinking, imaginative blocking, and difficulty in writing, whatever the actual tangle of rights and wrongs, one of our most gifted writers was impelled at the end of his life to image his career in just this way. The final pathos for "the imagination at play," as Terence Martin puts it in another context, is that at the end Poe "imagines our death."[10]

Our immediate concern, however, is with the center of Poe's artistic achievement, his ability to understand imaginatively the darker and sometimes the creative powers of the human mind, as he does in "A Descent into the Maelstrom." In this story and in Poe's fiction generally, the dominant powers are most often the inner and outer forces of chaos and irrationality. At the climax of "A Descent," however, just as the protagonist is about to be destroyed in the whirlpool, the counter forces of reason and imagination do help save him from that abyss of existence which also suggests the chaotic depths of the mind. Freudians might more particularly identify the smooth, funnel-like whirlpool with an entry through the mother-sea into the womb, an entry the protagonist is intensely curious about but which he also fears will destroy him until he finally emerges from this chaotic region of death and birth, a changed, suddenly aged new man. Certainly the rhythms of near death and a precarious new birth are involved, but the impulse toward and away from the womb is not the only revelation in this exploration of the depths. As another part of Poe's drama of mental powers, through luck, observation, reasoning, and above all a flash of intuition, the protagonist, we recall, is saved from inner and outer chaos. Since Charles Feidelson has emphasized that the loss of personal identity is often the price Poe's narrators pay for the "exciting knowledge" they crave and fear, we should stress that in "A Descent," Poe suggestively reveals the precarious, saving powers of reason and imagination as well as the destructive energies, impulses, and depths of the mind and universe, and our fascination with these inescapable depths and dangers.[11]

Richard Wilbur has observed that Poe often models his stories on the descent into the dream state, and another basic model for his fiction emerges in "A Descent."[12] In this story, Poe apparently transformed and universalized his own experience of alcoholic fugue states—the dizziness, the roaring in the ears, the descent into unconsciousness, and the emergence, interestingly enough through the agency of a water-cask, so that Poe puts to the uses of suggestive inner exploration not only the public interest in voyages of discovery but also his own more private concerns.

"The Purloined Letter" and the other tales of ratiocination are the obverse of works like "MS Found in a Bottle" and "A Descent into the Maelstrom." As Richard Wilbur and Edward Davidson have shown, the poetic mind's unequivocal mastery over both ordinary and extraordinary men and circumstances—this dramatizing of the superiority of the poetic power of imagination gives the Dupin stories much of their urgency, distinguishes them from the ordinary detective story, and constitutes a large part of their appeal.[13] Like the man in "A Descent," Dupin is a careful observer, so that he is not cut off from the outside world, but the important creative insights are achieved in the Gothically darkened chambers of his room and mind, "among recesses of thought altogether inaccessible to the ordinary understanding" ("The Murders in the Rue Morgue," IV, 148). Using Dupin's "truly imaginative" mind as his standard, Poe subjects to quiet ridicule those more routine mental habits the Inspector represents.

As a law officer, the Inspector is an authority figure, an embodiment of some of the dominant values of his nineteenth-century American society. He is thorough, diligent, practical, and commonsensical; he works hard, methodically, and dully. His approach is inductive and Baconian, as Poe defines these terms in *Eureka*. Part of the mechanism of the tales of ratiocination is to show the superiority of the poet over the inspector, to put the authority figure in the power of the poet, to reverse the ordinary relations and, in a world that devalues poetic power, to affirm that power at the expense of practical men of affairs. Through his imaginative, intuitive ability to perceive analogies, to respond to oblique hints, to place himself in the mind of another, and to see things "as a whole" (IV, 166), as the esemplastic imagination should, the poet surrogate easily wins the gold at the expense of the respectable police official and the influential politician. In "The Purloined Letter" an inverted letter appropriately contributes to the success of this disguised man of letters. In "The Murders in the Rue Morgue," in addition to the conflict with the Inspector, another main source of interest is the contest between the intuiting, reasoning mind and the brute horror of things, a contest the imaginative mind controls from start to finish.

To show the superiority of the poet and his imaginative powers, Poe also carries the attack into the citadel of science by arguing strongly against the supremacy of mathematics as a means of getting at "general truth" ("The Purloined Letter," VI, 44). Dupin, like Poe himself, has mathematical and analytical gifts, because on Poe's mature view of the mind "the *truly* imaginative are never otherwise than analytic" ("The Murders in the Rue Morgue," IV, 150), but the imaginative power is the comprehensive one.[14] Because the Minister D—— is also a poet and mathematician, he is, as his initial suggests, a double of Dupin and is thus sympathetically treated until the surprising and unprepared-for turn against him in the final paragraphs of "The Purloined Letter," a turn that cannot be fully explained by Poe's need to end the story in an interesting way. Is it that Poe, reacting against the prevailingly low estimates of the poet and against criticisms of himself as a failure and "an unprincipled man of genius" (VI, 52), turns these charges against the Minister D—— in his role as successful man of affairs and, using the dreadful Thyestes myth, punishes the successful man as a failure? Or is it that Poe, who has elevated the imaginative powers through Dupin, also partly accepts the conventional negative judgment and expresses it through the final treatment of the double, the Minister D——?

Whatever his reservations, however, at the center of the tales of ratiocination Poe dramatizes the triumph of the powers of imagination. More characteristic, and more characteristically "psychological," are Poe's stories about the destructive, not the creative, powers of the human mind, as in his studies of the cruel dynamics of obsession and self-punishment. The punitive animosities turned against others in "The Cask of Amontillado" and "Hop-Frog" also turn inward against the self in "The Black Cat" and "The Tell-Tale Heart." In "The Black Cat" even more powerfully than in "The Masque of the Red Death," Poe also dramatizes his insights into the unconscious tendency of the mind to protect itself by rigidly suppressing threatening inner forces. Poe, moreover, knows that the mind can endow a neutral object like a cat with a charge of significance revealing the deepest strains in the character, and in "The Black Cat" he brilliantly suggests the inner dynamics, the underlying fear, hatred, and guilt that animate the narrator's terrified obsession with a common-place animal. The story suggests that these unacknowledged feelings are among the causes of the narrator's alcoholism, a disease that finally intensifies and releases his mad, destructive tendencies, so that Poe's view about himself—that the madness caused the drinking, and not the reverse—receives powerful imaginative confirmation.

The evil the narrator personifies in the black cat may be metaphysical and is certainly personal: by the end of the story, we are made to realize that, in cutting out the eye of the black demon, the narrator is also irrationally slashing and seeking to destroy his own demons, his own unacknowledged impulses and affinity with evil; he is expressing that mingled guilt and hatred of the unacknowledged dark powers in his own nature which he generalizes into the principle of perverseness, the "unfathomable longing of the soul *to vex itself*—to offer violence to its own nature" (V, 146). In contrast to the author's imaginative understanding, the narrator consistently suppresses his awareness of the specific nature of this dark, threatening side of his personality, and in cutting out the eye of the black cat, perhaps he is also irrationally seeking to "root out" and deny his own unacceptable insights into his nature. To the even more basic extent that the cat as witch is also a surrogate for his wife—the climax of the story strongly suggests this unconscious connection—the narrator, in blinding the cat, is also expressing his hatred for his wife and his guilty sense that, unless he prevents it, she will see into him. The narrator never consciously admits this guilt and hatred, but his feelings emerge at first in his abusive language and at the end in murder.

The narrator has endowed the black cat with a complex significance he does not consciously recognize. No wonder, after he hangs the animal, he fears he has committed an ultimate sin, unforgivable even by the infinite mercy of God, surely an excessive reaction if the cat is simply a cat or even a mysterious embodiment of metaphysical evil but understandable if the narrator unconsciously feels he has acted out the murder of his wife from obscure, unmentionable motives.

Poe continues to demonstrate his imaginative grasp of these unconscious processes by suggesting that the destructive fire in the narrator's bedroom is either an act of unconscious self-punishment, an act of supernatural vengeance, or perhaps both, since the correlation between the irrational, dark tendencies of the mind and analogous forces in the universe is developed in "The Black Cat," as it is in different ways in "The Fall of the House of Usher" and "The Descent into the Maelstrom." The narrator later encounters the double of his black cat—or is it the mysterious reincarnation?—or is the suggestion that he is pursued by the dark powers another indication of the narrator's sense of guilt and self-hatred? In any case, the narrator is again attracted to the cat, not surprisingly in view of the complex role the animal plays in his inner life.

As part of that role, the cat functions as a surrogate for the narrator's wife. Poe has a particularly sure understanding of the way we can displace onto a neutral object the feelings we are unable to admit we feel toward a human being. Through a series of humanized details that apply as much to a docile, affectionate wife as to a cat—the cat covers him with "loathsome caresses," is annoyingly underfoot, is fond of the narrator, to his disgust and annoyance—Poe suggests that the narrator is obscurely, powerfully disturbed by his wife's sexual intimacies and by her interference with his freedom. The resulting murder is pervasively in the back of the narrator's mind, since the gallows he immediately projects onto the cat's white spot suggests his guilt feelings for the murder to come as well as for the earlier hanging. The "absolute dread" the cat inspired, moreover, although it may have supernatural implications, also has origins in the narrator's unacknowledged hatred of his wife—Poe has indicated some of the sources—and in his unconscious recognition and fear of his own feelings and capacities for violence. The depth and complexity of the narrator's emotions come to a focus in the image of the black cat, its "hot breath" and "vast weight" bearing down on him, the black cat "an incarnate Nightmare that I had no power to shake off" (V, 151) and a memorable instance of Poe's ability to embody his psychological insights in a powerful symbol. Poe uses the image to suggest the intolerable burden of guilt, fear, hatred, and sexual threat which oppresses the narrator. In the narrator's final attempt to rid himself of his burden by attacking the symbol of his distress, his wife interferes, his feelings of hatred and revulsion turn from the surrogate to their real object, and the narrator's inner demons perform their fatal deed.

The feelings of guilt and self-hatred, evident throughout the narrative, become dominant after the murder, and in the final scene the narrator thus helps to bring about his own punishment and destruction. In having the narrator accidentally wall up the black cat, Poe continues until the end to develop the story's suggestive ambiguity. The "accidental" oversight is another example of unconscious suppression and hatred—a cat would be obvious in such confined quarters—but the "accident" may also be the result of the dark powers without reinforcing the dark powers within. Or is Poe again engaging with the troubled borderline between religion and psychology by having his narrator suggest quasi-religious and metaphysical explanations as a mask for personal disorder? In any case, the concluding image of the decayed, gore-clotted corpse and the "seducing" beast, "with red extended mouth and solitary eye of fire" (V, 155) brings to a suggestive focus Poe's insights into the disturbing power of blocked sexuality, guilt, and demonic hatred. In view of Poe's achievement in "The Black Cat," it would be unwise for criticism to concentrate on the "unfathomable" metaphysical faculty of perverseness and to overlook or minimize Poe's unusually specific and profound understanding of the processes of obsession, displacement, hatred, and self-hatred.[15]

In a closely related story, "The Tell-Tale Heart," in having the narrator focus on another apparently trivial detail, the old man's eye, Poe shows both his ability to vary one of his major symbols and, even more important, his advanced understanding of irrational motivation, of the charge of unrecognized significance and underlying anxiety, dread, and terror that animate such apparently meaningless obsessions.

Without being at all mechanical, Poe establishes that the old man's eye is repulsively ugly. But traditionally the eye is the source of insight and particularly of insight into the ideal and the beautiful, those two categories stressed in Poe's aesthetics and connected with the eyes and vision in stories like "Ligeia." The narrator reacts as powerfully as he does because the old man's eye, filmed over as it is, suggests that these important regions are inaccessible, or at least that the old man is shut off from them. The film over the old man's eye also suggests the infirmity and disease of old age and impending death. In getting rid of the eye, the narrator is irrationally trying to do away with ugliness, his anxiety about mortality, and the metaphysical as well as the psychological dread that existence is meaningless, on the grounds that the ideal and the beautiful make for meaning, as they do in Poe's outlook. If the figure of John Allan lurks in the distant background, we can understand some of the personal sources of this detail, since Allan must certainly have called into question the meaning of Poe's life and central commitments. Blind as the eye is, it still keeps watch, and to destroy it is to destroy all it represents.

Poe also knows about the hate that is inseparable from love, since the narrator "loved the old man" (V, 88) in a singularly destructive way. As in "The Cask of Amontillado," the narrator controls and tortures his elderly antagonist, at the same time that he himself is dominated by his own irrational terror and hatred. The story is compelling partly because the narrator's lucidity and control, mirrored in his prose style, are combined with his profound irrationality and a progressive revelation of basic anxiety, terror, and dread. In powerful episodes Poe keeps attention focused on the eye and its double, the eye of the lantern, so as to develop the depth of the narrator's madness, to unify the story, and to intensify the sense of terror and mystery as well as suggest the strange connection between the old man and the narrator.[16]

Killing the old man, destroying the "pale blue eye," does not remove the sources of the narrator's underlying dread. The punitive hatred and fear directed against the old man are intensified by the guilt of murder and turn inward against the narrator himself. "When people hate with all that energy," an Evelyn Waugh character says, "it is something in themselves they are hating." To the extent that the eye embodies the narrator's own fears and tendencies, to the extent that he has irrationally identified himself with his victim, to the extent that the relation has powerful Oedipal reverberations, to that extent the narrator has already destroyed part of himself. At the end, the narrator is responsive enough to the claims of the heart, to the claims of affection, life, and benevolence, so that he punishes himself, but these positive qualities are not integrated into his being and in this seriously split self the claims of affection take the form of punitive guilt feelings—their complex sources have been suggested—and they express themselves in an act of final self-destruction.

In "The Tell-Tale Heart" and in most of Poe's best fiction, the sense of general relevance we ask for in major art comes from this imaginative understanding and probing of significant human tendencies, powers, and disturbances ordinarily suppressed and obscured. These stories can, of course, become metaphors for the realities and horrors of social, political, religious, and epistemological situations, so that their human relevance is first but not exclusively psychological.

Poe, for example, provides an anatomy of psychological paralysis, of the consciousness claustrophobically trapped in its own irrational depths and struggling vainly to free itself from unnamed, threatening forces, as in "The Pit and the Pendulum" or the scenes in the hold of the ship in *Pym*. Elsewhere, hostility flares out and a Fortunato or a group of natives are killed. Sometimes reason and the creative imagination are in control, as in "The Purloined Letter," but more often the inner and outer forces of chaos threaten and dominate, annihilation in the abyss is close, the walls move in and we seem powerless to stop them, and the inner world Poe characterized so precisely begins to seem a paradigm of the public world we read about in our daily newspapers. He was "Our Cousin, Mr. Poe," for Allen Tate, and on both public and psychological grounds perhaps after all he is our cousin, too.

In establishing bonds of kinship, we may, however, seize too eagerly on those elements in *Eureka* and in Poe's aesthetics which emphasize the positive religious and aesthetic values of union with Divine Beauty and Unity and we may imply that in Poe's imagined world these positive elements balance or overbalance the exploration of internal terror, destruction and self-destruction, cruelty, obsession, chaos, and dread. As a recent critic has put it, "life is, in Poe's vision, the thing to be defeated, to be transcended, or to be evaded in acts of an aesthetic character. These acts are simultaneously the destruction of the self and the creation of the perfect poem."[17] I would urge, however, that, except for the Dupin stories, some of the comic tales, and possibly "A Descent into the Maelstrom," the emphasis on destruction and terror overwhelmingly predominates in Poe's best work and that, moreover, we should not confine our reading of Poe's fiction to the religious and aesthetic terminology of *Eureka* and the critical essays—to a vocabulary of Beauty, Divinity, and aesthetic perfection painfully achieved through personal or universal annihilation, disintegration, and catastrophe. To limit ourselves or to give our main emphasis to Poe's explicit vocabulary and concepts will prevent us from responding to the full range of Poe's precise, profound, and disturbing revelations of our shared mental powers. Because of our present understanding of Poe's theory, we are in a position to begin reading again for their telling psychological insights a body of fiction we had assumed to be badly overinterpreted and hence closed to a psychological approach. Since Poe is primarily successful as the cosmographer of the troubled, destroying, and creating self, our critical approach might well keep actively in touch with these dimensions of Poe's success.

Notes

1. The classical psychological study of Poe is Marie Bonaparte, *The Life and Works of Edgar Allan Poe: A Psychoanalytic Study* (London, 1949). Although it is too rigid in many ways, Marie Bonaparte's book is sensitive to basic impulses in Poe's imagination and seems to me to deserve renewed attention, in contrast to David M. Rein, *Edgar A. Poe: The Inner Pattern* (New York, 1960).

2. The development of Poe's critical theory is traced by Marvin Laser, "The Growth and Structure of Poe's Concept of Beauty," *ELH*, 15 (1948), 69-84. See also George Kelly, "Poe's Theory of Beauty," *American Literature*, 27 (1956), 521-536 and "Poe's Theory of Unity," *PQ*, 37 (1958), 34-44; and Joseph J. Moldenhauer, "Murder as a Fine Art: Basic Connections Between Poe's Aesthetics, Psychology, and Moral Vision," *PMLA*, 83 (1968), 284-297.

3. Edgar Allan Poe, *Eureka*, in *The Complete Works of Edgar Allan Poe*, ed. James A. Harrison (New York, 1909), XVI, 300. My quotations from Poe are from the Harrison edition and the citations will appear in the text.

4. Poe has a marked tendency to compartmentalize his interests and insights, and although the deepest personal sources of this tendency are outside our present concern, we should note that Poe regarded poetry as superior to and more refined than prose, so that he was apparently liberated to explore in detail in his prose fiction material he felt was unworthy of poetry and which he did not choose to discuss explicitly in his theoretical work. Nina Baym, "The Function of Poe's Pictorialism," *SAQ*, 65 (1964), 46-54, also concentrates on the split between Poe's theory and practice.

5. Poe develops his model of the mind—Intellect, Taste, the Moral Sense—in his review of Longfellow's "Ballads and Other Poems," *Graham's Magazine*, April, 1842. The faculty of perversity, first mentioned in "The Black Cat" a year later (August 19,

1843), is never assimilated into Poe's developed poetics. His summary statement of his mature poetics, "The Poetic Principle" (1846 ff.), uses the same three faculties as the Longfellow review.

6. See, e.g., R. W. B. Lewis, *Trials of the Word* (New Haven, 1965), p. 207 and Joseph P. Rappolo, "Meaning and 'The Masque of the Red Death,'" in *Poe: A Collection of Critical Essays*, ed. Robert Regan (Englewood Cliffs, N. J., 1967), pp. 134-144.

7. See, e.g., Moldenhauer; Rappolo; Kermit Vanderbilt, "Art and Nature in 'The Masque of the Red Death,'" *NCF*, 22 (1968), 379-389; Richard Wilbur, "Edgar Allan Poe," in *Major Writers of America*, ed. Perry Miller (New York, 1962, I, 373-380 and "The Poe Mystery Case," *NYRB*, 9 (July 13, 1967), 16, 25-28; Joseph M. Garrison, Jr., "The Function of Terror in the Works of Edgar Allan Poe," *AQ*, 18 (1966), 136-150; and Edward Davidson, *Poe: A Critical Study* (Cambridge, Mass., 1957).

8. "A Tale of the Ragged Mountains," V, 174. For Poe's account of his experiments with the state between waking and sleeping, see the *Marginalia* for March, 1846, XVI, 87-90.

9. Baym, p. 47.

10. "The Imagination at Play: Edgar Allan Poe," *KR*, 28 (1966), 209.

11. *Symbolism and American Literature* (Chicago, 1953), p. 36.

12. "Edgar Allan Poe," p. 378.

13. Wilbur, "Edgar Allan Poe," pp. 379-380 and Davidson, pp. 213-222.

14. A month before he published "The Purloined Letter" (Jan., 1845), Poe wrote in his *Marginalia* about "the silent analytical promptings of that poetic genius which, in its supreme development, embodies all orders of intellectual capacity" (Dec., 1844; XVI, 29).

15. For a related view of perverseness stressing Poe's moral concerns, see James W. Gargano, "'The Black Cat': Perverseness Reconsidered," *TSLL*, 2, (1960), 172-179.

In his review of Fouqué's *Undine*, which he overvalued as one of the world's greatest books, Poe responded enthusiastically to what he saw as an allegory on Fouqué's marital relations and troubles (*Burton's Gentleman's Magazine*, Sept., 1839; X, 30-39, and the *Marginalia* for Dec., 1844; XVI, 48-51). See also the favorable remarks in the review of *Twice-Told Tales* ([Nov., 1847], XIII, 149). "The Black Cat" probably has a biographical basis, too, and the discrepancy between the mild, delicate romance Poe praises in his criticism and the more profound and disturbing work he created in his fiction reminds us again that Poe's criticism is an imperfect guide to his creative work. The "purity" and "ideality" he commends in his review of *Undine* and in his poetics are not the dominant qualities of "The Black Cat" (or of "The Fall of the House of Usher," published in the same issue of *Burton's* as the *Undine* review). On the evidence of "The Black Cat," it is also questionable if the imp of the perverse is really a "saving" force in Poe's eschatology and psychology (Moldenhauer, p. 295).

16. For analysis of the psychological identification of the narrator and his victim, see E. Arthur Robinson, "Poe's 'The Tell-Tale Heart,'" *NCF*, 19 (1965), 369-378.

17. Moldenhauer, p. 297.

The Motive for Murder in "The Cask of Amontillado" by Edgar Allan Poe_____

Elena V. Baraban

Edgar Allan Poe's "The Cask of Amontillado" (1846) has never failed to puzzle its readers. The story is a confession of a man who committed a horrible crime half a century ago. Montresor lures Fortunato into the family vaults under the pretext that he needs Fortunato's opinion of the newly acquired Amontillado wine. In a remote niche of the crypt, Montresor fetters Fortunato to the wall and then bricks him in. The reader is perplexed by a seeming absence of the motive for this crime. Unable to find a logical explanation of Montresor's hatred for Fortunato, most commentators conclude that Montresor is insane. Such interpretation, however, seems to make certain details in the elaborate structure of the story unnecessary and this, in turn, goes against Poe's approach to composition.

In the essay "The Philosophy of Composition," written in the same year as "The Cask of Amontillado," Poe demonstrates that there are no details in his works that appear due to accident or intuition, and that his work proceeds "to its completion with the precision and rigid consequence of a mathematical problem" (166). While such an approach to creative writing has earned Poe an antipathetic reputation of the first "technocrat of art" from Theodor Adorno (193), it would find support with Russian Formalists. The Formalists' view of the form "as the totality of the work's various components" and their interest in analyzing the form by identifying the functions of the text's various components (Todorov 10-11) match Poe's ideas about writing. Indeed, "The Cask of Amontillado" could be among the Formalists' favorite texts, for the details in this story are like pieces of a mosaic, each of which serves the purpose of completing the whole. My hypothesis is that the story contains all the information necessary for finding an explanation for Montresor's heinous deed.

Although the subject matter of Poe's story is a murder, "The Cask of

Amontillado" is not a tale of detection, for there is no investigation of Montresor's crime.[1] The criminal himself explains how he committed the murder. Despite this explanation, "The Cask of Amontillado" is a mystery, for at its heart lies an intriguing question: "Why did he do it?" This question is different from the "Who's done it?" of a classical mystery, as the latter presents crime as a logical puzzle solved by a detective thanks to his intellect (Rahn 49-50). Nonetheless, in the absence of the figure of a detective, the central question of Poe's story compels the reader to perform an intellectual act of detection himself. Moreover, this question requires that the reader reverse the process of solving the mystery. Whereas a detective begins his investigation with defining motives for the crime, the reader of "The Cask of Amontillado" should decipher the circumstances described by Montresor in order to determine the motive for his murder of Fortunato.

Far from being a mediocre murderer, Montresor elaborates a sophisticated philosophy of revenge: "I must not only punish, but punish with impunity. A wrong is unredressed when retribution overtakes its redresser. It is equally unredressed when the avenger fails to make himself felt as such to him who has done the wrong" (848). A successful realization of this plan is questioned in criticism. G. R. Thompson, for example, argues that Montresor has failed to accomplish a perfect murder: "Montresor, rather than having successfully taken his revenge 'with impunity . . . has instead suffered a fifty-years' ravage of conscience'" (13-14). David Halliburton also gives a didactic reading of the tale: "If the walls erected by Poe's masons ('The Black Cat,' 'The Cask of Amontillado') are material, they are also existential: to take up mortar and trowel is to victimize the other, and through this process to bring about the victimization of oneself" (263).[2] According to Thompson, Montresor's words in the opening of the story, "you, who so well know the nature of my soul" (848), are probably addressed to Montresor's confessor, "for if Montresor has murdered Fortunato fifty years before,[3] he must now be some seventy to eighty years of age" (13-14).[4] Thompson uses the fact that Montresor's narration is actually a confession made on his deathbed to support the argument about Montresor's troubled conscience.

Without questioning the interpretation of Montresor's narration as taking place at his deathbed, I would still ask if the fact of this belated confession gives us sufficient ground to assume that Montresor has suffered pangs of conscience for fifty years. Following J. Gerald Kennedy, Scott Peeples quotes Montresor in support of the argument about Montresor's bad conscience: "Fifty years later, he still remembers his heart's 'growing sick—on account of the dampness of the catacombs,' but his heartsickness likely arises from empathy with the man he is leaving to die amid that dampness" (150). The quoted phrase, however, can hardly be used as evidence of the character's empathy towards his victim. In fact, it is one of the numerous instances of irony in Poe's text. Charles May notes in this regard, "Even if our hypothesis that Montresor tells the story as a final confession . . . is correct, the tone or manner of his telling makes it clear that he has not atoned, for he enjoys himself in the telling too much—as much, in fact, as he did when he committed the crime itself" (81). Indeed, the dash in the middle of the sentence—"My heart grew sick—on account of the dampness of the catacombs"—indicates a pause. When Montresor pronounces the first part of the phrase, the reader may believe that Montresor begins to feel sorry for the poor Fortunato. But when the narrator concludes that his heart is growing sick "on account of the dampness of the catacombs," it becomes clear that Montresor feels satisfaction about his monstrous deed even after fifty years. The narrator is perfectly aware of the effect the second part of his sentence produces on his listener (even if the whole narration is Montresor's last confession and his listener is a priest). It destroys any hope in Montresor's humanity and highlights once again that Montresor feels no guilt regarding the murder. A bit earlier in the text, Montresor recollects how, after laying the fourth tier of the masonry, he stepped back to listen to "the furious vibrations of the chain" produced by his poor victim: "The noise lasted for several minutes, during which, that I might hearken to it with the more satisfaction, I ceased my labors and sat down upon the bones. When at last the clanking subsided, I resumed the trowel" (853). Poe's character then is anything but Raskolnikov, the hero of Dostoevsky's *Crime and Punishment*, who confesses the murder he has committed because he is unable to overcome the excruciating feeling of guilt. Unlike Raskolnikov, Montresor is perfectly calm and rational in his account. He never expresses pity for his enemy or feels remorse for what he did. In the essay "Forms of Time and Chronotope in the Novel," Mikhail Bakhtin describes Montresor's tone as "calm, matter-of-fact, and dry" (200). This pitiless tone is partly responsible for the feeling of horror that seizes the reader at the end of the story. Indeed, while most contemporary detective fiction serves a didactic purpose by showing how criminals are caught, "The Cask of Amontillado" depicts a man who has successfully committed a premeditated murder and escapes punishment. Not only does Montresor feel no guilt, but he perceives his murder of Fortunato as a successful act of vengeance and punishment rather than crime.[5] Montresor presents himself as a person who had the right to condemn Fortunato to death; he planned his murder as an act of execution. Why did Montresor "punish" Fortunato?

For many, "The Cask of Amontillado" seems to start in the middle of Montresor's account: "The thousand injuries of Fortunato I had borne as I best could; but when he ventured upon insult, I vowed revenge" (848). J. R. Hammond argues that Montresor's revenge was caused by the thousand injuries he had received from Fortunato (89). Edward Wagenknecht makes a similar argument when he writes, "Poe carefully avoids specifying the 'thousand injuries' that [Montresor] has suffered, and there is an absolute concentration upon the psychological effect" (161). These interpretations are untenable, for Poe clearly contrasts injuries and insult in his story: the cause of Montresor's revenge was "insult," not "injuries." The narrator, however, never specifies the nature of this insult and thus puzzles Poe's commentators further (Hoffman 223). In the words of May, "The reader has no way of knowing what these 'thousand injuries' and the mysterious insult are and thus can make no judgment about whether Montresor's revenge is justifiable" (79). But is the reader indeed deprived of the possibility of judging whether the wrong done by Fortunato could warrant "capital punishment"?

Poe's intriguing silence about the nature of the insult that made Montresor murder Fortunato has given rise to explanations of Montresor's deed through insanity. Richard M. Fletcher, for example, maintains that Montresor's actions are irrational and that therefore he is mad (167). Other critics share this view. In an annotation to "The Cask of Amontillado," Stephen Peithman writes, "If there is any doubt that Montresor is mad, consider how he echoes Fortunato scream for scream, shrieking even louder than his victim" (174). In turn, Edward Hutchins Davidson writes,

> We never know what has made him hate Fortunato nor are we aware that he has ever laid out any plan to effect his revenge. . . . There is nothing intellectual here; everything is mad and improvisatory—and Montresor succeeds just so far as he is able to adapt himself to a mad, improvisatory world. (201-202)

Stuart Levine considers Montresor mad since he "murders because of an unnamed insult" (72). In Levine's opinion, "'The Cask' has no passage to tell the reader that the narrator is mad; the entire story does that" (80). Levine is certainly right in observing that there is no textual evidence of Montresor's insanity. Therefore, one may add, there is no reason to assume it.

The argument about Montresor's insanity rests upon the presupposition that insults ought to be differentiated and that only some of them are offensive enough to call for murder while others may be handled in a more civilized manner. The story, however, suggests a different interpretation of Montresor's action. A significant detail in Montresor's narration is the absence of an article in front of the word "insult." This absence implies that the nature of the insult need not be named at all, because this "insult" is semantically contrasted with the "injuries" that Fortunato had done to Montresor. While "injuries" presuppose rivalry of socially equal enemies, "insult" involves contempt: that is, treating the other as a socially inferior person. To insult is, by definition, "to exult proudly or contemptuously; to boast, brag, vaunt, glory, triumph, esp. in an insolent or scornful way; to assail with offensively dishonoring or contemptuous speech or action; to treat with scornful abuse or offensive disrespect" (*OED*, VII: 1057). Fortunato's disrespect of Montresor, regardless of the form it takes, is a sufficient basis for Montresor's vengeance. It follows then that the story does not start from the middle and that Montresor is not mad. Rather than implying the protagonist's insanity, the first paragraph of the story delineates the conflict between the characters as arising from their social roles.[6] A number of onomastic and semantic characteristics of the text indicate that "The Cask of Amontillado" is a story about the characters' power relations and their social status.[7]

Hammond maintains that both characters "lead socially active lives" (221-222). This reading, however, contradicts a notable detail of the story: Fortunato can remember neither the coat of arms nor the motto of the Montresors. The display of family insignia was an indispensable part in the life of a socially prominent nobleman. Since a rich and powerful man such as Fortunato cannot remember the Montresors' insignia, it is logical to assume that Montresor was not an active participant in the life of local aristocracy. Montresor's inability to recognize a secret sign of the freemasons made by Fortunato and the latter's remark, "Then you are not of the brotherhood" (851), also imply that Montresor is probably a bit of a recluse.[8] Fortunato is definitely more powerful than Montresor who admits to this himself "He [Fortunato] was a man to be respected and even feared" (848). Montresor's other remark, "You are happy, as once I was. You are a man to be missed" (852), provides further grounds to believe that Montresor is no longer as rich and socially conspicuous as he used to be.

Although not as wealthy and powerful as his enemy, Montresor probably has a better aristocratic lineage than Fortunato. The catacombs of the Montresors are extensive and their vastness genuinely impresses Fortunato. In the catacombs, surrounded by the remains of Montresor's ancestors, Fortunato realizes how powerful this family used to be. The protagonist's name, "Montresor" (my treasure) is a metaphor, for Montresor's noble ancestry is indeed his treasure.[9] Such assumption is all the more legitimate, since the word "treasure" usually refers to hidden riches and in Poe's tale, the hiding place is the catacombs underneath Montresor's palazzo. Furthermore, if Montresor has a better aristocratic lineage than Fortunato, the following lines become apprehensible: "Fortunato possessed himself of my arm. . . . I suffered him to hurry me to my palazzo" (849). It is not accidental that Montresor uses the verbs "to possess" and "to suffer" to describe his sensations. He "suffered" when his offender virtually led him to his palazzo because etiquette does not allow minor aristocracy the liberty of touching someone of more noble origin. At that point, however, Fortunato does not even remember that the Montresors "were a great and numerous family" (850). He is a *Fortunato*, someone who becomes rich and prominent by chance (Fortune), rather than through personal virtue. The name of this character may derive from Fortunatus, "a hero of a popular European tale" who receives from Fortune a purse which can never be emptied and who is enabled to indulge his every whim (Barnhart 1603). The fortuitous ground of Fortunato's social standing is uncovered in the course of Montresor's sophisticated revenge.[10]

Being a descendant of a powerful aristocratic family, Montresor could not possibly let Fortunato insult him with impunity. The Montresors' motto is "*Nemo me impune lacessit*" ("No one insults me with impunity"), and therefore, for Montresor, punishing his offender is a matter of honor, a matter of fulfilling his duty before his noble ancestry.[11] A description of the Montresors' coat of arms also provides a clue for uncovering the motive for Montresor's crime. "A huge human foot d'or, in a field azure; the foot crushes a serpent rampant whose fangs are imbedded in the heel" (Poe 851), which is the Montresors' coat of arms, is a *mise-en-abyme*, for the protagonist destroys Fortunato, who metaphorically represents the serpent that has dared to attack Montresor. Fortunato may use his power to "injure" Montresor, but since he comes from a less prominent family, he has no right to insult Montresor.[12] In other words, the conflict between the two characters arises from the sensation of incongruity between their current social standing and their right to prominence by virtue of their origin.

Although at first glance it appears Montresor acknowledges Fortunato's capability to distinguish fine wines, a careful textual reading uncovers how Montresor actually impugns Fortunato's ability, further revealing Montresor's sense of aristocratic superiority. Montresor exposes Fortunato's inadequacy in every possible way:

> He had a weak point—this Fortunato—although in other regards he was a man to be respected and even feared. He prided himself on his connoisseurship in wine. Few Italians have the true virtuoso spirit. For the most part their enthusiasm is adopted to suit the time and opportunity—to practice imposture upon the British and Austrian *millionaires*. In painting and in gemmary Fortunato, like his countrymen, was a quack—but in the matter of old wines he was sincere. In this respect I did not differ from him materially: I was skillful in the Italian vintages myself, and bought largely whenever I could. (848)

From this passage, we learn that while consciously practicing imposture upon tourists in matters of painting and gemmary, Fortunato genuinely considers himself knowledgeable in vintages. Montresor, however, does not share this opinion: he thinks that Fortunato's "connoisseurship in wine" is a delusion and thus calls it his "weak point." This passage is significant for understanding why Fortunato, who prides himself on his ability to distinguish vintages, says that Luchesi "cannot tell Amontillado from Sherry" (849). Burton R. Pollin interprets this passage as Poe's error: "Even if Poe had not made the error about the Spanish origin of amontillado, I fear that he would have found it difficult to differentiate between sherry and amontillado, everywhere defined as 'pale dry sherry'" (36). Rather than considering Fortunato's words, "Luchesi cannot tell Amontillado from Sherry" (849), as the author's error, it is crucial to view them as a subtle means of characterization of Fortunato as unworthy of his reputation of a connoisseur in wine. Apparently, Fortunato does not know that Amontillado is a sherry.[13] The reader can actually hear the mistake, which is otherwise unheard in a dialogue—namely, that Fortunato capitalizes the word "sherry" and uses it as a proper name rather than a generic term for several varieties of wine. Fortunato's mistake conveys his ignorance and arrogance.[14]

The seeming absence of the motive for Montresor's crime and its atrocity raise the question about the time of action in "The Cask of Amontillado." Some critics tend to read the story as a tale set in the Middle Ages or Renaissance. The carnival and the description of the family catacombs, also used as a wine cellar, would seem to strengthen such view. Nonetheless, two details in the story suggest that the action in "The Cask of Amontillado" takes place in the eighteenth or nineteenth century. Montresor wears a roquelaure, a cloak named after the Duke of Roquelaure (1656-1738). Roquelaure was a popular piece of clothing during the eighteenth century and the early part of the nineteenth (*OED*, XIV: 100), which means that the story is set no earlier than the eighteenth century but no later than the first half of the nineteenth century. Another detail that indicates the eighteenth or nineteenth century as the time of action in "The Cask of Amontillado" is a reference to wealthy tourists that visited the town.[15] Montresor calls them "British and Austrian *millionaires*" (848). A new class of *nouveaux riches*, of whom Fortunato was probably one, became socially prominent in the eighteenth and nineteenth centuries. In the earlier period, no nobleman would think of exercising "imposture" upon the bourgeoisie. In his study of the cultural and historical backgrounds of Poe's story, Richard P. Benton argues that the crime described by Montresor takes place right before the French Revolution, at the end of the eighteenth century. Since the key point in Benton's article is that the setting of the tale is French, he argues for the dating of the story before the Revolution because "both aristocratic privileges and the carnival had been abolished in France by 1796" (20). Although Benton's argument regarding the French setting of the story is debatable,[16] his interpretation of the conflict between Montresor, "a proud but relatively impoverished" aristocrat, and "the upstart Fortunato" is convincing (19). It is definitely a conflict that reflects social tensions of the capitalist period.

It seems that Montresor chose for his revenge "one evening during the supreme madness of the carnival season" (848) because his servants were not at home and because Fortunato was already exhilarated with wine[17] and was an easy prey for Montresor. The carnival setting is also important because the traditional carnival symbolism helps Montresor undermine Fortunato's position.[18] The "madness of the carnival season" (848) in Poe's story is "supreme" because carnival is not simply a temporary substitution of normal order by chaos, but its inversion. In *Rabelais and His World*, Bakhtin notes that during carnival festivities "the world [is] permitted to emerge from the official routine" (90). Jokes, excessive eating, drinking, and merry-making are tributes to "the honor of the time" (848). During carnival, identities are destabilized and traditional social hierarchy and etiquette collapse; the poor may be elected carnival kings, bishops, and popes, whereas representatives of the upper classes may disguise themselves as peasants, servants, or fools. It is not surprising then that Fortunato, a man of wealth and influence, is wearing a costume of a fool during the carnival: "He had on a tight-fitting parti-striped dress, and his head was surmounted by the conical cap and bells" (848). Fortunato's carnival identity is a significant detail in the story, for Montresor's plan is to make a fool of his enemy, to ensure Fortunato's engagement in "a tragic farce."[19] Hence, Montresor's sarcastic comment about Fortunato's looks: "How remarkably well you are looking to-day!" (848). Further, Montresor makes another pun about Fortunato's "foolish" looks: "And yet some fools will have it that his [Luchesi's] taste is a match of your own" (849). Having chosen the role of a fool, Fortunato becomes socially inferior to Montresor who is wearing a black silk mask and a *roquelaure*, a costume that makes him resemble an executioner.

Space symbolism in "The Cask of Amontillado" also serves the purpose of undermining Fortunato's social role. The action takes place in Montresor's palazzo, a space that is new to Fortunato. Fortunato's poor physical condition highlights his inadequacy. In a hostile space of Montresor's family catacombs,[20] the victim's gait becomes "unsteady," his coughing becomes longer, and he has to lean upon Montresor's arm (850-851).

For a long time, Fortunato does not notice that Montresor's words and actions have double meaning. Fortunato says that he will not die "of a cough," and the cunning Montresor agrees: "True—true" (852). "Producing a trowel from beneath the folds" of his cloak (851), Montresor mocks Fortunato's membership in the Order of Masons. Fortunato also misreads the double meaning of the word "Amontillado." Slowly making his way through the crypt, the foolish victim sees several signs testifying to a special meaning of "Amontillado." By making Fortunato try De Grave, Poe "no doubt means a pun on the word 'grave'" (Peithman 171).[21] The whole imagery of the crypt suggests that the word "Amontillado" is a metaphor and evokes the meaning of the root of this word—*mons, montis*.[22] The walls of the crypt "had been lined with human remains, piled to the wall overhead. . . . Three sides of this interior crypt were still ornamented in this manner. From the fourth the bones had been thrown down, and lay promiscuously upon the earth, forming at one point a mound of some size" (Poe 852). A mound of some size would be *monticula* or, by extension, *montilla*. Already fettered to the wall of the niche, Fortunato still does not understand the metaphoric meaning of the word "Amontillado." In the best tradition of fairy-tales, the culmination comes at midnight:

Now there came from out the niche a low laugh that erected the hairs upon my head. It was succeeded by a sad voice, which I had difficulty in recognizing as that of the noble Fortunato. The voice said—

"Ha! ha! ha!—he! he!—a very good joke indeed—an excellent jest. We will have many a rich laugh about it at the palazzo—he! he! he!—over our wine—he! he! he! "The Amontillado!" I said. "He! he! he!—he! he! he!—yes, the Amontillado." (853-854)

Critics have interpreted this passage in a number of ways. According to Levine, "Fortunato tries to laugh off the entire affair as a prank" (85-86). Since the character is not actually laughing but is simply saying "Ha! ha! ha!" in a "low" and "sad" voice, the scene produces the effect of horror. In addition to interpreting the scene as Fortunato's futile attempt to present Montresor's actions as a joke, critics maintain that Fortunato's laughter and his incessant repetition of the word "Amontillado" give Montresor ground to believe that his victim finally realizes that "Amontillado" is a pun. Charles W. Steele makes an informed argument in favor of the metaphoric meaning of "Amontillado":

Rendered in English, the term means "Montilla-fied" wine. No other meaning does have relevance. . . . The Italian past participles *ammonticchiato* and *ammonticellato*, signifying "collected or formed into little heaps" are from two derivative forms of the verb *ammontare* (to heap up; Spanish: *amontonar*, past part. *amontonado*). The *ch* (k) and the *c* (ch as in chill) of the Italian past participles positioned as they are in their respective words and spoken rapidly would both approach our *j*. The *ll* of *amontillado* (variously like the *li* of *million* and the *y* of *yes*) when pronounced emphatically gives roughly the same result. Thus an apparent identity of sound exists for the untrained ear. (As Poe was taught Italian and Spanish at the same time in 1826 at Charlottesville by Professor Blaettermann, a German, it is quite possible that he was not an expert on pronunciation.)

The implication of Montresor's pun may be understood as the pile of bricks he hastily threw to wall in Fortunato. As the climax of the story is reached, he causes his victim to repeat the word amontillado . . . a final time, as if to assure himself that his subtle and superior wit has been fully appreciated. (43)

According to Steele, Montresor gets an impression that Fortunato is able to understand the meaning of "Amontillado." If, as Kennedy writes, "for Montresor the drink has been from the outset a secret, figurative reference to death itself and in promising a taste of Amontillado, he has . . . been speaking of Fortunato's destruction" (141), the only way Fortunato may understand Montresor's pun is through devising associations between the name of the wine and Italian words. The name of the wine looks like the past participle of the Spanish verb *amontinallar.* Amontillado, thus, would mean "collected in a pile," "gathered in a mount," or "piled at the mountain." Although in modern Spanish there is no verb *amontinallar* (instead, there is the verb *amontonar*), in Old Spanish there was the verb *amontijar.* This means that it may not be necessary to explain similarities in the pronunciation of related Italian and Spanish verbs. Similarities in Romance languages allow us to believe that regardless of whether Fortunato knew Spanish, in the end of the story, he might realize that he himself is to become amontillado—a pile of bones gathered in a mount in Montresor's crypt.[23]

Whether Fortunato actually understands the reason behind Montresor's terrible vengeance—namely, that he is being punished for his arrogance and for insulting someone who is equal or superior to him— does not impede a successful completion of Montresor's plan. Montresor "punishes" Fortunato "with impunity" and escapes retribution. Moreover, in accordance with his plan, Montresor does not murder Fortunato secretly, but stages a spectacle of execution so that the victim knows who kills him.[24] If Fortunato does not understand why Montresor has decided to kill him, he may believe Montresor is a madman. Typically, some scholars who argue that Montresor is insane turn to the last scene in the story. John Rea, for example, maintains that

Montresor's action is "perversity, not revenge. If he had cared about re-venge, instead of echoing Fortunato, his last words would have been something about the insult that he says Fortunato has given him" (qtd. in Peithman 174). A careful examination of Montresor's last words, however, provides additional evidence in support of the thesis that the motive for Montresor's murder of Fortunato has been vengeance. The very last words in the story are, "Against the new masonry I re-erected the old rampart of bones. For the half of a century no mortal has dis-turbed them. *In pace requiescat!*" The sentence "*In pace requiescat!*" ("May he rest in peace") refers to Fortunato. The phrase is used in the Requiem Mass and during Last Rites, when, having listened to a dying person's confession, a priest forgives his/her sins. If Montresor's narra-tion is his last confession, he should look forward to being forgiven and to hearing "*In pace requiescat!*" ("May your soul rest in peace") from his priest. Instead, Montresor maliciously subverts his role as a repen-tant sinner when he says "*In pace requiescat!*" in regard to Fortunato. Not only does he deprive the poor man of a Catholic's right to the last confession, he is arrogant enough to abuse the formulaic expression used by priests to absolve dying sinners. The fact that Montresor uses this expression for finally pardoning Fortunato highlights his convic-tion that he has merely avenged himself for the wrong that Fortunato afflicted upon him fifty years ago.

From *Rocky Mountain Review of Language and Literature* 58, no. 2 (Fall 2004): 47-62. Copyright © *Rocky Mountain Review of Language and Literature.* Reprinted with permission of *Rocky Mountain Review of Language and Literature.*

Notes

I would like to thank Steven Taubeneck for discussing portions of this article with me. My special thanks go to the anonymous reviewers of this work whose insightful comments have led to significant improvements of both form and content.

1. Edgar Allan Poe has long enjoyed the reputation of the founder of contempo-rary detective fiction. In three of his short stories, the detective Chevalier C. Auguste

Dupin is the central character. See John Walsh (5, 82) on Poe's role in the development of modern detective fiction.

2. Other scholars who argue that Montresor has failed to commit the perfect crime because he has suffered the pangs of remorse are Thomas Pribek, Walter Stepp, J. Gerald Kennedy, Charles May, and Scott Peeples. Writing a few years after Thompson, Kennedy argues that Montresor's feeling of guilt overtakes his retribution (141-143). Peeples discusses Kennedy's interpretation in detail and supports his reading of "The Cask of Amontillado" (148).

3. This is clear from Montresor's words, "For the half of a century no mortal has disturbed them [the bones]" (854).

4. Peeples agrees with the interpretation of the tale as a deathbed confession (150). William H. Shurr also discusses Thompson's hypothesis regarding Montresor's audience in "The Cask of Amontillado." In support of this hypothesis, Shurr quotes Benjamin Franklin's tale published a few years before Poe's story. In the tale, a Frenchman whose name is Montresor is very ill. His confessor believes Montresor may die soon and suggests he "makes his peace with God." Shurr argues that Franklin's tale is one of the sources for the story by Poe (28-29).

5. The significance of the vengeance theme in "The Cask of Amontillado" cannot be overlooked. David S. Reynolds maintains that the story has biographical resonance with Poe's life: it "reflects Poe's hatred of two prominent New York literary figures, the author Thomas Dunn English and the newspaper editor Hiram Fuller" (93). Reynolds refers to earlier biographical studies of the story by Francis P. Demond and Marie Bonaparte: see Demond (137-146) and Bonaparte (505-506).

6. Much criticism focuses on Poe's use of symbols that enhance psychological portrayal of his characters. In the last decade, however, more studies have explored the immediate historical and social context of Poe's work: e.g., the reading of Poe's "House of Usher" by Leila S. May (387-396).

7. Some commentators suggest that the conflict between Montresor and Fortunato may be part of their blood feud. Such reading, however, cannot account for the fact that Fortunato willingly agrees to go to Montresor's residence to taste wine and talks with Montresor as if they were friends.

8. See a detailed discussion of the Freemasonic elements of Poe's story by Peter J. Sorensen (45-47); cf. Reynolds (99-100).

9. On the origins of the name Montresor, see E. Bruce Kirkham (23).

10. Graham St. John Stott provides a reading of the name "Fortunato" and of Poe's whole story in the light of the interpretation of God and virtue in Calvinism: "Fortunato means fortunate, wealthy, happy, or more generally, because of its derivation from the verb *fortunare*, blessed by the goddess *fortuna*, or random fate. Naturally, to embrace fortuna was unthinkable in the Reformed tradition. Fate was not random" (86). Montresor, according to Stott, is God's agent; he punishes Fortunato for representing ungodly ideas and qualities, the opposite of providence.

11. The motto of the Montresor family may also be translated as "Let no one have insulted me with impunity." Typically, the motto refers to "insult," not "injuries." The Latin verb "lacessere" means to "provoke," "ill-treat," "challenge," "harass," and "bully"; Latin equivalents for the verb "to injure" are "nocere" and "laedere."

12. Commentators have provided insightful interpretations of the Montresors' coat of arms including those who view the Montresors as represented by the serpent and those who argue that it is impossible to decide if the Montresor family is represented by the foot or by the snake. The latter interpretation is used in support of the argument that Poe's story is an exploration in the "circularity of revenge" (Kennedy 143). Peeples writes in this regard, "The Montresor family could be represented by the foot, which crushes its enemies, or the snake, which sinks its fangs into the heel of its adversary. . . . In either case, both the foot and the snake are injured, perhaps fatally (if the snake is poisonous); neither wins" (150). In Peeples' interpretation, the emphasis is on injuries. By contrast, if the Montresors' motto is to be taken into account ("No one insults me with impunity"), the emphasis in interpreting the coat of arms should be on retaliation.

13. Other principal types of sherry are Montilla, Manzanilla, Fino, and Vino de Pasto (Simon 483).

14. Burton R. Pollin refers to several sources on *Amontillado*: "For evidence that the name *amontillado* was applied to a fine, dry sherry in the 1840's see Richard Ford, *Gatherings from Spain* (London, 1906), chap. xiv, which concerns the production of sherry wines; the book dates from 1846, being revised from *The Handbook for Travellers in Spain* (London, 1845)" (Pollin 240-241). Pollin also refers to the book by Walter James: *Wine: A Brief Encyclopedia* (New York, 1960): 8.

15. A popular tourist destination, Italy attracted many international tourists from across Europe and North America throughout the nineteenth century especially during carnivals. The last chapters of *Smoke* (1867) by Ivan Turgenev are set during the carnival in Venice in the second half of the nineteenth century.

16. Although Montresor is a French name, the story is set in Italy. This is clear from the sentences, "He prided himself on his connoisseurship in wine. Few Italians have the true virtuoso spirit" (848). Other details that also testify to an Italian setting are "palazzo," "Italian vintages," and Italian names of Fortunato and Luchesi. These details help to counter the argument by Burton R. Pollin, Stanley J. Kozikowski, and Richard P. Benton, who maintain that the setting of the tale may be French. See Pollin (31-35), Kozikowski (269-277), and Benton (19-25).

17. Several commentators interpret the story as a tale about the evils of excessive drinking. Pollin mentions "self-destructive drunkenness" (25) as the basic idea that Poe borrowed from Hugo. According to Arthur Hobson Quinn, Fortunato's "craving for the wine has led him to his doom" (500). Jeffrey Meyers presents a similar argument: "There is a considerable amount of drinking in Poe's stories. He usually describes its negative effects, with a moral disapproval that suggests he shared contemporary attitudes and was passing judgment on his own disreputable behavior. In one story a victim is lured by the offer of fine Sherry and then permanently sealed up in a catacomb filled with Amontillado" (87). It is hard to believe that Fortunato, a wealthy and powerful man, would be "lured" by the offer of alcohol from his less powerful countryman. Fortunato follows Montresor in order to show his connoisseurship of wines.

18. In "Forms of Time and Chronotope in the Novel," Mikhail Bakhtin discusses the difference between the use of carnival imagery during the Renaissance and by authors of the later period (such as Poe). In "The Cask of Amontillado," the tropes of car-

nival are no longer used for asserting the "all-encompassing whole of triumphant life"; rather, they create "the denuded, sterile, and, therefore, oppressive contrasts" (199-200). Since Poe's characters, one a representative of the old aristocracy and the other a new "aristocrat," are most likely class enemies of the capitalist period, perception of the carnival by Poe's protagonist who feels himself as an outsider among the rising bourgeoisie cannot be the same as the carnival consciousness in Rabelais' *Gargantua and Pantagruel* (1532-1552), which Bakhtin discusses in *Rabelais and His World*.

19. A fool was always an important character in carnival performances. Fortunato, however, was not "engaged," and this gave Montresor a chance to arrange a special "performance" for the *unlucky* fool.

20. Used in the story in its original sense, the word "catacombs" refers to a subterranean cemetery of galleries with recesses for tombs.

21. Reynolds also notes that De Grâve is a pun that points to Fortunato's fate (97).

22. *Ad + montis* may mean "towards a mount."

23. The title of Poe's story may be read as a metaphor. One of the readers of this paper has drawn my attention to the fact that the word "cask" may be interpreted as part of the pun that points out to Fortunato's death. According to *OED*, in the past the word "cask" could mean "casket." In turn, in the nineteenth-century America the word "casket" began to be used in the meaning of "coffin" (*OED*, 941). If the word "cask" in Poe's story is to be associated with a coffin and if Amontillado is a pun on Fortunato's terrible death, then the title "The Cask of Amontillado" may in fact stand for "The Casket of Fortunato."

24. The mask that Montresor is wearing highlights the association of the murder with execution. Executioners used to wear masks so that relatives or friends of the condemned could not find them.

Works Cited

Adorno, Theodor. *Aesthetic Theory*. Trans. C. Lenhardt. London: Routledge & Kegan Paul, 1984.

Bakhtin, Mikhail. "Forms of Time and Chronotope in the Novel." *The Dialogic Imagination*. By Mikhail Bakhtin. Trans. Caryl Emerson and Michael Holquist. Austin: University of Texas Press, 1996. 84-259.

_____. *Rabelais and His World*. Trans. Helene Iswolsky. Bloomington: Indiana University Press, 1984.

Barnhart, Clarence L., ed. *The New Century Cyclopedia of Names*. New York: Appleton-Century-Crofts, Inc., 1954.

Benton, Richard P. "Poe's 'The Cask of Amontillado': Its Cultural and Historical Backgrounds." *Poe Studies* 29.1 (June 1996): 19-27.

Bonaparte, Marie. *The Life and Works of Edgar Allan Poe: A Psycho-Analytic Interpretation*. London: Hogarth, 1971.

Davidson, Edward Hutchins. *Poe, A Critical Study*. Cambridge: Harvard University Press, 1957.

Demond, Francis P. "'The Cask of Amontillado' and the War of the Literati." *Modern Language Quarterly* 15 (1954): 137-146.

Fletcher, Richard M. *The Stylistic Development of Edgar Allan Poe*. The Hague: Mouton, 1973.

Halliburton, David. *Edgar Allan Poe: A Phenomenological View*. Princeton: Princeton University Press, 1973.

Hammond, J. R. *An Edgar Allan Poe Companion: A Guide to the Short Stories, Romances, and Essays*. London: Macmillan, 1981.

Hoffman, Daniel. *Poe Poe Poe Poe Poe Poe Poe*. Garden City, NY: Doubleday, 1972.

Kennedy, J. Gerald. *Poe, Death, and the Life of Writing*. New Haven: Yale University Press, 1987.

Kirkham, E. Bruce. "Poe's 'Cask of Amontillado' and John Montresor." *Poe Studies* 20.1 (June 1987): 23.

Kozikowski, Stanley J. "A Reconsideration of Poe's 'The Cask of Amontillado.'" *American Transcendental Quarterly* 49 (Summer 1978): 269-280.

Levine, Stuart. *Edgar Poe: Seer and Craftsman*. DeLand, FL: Everett/Edwards, 1972.

May, Charles. *Edgar Allan Poe: A Study of the Short Fiction*. Boston: Twayne, 1991.

May, Leila S. "Sympathies of a Scarcely Intelligible Nature: The Brother-Sister Bond in Poe's 'Fall of the House of Usher.'" *Studies in Short Fiction* 30 (1993): 387-396.

Meyers, Jeffrey. *Edgar Allan Poe: His Life and Legacy*. New York: Charles Scribner's Sons, 1992.

The Oxford English Dictionary. 2nd ed. Ed. J. A. Simpson and E. S. C. Weiner. Oxford: Clarendon Press, 1989.

Peeples, Scott. *Edgar Allan Poe Revisited*. New York: Twayne, 1998.

Peithman, Stephen. "The Cask of Amontillado." *The Annotated Tales of Edgar Allan Poe*. Ed. Stephen Peithman. Garden City, NY: Doubleday and Co., Inc., 1981. 168-174.

Poe, Edgar Allan. "The Cask of Amontillado." *Poetry and Tales*. By Edgar Allan Poe. New York: The Library of America, 1984. 848-854.

_____. "The Philosophy of Composition." *Poe's Poetry and Essays*. Introduction by Andrew Lang. New York: E. P. Dutton and Co., Inc., 1955. 163-177.

Pollin, Burton R. "*Notre-Dame de Paris* in Two of the Tales." *Discoveries in Poe*. Notre Dame: University of Notre Dame Press, 1970. 24-38.

Pribek, Thomas. "The Serpent and the Heel." *Poe Studies* 20.1 (June 1987): 22-23.

Quinn, Arthur Hobson. *Edgar Allan Poe: A Critical Biography*. London: Appleton Century Co., 1992.

Rahn, B. J. "Seeley Regester: America's First Detective Novelist." *The Sleuth and the Scholar: Origins, Evolution, and Current Trends in Detective Fiction*. Ed. Barbara A. Rader and Howard G. Zattler. Contributions to the Study of Popular Culture Series. No. 19. New York: Greenwood Press, 1988. 47-61.

Reynolds, David S. "Poe's Art of Transformation: 'The Cask of Amontillado' in Its Cultural Context." *New Essays on Poe's Major Tales*. Ed. Kenneth Silverman. New York: Cambridge University Press, 1993. 93-113.

Shurr, William H. "Montresor's Audience in 'The Cask of Amontillado.'" *Poe Studies* 10.1 (June 1977): 28-29.

Simon, Andre Louis. "Sherry." *Chambers's Encyclopaedia*. New Revised Edition. Vol. XII. Oxford: Pergamon Press, 1966. 482-483.

Sorensen, Peter J. "William Morgan, Freemasonry, and 'The Cask of Amontillado.'" *Poe Studies* 22.2 (December 1989): 45-47.

Steele, Charles W. "Poe's 'The Cask of Amontillado.'" *Explicator* 18.7 (April 1960): 43.

Stepp, Walter. "The Ironic Double in Poe's 'Cask of Amontillado.'" *Studies in Short Fiction* 13 (1976): 447-453.

Stott, Graham St. John. "Poe's 'The Cask of Amontillado.'" *Explicator* 62.2 (Winter 2004): 85-89.

Thompson, G. R. *Poe's Fiction: Romantic Irony in the Gothic Tales*. Madison: University of Wisconsin Press, 1973.

Todorov, Tzvetan. "Some Approaches to Russian Formalism." *Russian Formalism: A Collection of Articles and Texts in Translation*. Ed. Stephen Bann and John E. Bowlt. New York: Barnes & Noble Books, 1973. 6-19.

Wagenknecht, Edward. *Edgar Allan Poe: The Man Behind the Legend*. New York: Oxford University Press, 1963.

Walsh, John. *Poe the Detective: The Curious Circumstances Behind "The Mystery of Marie Rogêt."* New Brunswick: Rutgers University Press, 1968.

The Problem of Realism in "The Gold Bug"_____

J. Woodrow Hassell, Jr.

While one cannot deny the truth of Professor Fagin's description of Poe's narrative genius as that of "a poet whose native idiom was figurative language, whose mind habitually thought in rich imagery, at once luxurious, indefinite, and romantic,"[1] the thoughtful reader of the tales of ratiocination cannot fail to notice the contribution of a very different kind of artistic personality, that to which Hervey Allen refers as the "Perfect Reasoner" and the "Perfect Logician."[2] In this article I propose to study "The Gold Bug" as a product of the collaboration of the Poet and the Reasoner.

I

As Professor Wimsatt has demonstrated, "The Gold Bug" was the brilliant climax to Poe's cryptographic writings, and its purpose was to capitalize upon the curiosity about ciphers which he had carefully nurtured in the readers of *Alexander's Weekly Messenger* and *Graham's Magazine*.[3] The germ from which the story originated, then, was Poe's desire to reveal in spectacular fashion the methodology of solving a simple substitution cipher. The inspiration was clearly that of the Reasoner.

While ciphers appeal to the imagination, their solution involves a fundamentally rational procedure, similar to that used in attacking a mathematical problem. It follows, therefore, that while a narrative based upon the solution of a cipher need not be completely realistic in every particular, it must at the very least be credible as a record of fact. The author of such a tale must be most careful to fulfil the demands of verisimilitude.

In spite of this limitation, it was the Poet who supplied the main outline of the tale and many of its details: the accidental discovery of the parchment and of the secret writing on it; the complicated clues in

Kidd's memorandum, with its references to such romantic details as the "Devil's seat," the "Bishop's hostel," the skull in the tulip tree, etc.; and the buried treasure. The result is a romantic narrative, in which realism and fantasy are in general nicely blended, but in which they are also sometimes in conflict. Possibly the most salient feature of Poe's art in "The Gold Bug" is the consummate skill with which he concealed this conflict and gave an appearance of reality to the fanciful elements of the story.

II

As the outlines of the tale crystallized in his mind, Poe seems to have perceived at once the problem of verisimilitude which he faced and to have prepared to disarm the potential suspicions of his readers.

In the first place, he must have been uncomfortably aware that the discovery of the parchment and its message was based upon a chain of all too fortuitous circumstances, a series of coincidences which must be rendered credible at all costs.

The Poet and the Reasoner attacked the problem with a two-pronged assault. It was the former, no doubt, who suggested the introduction of the theme of the gold bug, which from its initial role of motivating Legrand's discovery of the parchment is developed into the symbol of a kindly fate, which has foreordained his acquisition of the treasure. Thus the events of the tale are presented in an atmosphere of a kind of inevitability.

But this was not enough. Poe was fully aware that the chain of circumstances must be presented in such a way as to minimize their fortuitous character, and this he has done with great skill.

At the very beginning of the narrative, when the detail has no apparent significance, Poe raises the issue of the unusual frigidity of the weather. The reader sees nothing at which to cavil and accepts. Thus the process of legerdemain commences.

Next Legrand looks in his writing desk for paper but finds none.

Now rare indeed is the writing table which is totally destitute of paper of any kind; but the situation is possible, and in any event the attention of the reader is concentrated upon the beetle, a sketch of which Legrand is about to draw.[4] He accepts again, all the more readily when Legrand, like most men, is able to find in his pocket a rumpled piece of what appears to be paper. (Note how subtly Poe suggests paper, without committing himself irrevocably, by describing it as "what I took to be very dirty foolscap." Jupiter unwittingly adds to the deception by referring to the parchment as "paper" on the occasion of his visit to Charleston.)

Finally, Wolf, the great Newfoundland, enters and realistically enough leaps upon the shoulders of his friend, the Charlestonian, who by now holds the drawing made by Legrand on the "fools-cap."

A few paragraphs further on, the narrative is interrupted. It is only much later that the reader is permitted to realize that these seemingly innocent details, which his mind has now been conditioned to accept as plausible, are the basis for the discovery of the writing on the parchment.

But if Poe has succeeded in making the parchment theme credible to a passive reader, the analytical one is not long in recognizing that it is fundamentally unrealistic. When Jupiter found it, the parchment had clearly been on the beach for a long time. Indeed, Poe indirectly says as much when he establishes a connection between the boat, which "seemed to have been there for a very great while," and the parchment. But one can hardly be expected to believe that a message written in ink upon a piece of parchment which has been exposed for even a short time to the rain, to the heat of the sun, to the abrasion of constantly shifting sands, and to the chemical action of sea water could remain legible.

This criticism is all the more valid if, as Poe implies, the ink used by Kidd was "regulus of cobalt, dissolved in spirit of nitre." The union of those chemicals produces cobalt nitrate, $Co(NO_3)_2$, which is readily soluble in water. Even if one can accept the unlikely hypothesis that the lettering on the parchment was intact when Jupiter picked it up, Legrand's washing it with warm water could scarcely have failed to obliterate the message. Consequently, there can be little doubt that Poe had had no practical experience with invisible inks when he composed "The Gold Bug."[5]

Thus, it must be considered as certain that Poe did not know of this weakness in the motif of the parchment on the beach. He realized, of course, that parchment is extremely durable; and inexperienced as he was with invisible inks, he very probably took it for granted that the ink used on the parchment was as indelible as the latter was imperishable. Certainly that is the assumption which he expected his readers to make, and it is not unlikely that the vast majority has done so.

While in this particular instance Poe did so unconsciously, he used here one of his most effective techniques for producing a pseudo-realistic effect, that of linking an unreal detail to a highly realistic one in such a way as to persuade the reader of the validity of the former.

There is still another violation of realism in Poe's treatment of the parchment theme. Legrand made his drawing of the bug with ordinary pen and ink. Is it not astonishing that the visitor, who saw, not the sketch of the insect but the reddish outline of the skull, failed to detect the sudden apparent change in the color of the ink?

Poe seems to have been aware of this problem, which placed him in a quandary. To have permitted the friend to realize that what he was examining was not the picture drawn by Legrand would have been to disclose prematurely a detail which Poe rightly felt should be reserved for later revelation. Therefore, he very ingeniously shifts the reader's attention away from the *color* of the sketch to the heated discussion between Legrand and his visitor regarding its *form*, and in so doing gives plausible motivation to Legrand's discovery of the skull on the parchment. A very clever coup!

In both these instances, the Prestidigitator has succeeded in turning the attention of the reader away from details which could prove embarrassing if examined too closely.

III

Thus far this study has dealt with problems in realism of which Poe seems to have been aware for the most part and for which he made provision very skillfully. In the following sections, I propose to present further examples of how he strove to give an air of verisimilitude to his story, and also some instances of failure to be realistic of which Poe was not conscious. Finally, I shall discuss some miscellaneous details of the narrative which bear upon the problem of its realism.

In the passage describing the solution of the cipher, it is the Reasoner who holds the spotlight, and his performance is truly remarkable. Wimsatt has not exaggerated when he says, "Legrand's explanation of how he solved the cipher is a fine feat of exposition. . . . The writing of this kind of prose was . . . one of Poe's most impressive gifts."[6] Cryptanalytic experts also consider the passage a classic. Witness Mrs. Gaines's statement that it is a "gem of cryptanalysis, equal to any modern specimen."[7]

However, the passage is far more than an example of brilliant expository writing; it also highlights a technique used by Poe with telling effect throughout the last part of "The Gold Bug." Legrand's discussion of his solution of the cipher gives a powerful impression of precision, orderliness, and logical and realistic method in dealing with a real problem, an impression which is reinforced by his methodical shrewdness in deriving from the decrypted cipher the directions for finding the treasure and in pursuing these clues to a successful conclusion. Thus the dominating personality of Legrand, the apostle of common sense, logic, and realistic observation, is used by Poe to impart an atmosphere of realism to the final section of the tale.

Artistically effective as the passage undoubtedly is, it nevertheless reveals under close examination that the Perfect Reasoner was not quite so expert a cryptographer as he believed himself to be—or as he would have wished his readers to consider him—for it includes errors of detail, hence minor failures in realism.

Possibly the most obvious mistake in "The Gold Bug" occurs in the table showing how many times each symbol of the cryptogram appears in the cipher text: the character "(" is omitted altogether.[8] As Professor Mabbott has indicated, the error is multiplied in texts of "The Gold Bug" which are based on the handwritten corrections of the author in the J. Lorimer Graham copy of the 1845 edition of Poe's Tales.[9]

There is, however, an additional error in the table, one which has not been the subject of comment. To illustrate it clearly, I shall reproduce the table as given in the *Dollar Newspaper*[10] and in the 1845 edition of the *Tales*:[11]

	Of the character	8	there are	33.
		;	"	26.
		4	"	19.
‡		)	"	16.
		*	"	13.
		5	"	12.
		6	"	11.
†		1	"	8.
		0	"	6.
9		2	"	5.
:		3	"	4.
		?	"	3.
		¶	"	2.
		— .	"	1.

One must consider that a cryptographer dealing with an unknown cipher cannot take it for granted that a single cipher character will necessarily represent one plain language letter, since there are systems in which groups of two or more symbols stand for a given letter of the alphabet. One may even find ciphers in which sometimes one and sometimes groups of two or more cipher characters are used to represent single letters of the text.

But taken in its context, Legrand's statement, "Of the character 8 there are 33," can mean only that the symbol 8 is the cipher substitute for a letter of the English alphabet. When, three lines below, he observes, "Of the character ‡) there are 16," he would appear to imply that the two symbols *taken together* constitute a unit standing for a single letter of the alphabet. The same consideration applies to the remarks concerning the characters † 1, 9 2, : 3, and ——. .

That such a meaning is not correct may readily be ascertained from the cryptogram itself, where these symbols do not always appear in adjacent positions; in some instances, never. Furthermore, Poe himself later indicates that † alone represents the letter *d*.

The explanation is that the author has listed together those cipher symbols which appear the same number of times. For example, 9 and 2 each have five occurrences. Thus, while Poe's actual count was correct, the form in which he presents it in the table is misleading and technically inaccurate.

That this double symbol error should have occurred is strange, because there is no virtue whatsoever in listing together the symbols which appear the same number of times, *unless one wishes to make the table more compact.*[12]

That the man who set the type for "The Gold Bug" in the *Dollar Newspaper* edition was concerned with spatial limitations is indicated by the way in which he dealt with the conclusion of Legrand's letter to his friend in Charleston. The concluding salutation and the signature are placed on the same line, as follows: "Ever, (*sic*) yours, WILLIAM LEGRAND."[13]

Therefore, it may well be that what I have called the double symbol error was not the work of Poe at all, but rather that of the typesetter, who set the symbols double in order to save space where there seemed to be only repetition of statement.

Be that as it may, Poe seems to have been indifferent to the possibility of error in his frequency table, since when he inserted the penciled corrections in the J. Lorimer Graham copy of the *Tales*, he made only one minor emendation in the table.

The mistakes in the frequency table are of interest in what they indicate regarding the limitations of the Reasoner; but since they are inconspicuous and detract but little, if at all, from the effectiveness of Poe's discussion of ciphers, the worst which can be said of them is that they indicate carelessness about minor details.

An error of a more serious type, from the pedagogical point of view, occurs in Legrand's remarks about ciphers. He says, ". . . in English, the letter which most frequently occurs is *e*. Afterward, the succession runs thus: *a o i d h n r s t u y c f g l m w b k p q x z* . . ."

Wimsatt has pointed out that this listing is an unwarranted and careless combination of two frequency groups, one of vowels and the other of consonants, which Poe found in Rees's *Cyclopaedia*.[14] How faulty it is can be observed by comparing it with the table given in Mrs. Gaines's authoritative text:[15]

POE   :   E A O I D H N R S T U Y C F G L M W B K P Q X Z
GAINES :   E T O A N I R S H D L C F U M P Y W G B V K X J Q Z

Some of the inaccuracies in Poe's order may be of negligible importance, but failure to recognize that the letter *T* is in almost all English texts the letter of second highest frequency would certainly handicap a fledgling cryptographer.[16]

Since Poe intended "The Gold Bug" to be a lesson in cryptography, the revelation of how to solve a cipher which had been so eagerly awaited by the readers of his magazine articles, the errors in Poe's letter order are more serious than those of the frequency table, because they involve inaccuracies in cryptographic principle. On the other hand, as failures in realism they are too inconspicuous to disturb the ordinary reader.

IV

The solution of the cipher produced the following text: "A good glass in the Bishop's hostel in the Devil's seat—forty-one degrees and thirteen minutes—northeast and by north—main branch seventh limb east side—shoot from the left eye of the death's head—a bee-line from the tree through the shot fifty feet out."[17]

In spite of the presence of such romantic expressions as "the Bishop's hostel" and "the Devil's seat," the memorandum is not in general subject to the charge of unrealism. It is, in fact, a very concise statement of the clues for finding the buried treasure; and much of its phraseology is, as Poe indicates, precisely the language which one would expect a seafaring man to use.

The only clearly unrealistic detail is the angular measurement, "forty-one degrees and thirteen minutes." It is significant that when Poe made his penciled corrections to the story, he changed it to read "twenty-one degrees and thirteen minutes." His reason for making the change is not hard to discover.

Considered from a mathematical point of view, the actions of Legrand in the Devil's seat created a definite geometrical figure, the triangle given below:

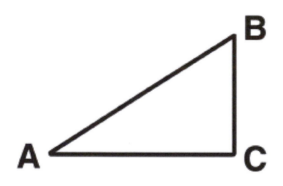

In the figure, A represents the eye of Legrand; B the skull; and C the intersection of a vertical dropped from the skull to the horizontal line passing through point A. Line BC is the vertical distance between A and B; line AC the horizontal distance.

Regardless of the dimensions of the triangle, if angle BAC is 41°13′, line *AC* will always be longer than line *BC*, but the proportionate difference will never be great. In other words, if Legrand's angle of sight was 41°13′, the skull was almost as far above the Devil's seat as it was distant from it horizontally.

While not detailed, Poe's description of the topography of the area tends to preclude such a situation. The pertinent passages of the text, while agreeing that the skull was above the Devil's seat, all seem to indicate that it was much farther away horizontally than vertically. Therefore, it becomes apparent that the angular reading of 41°13′ is inconsistent; but if it is given as 21°13′, the difficulty is eliminated, since then the horizontal distance will increase at a much more rapid rate than the vertical.

It may be that when he originally composed the tale Poe did not formulate a precise mental picture of the vista extending before Legrand, but that later he did so and thus came to realize the desirability of changing the angle. In any event, Poe is to be credited with correcting this inconsistency.

V

Having located the skull, Legrand summons his friend; and the three men, Legrand, the Charlestonian, and Jupiter, proceed to the tulip tree. Although the death's head now becomes a "prop" of the first importance, Poe gives relatively few details regarding it. Among those which he does supply are the following:

1. It is attached to the limb with one large nail.

2. The beetle is easily passed through the eye socket of the skull and then falls unimpeded to the ground.

Of the validity of these two details there are grounds for serious doubt, especially in view of Poe's contention that the skull must serve as so completely accurate a reference point that a variation of even two and a half inches is not permissible.

To have the skull affixed to the limb with only one nail is inconsistent with this premise. Even if originally it had been tightly attached to the wood, the movement of the limb in the wind and the erosive effects of the weather could scarcely have failed to produce a loosening effect which would have permitted the skull to rotate about the axial nail. To have made it a truly accurate indicant, Poe should have used at least two nails.

Furthermore, Poe makes no provision for the fact that unless the skull had been specially prepared in advance, it would have been impossible for Jupiter to pass the bug through the eye socket and then to let it fall freely to the ground. Of course, the skull could have been cut in one of several ways so as to permit the passage of the beetle. Indeed, Poe may have envisioned it as having been prepared in such a way as to fit the limb tightly and at the same time to leave openings under the eye sockets through which the bug could be passed. (Under these conditions one nail might possibly have sufficed to hold the skull securely in place.) But of these matters he makes no mention.

Probably these problems in realism did not occur to Poe. Just as his visualization of the general locale of his story, except for that of Sullivan's Island, was vague, so I believe that he neglected to picture to himself in detail the sight which greeted the astonished eyes of Jupiter when that worthy Negro came to the end of the limb. On the other hand, it is possible that Poe may have been aware of the problems in question but supposed that it would make his story very clumsy indeed to supply a detailed description of the appearance of the skull and of its position on and means of attachment to the limb. In any event, he very cleverly avoids the necessity of supplying such details by keeping the skull out of sight of everybody except Jupiter, whose state of mind is so confused that he cannot distinguish his right eye from his left.

Whatever objections may be raised against Poe's treatment of the skull, we must take his word that the beetle passed through the right eye socket, dropped to the ground, and thus established a reference point. Since this was in error by about three inches, Poe says, the three men almost failed to find the treasure; but finally Legrand divines Jupiter's mistake, shifts the peg, and locates the chest.

Here the Reasoner was once again at fault. As has been demonstrated, the difference of three inches could not have had the importance which Poe attributed to it. It really makes no difference through which eye of the skull Jupiter put the bug.[18]

This error was clearly the result of carelessness. Once again there was a specific problem in mathematics which Poe simply did not trouble himself to work out. Had he done so, he could easily have adjusted the dimensions of the geometrical figure so as to present the situation realistically. Since few readers have cared to investigate the matter, this instance of unrealism has passed almost completely unnoticed.

VI

There remain a few loose threads to be gathered in. Mention has already been made of the important artistic role of the gold bug. Its genesis is also of interest, especially since it is an interesting example of cooperation between the Poet and the Reasoner. For a more detailed account, I shall refer the reader to the pertinent works of Professor Smyth[19] and Hervey Allen.[20] Suffice it to say here that the beetle of "The Gold Bug" is a composite of two genuine entomological specimens, the so-called "Click Beetle" (*alaus oculatus*), and the "Gold Beetle" (*callichroma*). Thus the results of the careful observation of the Reasoner have been combined by the Poet to create a fictitious insect, which, however, is not so far removed from reality as seriously to shock even a professional entomologist.

Turning from the beetle to the tulip tree, we find a very minor error. In somewhat pedantic style, Poe refers to it as "*Liriodendron Tulipiferum*." The correct spelling is, of course, "*Liriodendron Tulipifera*." The misspelling is perhaps hardly worthy of note, except that it is amusing to find Poe, while assuming the learned manner of a professor of botany, falling into so egregious an error.

Finally, a brief discussion of Poe's description of the setting of his story is in order. That of Sullivan's Island is relatively detailed and clear and may well be considered an accurate portrayal of the island as it appeared during the period of Poe's military service at Fort Moultrie. However, the description of the mainland is, as has been noted, quite vague, precisely because it is purely fictitious and because Poe did not create for himself a precise visualization of the imaginary area.

In presenting to his readers the "high grounds on the shore of the mainland" and the "hills upon the mainland," Poe deliberately violated the demands of realism.[21] In so doing the Poet took an artistic "calculated risk," for an accurate description of coastal South Carolina would have forced him to dispense with such attractive romantic details as the "Bishop's castle," the "Devil's seat," and the hill where the treasure was buried.

VII

In general, the separate roles of the Poet and the Reasoner in the composition of "The Gold Bug" are not difficult to trace. It was clearly the latter who originated the plan to write a story centered about the solution of a cipher, who created the character of William Legrand, and who took charge of those parts of the tale in which Legrand describes how he "broke" the cipher and went on to locate the treasure. Equally obviously, it was the Poet who composed the rest of the narrative, introducing much that is fanciful into its structure. The problem in realism which Poe faced was to create from these sometimes conflicting elements a plausible and consistent narrative unit.

His approach to the problem was twofold: characteristically, he first sought to create a mood and atmosphere in which the plot of the tale would most readily seem credible; and secondly, he employed special measures to deal with specific difficult situations.

As we have seen, the powerful personality of Legrand and the symbolic role of the bug both contribute most effectively to the verisimilitude of the tale. Poe further enhanced its plausibility by introducing a number of strikingly realistic details into the tale. His description of the skull as presenting a white target against the dark foliage of the tree is an example. Also worthy of note in this connection is the soundness of the motivation of the actions of the three men.

In spite of these measures and despite the fact that the Poet and the Reasoner frequently worked together in harmony—the synthesis of the gold bug is a striking example—the demands of the former sometimes produced problems in realism for which special provision had to be made. We have observed the amazing feats of legerdemain with which Poe solved them. The one problem with which the skill of the sleight of hand artist was not able to cope was the insistence of the Poet that the South Carolina mainland must be depicted as hilly. Here Poe had to make a choice, which even Charlestonians will agree was a happy one.

There are other problems of realism in "The Gold Bug," for which the author made no provision simply because he was unaware of their existence. Since most of them are technical and hence inconspicuous, and since they produce no serious inconsistencies in the tale, they are of little artistic importance. However, they are of interest in what they reveal of Poe's limitations.

In general they indicate that in dealing with minor or technical details, he tended sometimes to be careless.

The cryptographic mistakes suggest that Poe was not a profound student of the subject and that his approach to cipher solution was more intuitive than methodical. They also reveal him to have been a *poseur*, in that the air of authority with which he wrote on cryptography is not justified by his actual knowledge of it.[22]

The misspelling of the scientific name for the tulip tree is another example of the limitations of Poe's pretended erudition, but more conclusive still is his treatment of the invisible ink theme.

Of the two mathematical errors little more need be said. They are probably the result of hasty composition, and Poe must be credited with the correction of the more obvious one, that of the angle of 41°13′.

VIII

When one considers the many divergent and sometimes conflicting elements which have gone into the structure of "The Gold Bug," one cannot fail to admire the skill with which Poe has fused them into a plausible and coherent unit. Errors and inconsistencies are present, to be sure; but, as Professor J. O. Bailey has justly remarked, "The perfectly fascinating hocus-pocus that makes up the art of 'The Gold Bug' is all the more remarkable because it is indeed hocus-pocus, evident to anyone who undertakes to weigh and measure what Poe pretends to weigh and measure so carefully." And, one might add, the supreme proof of the brilliant art of the tale lies precisely in the fact that its readers have been so charmed that almost none has even thought of inquiring too closely into "what Poe pretends to weigh and measure so carefully."[23]

From *American Literature* 25, no. 2 (May 1953): 179-192. Copyright © 1953 by Duke University Press. Reprinted by permission of Duke University Press.

Notes

1. N. Bryllion Fagin, *The Histrionic Mr. Poe* (Baltimore, 1949), p. 213.

2. Hervey Allen, *Israfel* (New York, 1934) pp. 408, 410.

3. W. K. Wimsatt, Jr., "What Poe Knew about Cryptography," *PMLA*, LVIII, 778-779 (Sept., 1943)

4. The necessity for sketching the bug is also plausibly motivated.

5. Wimsatt's implied theory (*op. cit.*, p. 775, n. 98) is probably correct.

6. *Ibid.*, p. 779.

7. Helen F. Gaines, *Elementary Cryptanalysis* (Boston, 1944), p. v.

8. See the table, which is reproduced in its original form.

9. Hervey Allen and Thomas O. Mabbott (eds.), *The Gold Bug* (Garden City, 1929), pp. 67-68, 85-86.

10. Edgar Allan Poe, "The Gold Bug," *Dollar Newspaper*, I, No. 23, 1, 4 (June 28, 1843).

11. Edgar Allan Poe, *Tales* (New York, 1845). My immediate source, which reproduces the text in question, is the following: *The Complete Poems and Stories of Edgar Allan Poe*, ed. A. H. Quinn and E. H. O'Neill (New York, 1946), I, 470-471.

12. For the standard procedure for making a frequency count, see Gaines, *op. cit.*, pp. 74 and 77.

13. *Ed. cit.*, p. 1.

14. *Op. cit.*, pp. 771-772.

15. *Op. cit.*, p. 219.

16. *Ibid.*, p. 75.

17. This is the reading to be found in all editions of "The Gold Bug" through 1845.

18. Theda Gildemeister (ed.), *The Gold Bug* (New York, 1902), p. 95.

19. Ellison A. Smyth, Jr., "Poe's *Gold Bug* from the Standpoint of an Entomologist," *Sewanee Review*, XVIII, 67-72 (Jan., 1910).

20. *Israfel*, pp. 174-177.

21. *Ibid.*, pp. 171-172, 178.

22. See Wimsatt, *op. cit.*, pp. 776-778.

23. Grateful acknowledgment is made of the invaluable contributions to this article of the following gentlemen: Professors J. O. Bailey and Alfred G. Engstrom of Chapel Hill, N. C.; Professors W. E. Hoy, M. B. Seigler, and J. W. Bouknight, and Dr. William M. Corbett of Columbia, S. C.

The Self-Consuming Narrator in Poe's "Ligeia" and "Usher"

Ronald Bieganowski

In his analysis of the dialectical dimensions to literature, Stanley Fish argues for a transfer of attention from the content of art (that it reflects, contains, or expresses Truth) to its effects: "from what is happening on the page to what is happening in the reader. A self-consuming artifact signifies most successfully when it fails, when it points away from itself to something its forms cannot capture."[1] This proposal has led to fresh and stimulating readings of a number of texts. It can also, I believe, help clarify some very elusive tales of Edgar Allan Poe: Poe appears to have created self-consuming narrators in "Ligeia" and "The Fall of the House of Usher." These narrators focus attention less on what they would seem to point to (Beauty, Truth) and more on what happens in them as they attempt to express the ineffable.[2] These works represent two of Poe's most read and talked about stories, perhaps two of the best known stories in American literature.[3] Though not presuming to have discovered a final interpretation, I do have a sense that Poe is much more obvious in these stories than has been commonly recognized and that, in a relatively simple structure, Poe's "The Imp of the Perverse" helpfully reveals his self-consuming narrator at work.

In "The Imp of the Perverse," Poe shows the power language has on the narrator as well as on the reader. The impact of the story on the reader follows the impact of "a rough voice" resounding in the narrator's ears. The story's second part, where the narrator tells of his successfully undetected murder of a friend and his subsequent confession, clearly illustrates the general description of "perverseness" given in the first part. Poe then concludes a general analysis of the soul's faculties and impulses:

> We stand upon the brink of a precipice. We peer into the abyss—we grow
> sick and dizzy. . . . By slow degrees our sickness, and dizziness, and horror,

become merged in a cloud of unnameable feeling. By gradations, still more imperceptible, this cloud assumes shape, as did the vapor from the bottle out of which arose the genius in the Arabian Nights. But out of this *our* cloud upon the precipice's edge, there grows into palpability, a shape, far more terrible than any genius, or any demon of a tale, and yet it is but a thought, although a fearful one, and one which chills the very marrow of our bones with the fierceness of the delight of its horror. It is merely the idea of what would be our sensations during the sweeping precipitancy of a fall from such a height.[4]

The sequence outlined here—"cloud of unnameable feeling" to "shape" to "palpability"—describes the dynamic growth of "merely the idea of what would be our sensations" into a creature more powerful ("terrible") than "any demon of a tale." According to the story's analysis of the soul's faculties, the human imagination creates a tangible, readily perceptible being. In part two, the narrator's story shows him as a victim of his own imagining when he consciously rejects making an "open confession" to the murder. "No sooner had I spoken these words, than I felt an icy chill creep to my heart." The thought, words, chill assume a shape: "some invisible fiend, I thought, struck me with his broad palm upon the back. The long imprisoned secret burst forth from my soul."

The imagining, then verbal expression, create the fiend that overtakes the narrator's reason; it touches his soul in one of its hidden, inarticulate impulses. His language, not attempting to express or contain Truth, represents his own experience, experience that he would not have if it were not for his own words. His experience follows, flows from, his language. Language here creates experience. Even the murder plot comes from "reading some French Memoirs" where, as the narrator says, "The idea [of a poisoned candle] struck my fancy at once."

For the reader of "The Imp of the Perverse," experience necessarily follows upon the word as it does for all readers. As the reader moves line by line further into Poe's text, the mere thought or idea of perverseness begins to take a shape, almost a palpable one when the frame of reference shifts from a consideration of the soul's forces to the reader's implied question. Shortly after using the example of the brink of a precipice, Poe replaces the "we" of that section with a narrative "I" addressing the reading audience's "you." "I have said thus much, that in some measure I may answer your question, that I may explain to you why I am here, that I may assign to you something that shall have at least the faint aspect of a cause for my wearing these fetters, and for my tenanting this cell of the condemned." For us readers, the discourse has turned from what appeared to be exposition to direct address by a narrator assuming a particular shape because of the question presumed to be within the reader. I certainly did not know that I had a question; I had no thought of the narrator being anywhere in particular. As the text turns on me the reader, giving me ideas, there begins to take shape a genius much like the vapor in the Arabian Nights, much like the imp of the perverse. Language in this fictive mode creates an almost palpable character out of the narrator right before our eyes.[5] Though describing the spirit of perversity, Poe also suggests the spirit of fiction. "We might, indeed, deem this perverseness a direct instigation of the arch-fiend, were it not occasionally known to operate in the furtherance of good" (p. 829). The good: every time we read a story, especially one of Poe's.

The event that this story is begins to unfold, then, in the description of what happens to the reader in the process of following the text. What happens to the reader reveals what happens to the narrator. And what happens to the narrator suggests the process the reader undergoes in the reading of Poe's story: a circle, to be sure, but rippling concentrically from the words of Poe's text. Just as the reader becomes an active mediator containing the psychological effects of the story's utterance, so the narrator's imagination records a series of psychological effects that constitute the action of Poe's text. To an important extent, some of Poe's most memorable stories record in vivid fashion the sequence of responses experienced by the narrator.[6] The stories describe what happens to the narrators as each responds to an utterance, to the words "I am safe . . . if I be not fool," to "that sweet word alone," Ligeia, or to a letter, a MS. "that admitted of no other than a personal reply." Poe's narrators exemplify the kind of reader the stories require because the narrators themselves are engaged by the power of language.[7] Among Poe's stories, "Ligeia" offers a clear, important instance of this strategy and becomes, in turn, particularly suggestive of a way of reading "Usher."

II

"Ligeia" begins with the narrator trying to overcome his faint memory with the incantation of his beloved's name:

> Ligeia! Ligeia! Buried in studies of a nature more than all else adapted to deaden impressions of the outward world, it is by that sweet word alone— by Ligeia—that I bring before mine eyes in fancy the image of her who is no more. And now, while I write, a recollection flashes upon me. . . . (p. 262)

To a large extent, these lines summarize the basic action of the story: the narrator in uttering "Ligeia" brings before imagination's eye the image of Ligeia. It is, of course, the dynamic process of literary art. In a text containing a narrator particularly self-conscious of narrating, the story becomes an illustration of what verbal utterance does to its narrator as well as to its reader.

Following the surface events, the story can be divided into two parts, the speaker's recollections first of Ligeia and then his recollections of Rowena. In the first part, the narrator recalls Ligeia's beauty, learning, passion as well as his own intense feelings for her. What Ligeia stands for has certainly been much discussed.[8] What has not been widely noticed is that the narrator, in straining to remember, relies on such linguistic metaphors as the power of language, of text and utterance, to restore, if only for a moment, his lost Ligeia. From the very outset of the story, he has declared the power of the sweet word, Ligeia. He dismisses "expression" of her eyes as "word of no meaning" (p. 264). Among the circle of analogies expressive of Ligeia's eyes that aroused a sentiment comparable to gazing into her eyes, he was reminded of that sentiment "not unfrequently by passages from books" (p. 265). The text from Joseph Glanvill stands out in particular. For all the notice given to the Glanvill statements about will power, a clearly significant force, it seems to me of first importance that the quotation is a text expressive of Ligeia, words particularly affecting the narrator. There is "some remote connection between this passage in the English moralist and a portion of the character of Ligeia." Not only the expansion of her eyes and melody of her voice, but "the fierce energy . . . of the wild words which she habitually uttered" demonstrated her passion (p. 266). As his maternal instructor, his muse, she made language vibrant and bright. At her decline, language loses its vibrance: "wanting the radiant lustre of her eyes, letters, lambent and golden, grew duller than Saturnian lead" (p. 267). The description of Ligeia's last moments appears to be a record of his response to her utterances, a record of the power of her language to move him with feeling. The verses she composed not only describe "a play of hopes and fears," "the tragedy, 'Man,'" but also become a means of recalling her genius—a verbal form capable of repetition and so of recall.

Part one shows the narrator, in search of Ligeia among his memories, particularly dependent on utterance as the resource for bringing her image before his fancy. To neglect what the narrator does here (to recall Ligeia from his memory through particular recourse to verbal forms) for the sake of investigating the motives for such persistence or identifying what Ligeia stands for, though substantive issues, is to miss the story on an important level. Part two becomes an illustration in relatively concrete circumstances of what is outlined as the narrator's process in part one.

The memories connected with the English abbey are identified with the narrator's feelings of loss. In parallel with part one, he probes his memory: "I minutely remember the details of the chamber." The presence of Rowena drives his memory back to Ligeia. He "revelled in recollections" of her: "Now, then, did my spirit fully and freely burn with more than all the fires of her own. . . . I would call upon her name, during the silence of the night, or among the sheltered recesses of the glens, as if . . . I could restore her to the pathway she had abandoned . . . upon earth." In calling her name, the narrator, repeating what he did in part one, relies on the power of the word as if he could restore her—and he does restore her with the fictive power of language. The force of fiction relies precisely on such a sense of the imagined world as if it were the world of experience.

In detailing the process of his deathbed watch, he describes a process starting with his intense longing, with the thought of Ligeia; he notes sounds ("inarticulate breathings" of the wind), passes "some palpable although invisible object," hears a "gentle foot-fall," and imagines seeing "three or four large drops of a brilliant and ruby colored fluid"; finally the thought appears to take shape, becomes palpable, reaching full presence in the utterance of her name—the last word of the text, the word that is the story—"Ligeia." The story ends where it began: with the sweet word, bringing before the narrator's fancy the image of her who is no more.

This narrator shares the experience of the speaker in "Imp." A cloud of unnameable feeling, a thought, an idea assumes form, growing to palpability, a shape comparable to the genius of the Arabian nights, to any demon of a tale. The flow of the story begins with the single word, which action stirs all memories of what Ligeia has come to represent for the narrator. The feelings, memories, thoughts surrounding the name coalesce into the image represented by the name, the story, the word "Ligeia."

This kind of experience shown in the story of the narrator's imagining Ligeia suggests what Poe's text does to its readers. In creating a storyteller as especially self-conscious of telling the tale, the text calls attention to itself as narration, as an action going on in the present time of its being read. Such an observation can be so true that it becomes transparent in its obviousness and thus the full effect—the reader's experience of the narrator's self-consuming as well as the reader's own—is missed.

The story opens with the calling of Ligeia's name followed immediately by the narrator's self-conscious statement, "While I write, a recollection flashes upon me. . . ." In the midst of the story, he calls attention to his act of narrating. Regarding Ligeia's wild longing for life, he says, "I have no power to portray—no utterance capable of expressing" (p. 268). Concerning the English abbey, he decides "I must not pause to detail." Other memories of that place are "not now visibly before me." But he reminds the reader, "I have said that I minutely remember the details of the chamber" (p. 270). The third to last paragraph emphatically calls attention to the act of narrating going on before the reader's eyes. The paragraph opens: "And again I sunk into visions of Ligeia—and again, (what marvel that I shudder as I write) *again* there reached my ears. . . ." The paragraph ends: "Let me hurry to a conclusion."[9]

This self-conscious narration suggests the nature of the reader's experience: the resurrection of Ligeia is a linguistic event, an event reenacted through the recall of fiction. The writing or telling or reading brings Ligeia to life again. As the reader's experience parallels that of the narrator's shudder and horror, so what happens to the narrator, what the text does to the narrator, becomes the point of the story: it brings before the reader's fancy the image of Ligeia. The reader, engaged by Poe's words and perhaps even straining for some verifiable truth, is led by the text to actively experiencing the creation of the imagined Ligeia, and that experience becomes Poe's fiction—Ligeia.

III

Recognizing Poe's texts as utterances that affect the narrator as well as the reader can help reveal "The Fall of the House of Usher" as a subtle variation on the patterns established in "Imp" and "Ligeia." This story contains a spirit of perverseness in at least the burial of Madeline; Roderick totters, much like the narrator in "Imp," on the brink of the irrational; his poem, "The Haunted Palace," describes the overthrow of the "monarch Thought's domain." More important, the narrator, from the inciting incident on, has been led through the story's events by Roderick's imaginative creations: his letter, music, painting, poetry, his "fantastic yet impressive superstitions." When we trace what happens to the narrator, the story appears to be a series of utterances taking on palpable shape for the narrator, ultimately becoming the very House of Usher and its fall.[10]

In the middle of the final stormy night, the narrator tries to pass the dark hours with Roderick by reading from the "Mad Trist." Each of the readings from the text is followed by sounds and actions from within the house that duplicate what have been described in the "Mad Trist." After the second reading, the narrator is amazed by the sounds he hears from the distant parts of the house "the exact counterpart of what my fancy had already conjured up for the dragon's unnatural shriek as described by the romancer." Canning's text creates the narrator's experience. The other quoted text in the story, Roderick's "The Haunted Palace," predicts what the narrator describes as the tottering of Usher's "lofty reason upon her throne." Earlier in the story, Roderick's speaking of his sister seems to evoke a vision of Madeline: "While he spoke, the lady Madeline (for so was she called) passed slowly through a remote portion of the apartment. . . ." (p. 323). The speaking calls her forth. The inciting incident of the story's action arises from the singular summons of Roderick's letter to the narrator, a letter "which, in its wildly importunate nature, had admitted of no other than a personal reply." Because of "the apparent *heart* that went with his request," the narrator cannot hesitate in answering Roderick's letter. The story's final action, the dank tarn silently closing over the fragments of the "*House of Usher*" (Poe's emphasis for the story's last words), follows "a long tumultuous shouting sound like the voice of a thousand waters." As the tarn's waters become silent, the House of Usher (family, mansion, and fiction) as utterance is no more.

Appropriately the story ends in silent waters, an archetypal source for the story itself.[11] While Roderick's written word starts the narrator on his journey through a "soundless day," it is the reflected image of the house in the tarn that represents the narrator's destination. Twice in the opening pages, the narrator contemplates the house's reflection in the surface of the water. Instead of the incantation in "Ligeia," these repeated sightings produce the house. He distinguishes the reflected image from the house's "real aspect," the dreary sensation of its appearance in "everyday life." To relieve the insufferable gloom he attempts to goad his imagination into something of the sublime. To counter the effect of "the hideous dropping off of the veil" that facing natural objects requires, the narrator rearranges the particulars of the scene, so veiling nature with poetic sentiment.

> I reined my horse to the precipitous brink of a black and lurid tarn that lay in unruffled lustre by the dwelling and gazed down—but with a shudder even more thrilling than before—upon the remodelled and inverted images of the gray sedge, and the ghastly tree-stems, and the vacant and eye-like windows.
>
> Nevertheless, in this mansion of gloom I now proposed to myself a sojourn of some weeks.

His second description of the house before entering it ends with his eye following the "barely perceptible fissure" until "it became lost in the sullen waters of the tarn." Beginning with the mere idea of teasing the physical appearance of the mansion into "aught of the sublime," the narrator childishly, as the text suggests, (impishly?) gazes at the reflected, watery appearance of the house. Hovering at the "precipitous brink" of the tarn, the cloud of feeling assumes a form, a palpable shape, so much so that the narrator can announce that "in this mansion," into the image mirrored in the water, will he travel through

---

fancy. In what today could be likened to a cinematic effect, Poe shows the narrator, at the beginning of the story's action, staring into the waters with the reader, as it were, looking over the narrator's shoulder. With more intense scrutiny of the reflected image, the narrative tightens its focus on the specific details shimmering in the water, and the action appears to begin but is really a continuation of what began with the story's first sentence. Only at the end does the narrative focus lengthen to reveal that for the duration of the story the narrator, still standing at the tarn's edge, has been contemplating the image of the house reflected in the water.

After recalling the "childish experiment" of looking into the tarn and later shaking off "what *must* have been a dream," the speaker crosses over in imagination to the Gothic archway of the hall. He then proceeds to enter the House of Usher: "A valet, of stealthy step, thence conducted me, in silence, through many dark and intricate passages in my progress to the *studio* of his master. Much that I encountered on the way contributed, I know not how, to heighten the vague sentiments of which I have already spoken." This valet to a family with a "passionate devotion to the intricacies . . . of musical science" silently conducts the narrator through intricate passages to Roderick's study, a wild composition representing his imaginative state. Without musical score or baton, the valet conducts the narrator through Usher's creation, appearing as self-consuming narrator to the teller of the story. The narrator in turn, of course, leads the reader into the fictive house.

The story has been a journey into the realm of the narrator's disembodied imagination where imps, Ligeia, and Ushers become palpable for the duration of the text. The narrator, as obviously the reader, has been led by the imagination's power to create images more thrilling than the physical world. What idea, word, or utterance does to the narrator becomes the first point of Poe's stories. For the narrator, this text records the fall of the House of Usher, Madeline's toppling Roderick, while for us readers it records the arousal of these images. "Usher" has become a dialectic within our imaginations of us/her created by Poe's words. As the valet conducts the narrator further into the imagined world stirred by the reflection in the tarn so Poe's narrator leads (ushers) readers to actively engaging their interior worlds of fancy. And the readers have been staring at their own images of Poe's fiction much as the narrator has been transfixed by the reflections in the tarn.

IV

Seeing Poe's readers as actively mediating presences suggests a new perspective to the stories: as a set of responses by the narrator to the creative, imaginative, poetic word. The reader represents Poe's ideal narrator, and Poe's narrator represents his ideal reader. These stories portray a thoroughly imagined world, "the spirit's outer world," as Poe describes it in one of his "Marginalia." And the valuable result here is the refusal to settle for an identification of what constitutes Poe's spiritual world as the entire substance of his fiction. Rather, the exciting experience is to recognize as essential to Poe's fiction the process of discovering that spiritual realm, and this self-consuming process becomes the structure and substance of these stories.

"Ligeia" and "Usher" show us narrators intensely preoccupied with images reflecting their sense of the beautiful, which preoccupation displaces all else including themselves in the stories. As the narrators become fixed on their experience of the imagination's power, specifically the power of language, their narrations take on a life of their own, thus engaging the reader with the power of Poe's words. In the context of these stories, the narrators become self-consuming precisely in the action of trying to tell of their experience which necessarily calls attention to each attempt to express the ideal. Poe's narrators appear to mediate between the mundane and the sublime, present dreariness and recollected excitement (Poe's terror), the unpoetical and poetical, the text and the reader. Richard Wilbur, in his analysis of Poe's stories as journeys toward the inner, spiritual self, concludes that "Usher" is "a triumphant report by the narrator that it *is* possible for the poetic soul to shake off this temporal, rational, physical world and escape, if only for a moment, to a realm of unfettered vision."[12] These stories record the narrators pursuing glimpses of Beauty in the momentary intimations suggested through language, with the reader experiencing the poetic vision.

In his description of the artist's attempt to recollect Beauty, Poe provides an apt description of these narrators and so of his readers. For Poe, a Platonic sense of the Beautiful abides in the human imagination as a recollection of existence prior to the soul's birth as well as a pre-science of eternity. For such an artist and narrator, the beauty of nature and of one's beloved become delightful because they offer some particular, partial manifestation of the ideal. Reflected images double the intensity of such beauty. Poetic language also duplicates such manifestations: "as the lily is repeated in the lake, or the eyes of Amaryllis in the mirror, so is the mere oral or written repetition of these forms, and sounds, and colours, and odours, and sentiments, a duplicate source of delight."[13] And the reader's imagination redoubles these reflections, further intensifying the delight. These perceptions of beauty become "a class of fancies, of exquisite delicacy" that offer "a glimpse of the soul's outer world."[14] Such fancies occur at the "very brink of sleep," between the waking world and the world of dreams. These fancies hold the artist's entire attention because they point toward the ideal. And so, significant for the artist and narrator is the power of words. In his dialogue, "The Power of Words," Poe has Agathos speak of "the *physical power of words*."[15] Poe himself declared, "so entire is my faith in the *power of words*, that at times, I have believed it possible to embody even the evanescence of fancies such as I have attempted to describe."[16] These stories show Poe's narrators seeking to embody in words—Ligeia, Usher—their evanescent fancies of beauty and finally failing because they cannot capture the ideal. But these narrators signify most successfully precisely because they so fail and self-consume.

Notes

1. *Self-Consuming Artifacts* (Berkeley: Univ. of California Press, 1972), p. 4.

2. G. R. Thompson and Patrick F. Quinn, in their debate over Poe's narrators especially in "Usher," make many thoughtful, suggestive observations concerning the stories and Poe's fiction. Their disagreement, however, rests to an important extent upon their concern with the narrator's reporting details verifiable according to norms outside the story's action, according to some objective or rational criteria. My suggestion here is that the narrator reports the effects on him of images created through language or the tarn's mirror surface. See G. R. Thompson, *Poe's Fiction: Romantic Irony in the Gothic Tales* (Madison: Univ. of Wisconsin Press, 1973) and his "Poe and the Paradox of Terror: Structures of Heightened Consciousness in 'The Fall of the House of Usher'" as well as Patrick F. Quinn, "A Misreading of Poe's 'The Fall of the House of Usher,'" and his "Usher Again: Trust the Teller" in *Ruined Eden of the Past: Hawthorne, Melville, and Poe*, ed. G. R. Thompson and Virgil L. Lokke (West Lafayette: Purdue Univ. Press, 1981).

3. *Edgar Allan Poe: Modern Critical Views*, ed. Harold Bloom (New York: Chelsea House, 1985); *Critics on Poe*, ed. David B. Kesterson (Coral Gables: Univ. of Miami Press, 1973); Robert L. Marrs, "'The Fall of the House of Usher': A Checklist of Criticism Since 1960," *Poe Studies*, 5 (1972), 23-24; *Twentieth Century Interpretations of Poe's Tales: A Collection of Critical Essays*, ed. William L. Howarth (Englewood Cliffs, N.J.: Prentice-Hall, 1971); *Twentieth Century Interpretations of "The Fall of the House of Usher": A Collection of Critical Essays*, ed. Thomas Woodson (Englewood Cliffs, N.J.: Prentice-Hall, 1969); *Poe: A Collection of Critical Essays*, ed. Robert Regan (Englewood Cliffs, N.J.: Prentice-Hall, 1967).

4. "The Imp of the Perverse," *Edgar Allan Poe: Poetry and Tales*, ed. Patrick F. Quinn (New York: Library of America, 1984), p. 829. All subsequent references to fiction are from this volume.

5. In "The Power of Words," Poe has his two speakers discuss the "*physical power of words*" (Poe's emphasis), p. 825.

6. Charles Feidelson, Jr., recognizes "The wonder and the horror of the images that assail the narrator and preoccupy Roderick" in "Poe as Symbolist," *Twentieth Century Interpretations*, ed. Woodson, p. 77. Also see James W. Gargano, "The Question of Poe's Narrators" in *Poe*, ed. Regan, pp. 164-71. Also, of course, the Thompson-Quinn debate.

7. James M. Cox suggests that the stories embody a kind of self-consciousness when he describes them as "wrecking the forms [gothic and romantic] upon which they prey." "Edgar Poe: Style as Pose," *Twentieth Century Interpretations*, ed. Woodson, p. 114.

8. Maurice J. Bennett, "'The Madness of Art': Poe's 'Ligeia' as Metafiction," *Poe Studies*, 14 (1981), 1-6; Joseph M. Garrison, Jr., "The Irony of 'Ligeia,'" *Emerson Society Quarterly*, 60 (1970) Supplement, 13-17; Claudia C. Morrison, "Poe's 'Ligeia': An Analysis," *Studies in Short Fiction*, 4 (1967), 234-44; John Lauber, "'Ligeia' and Its Critics: A Plea for Literalism," *Studies in Short Fiction*, 4 (1966), 28-32; Roy P. Basler, *Sex, Symbolism, and Psychology in Literature* (New York: Octagon, 1967), pp.

143-59; Paul John Eakin, "Poe's Sense of an Ending," *American Literature*, 45 (1973), 1-22; James Schroeter, "A Misreading of Poe's 'Ligeia,'" *PMLA*, 76 (1961), 397-406.

9. Poe revised "Ligeia" several times, the most extensively for New York *New World*, 15 February 1845, according to Thomas Ollive Mabbott, *Collected Works of Edgar Allan Poe, II: Tales and Sketches, 1831-1842* (Cambridge: Harvard Univ. Press, 1978), p. 309. In that particular revision, Poe adds the repetitive, second Ligeia in the story's first paragraph as well as a few phrases calling explicit attention to utterances of Ligeia and to self-conscious expressions of the narrator. Earlier revisions eliminated several instances of the proper name, replacing it with the pronoun. The overall effect of Poe's revising would seem to be a heightening both of deliberate use of the proper name and of the narrator's self-consciousness. Mabbott concluded: "The story was revised with greatest care. It must be regarded as a thoroughly conscious and complete work of art" (p. 306).

10. Charles Feidelson, Jr., identifies the subject of "Usher" to be aesthetic sensibility in "Poe as Symbolist."

11. Georges Poulet sees the House of Usher as existing "only in the dense vapor issued from the ground. It has, so to speak, created its own space"; "When sinking into its own pool, the House of Usher disappears into itself." "The Metamorphoses of the Circle," *Twentieth Century Interpretations*, ed. Woodson. See also Thompson, *Poe's Fiction*, p. 90.

12. "The House of Poe," in *Poe*, ed. Regan, p. 110, also p. 108.

13. "The Poetic Principle," p. 77.

14. "Marginalia," March 1846, *Edgar Allan Poe: Essays and Reviews*, ed. G. R. Thompson (New York: Library of America, 1984), p. 1383.

15. "The Power of Words," p. 825.

16. "Marginalia," p. 1384.

Poe's Re-Vision:
The Recovery of the Second Story_____

Cynthia S. Jordan

I

While the longstanding debates over Hawthorne's treatment of women characters have been reinvigorated and refined by feminist critics in the last fifteen years or so, feminist criticism has as yet had little to say about Poe's women-centered fictions.[1] This lack of attention might have surprised—or more probably, annoyed—the egotistical Poe, since he himself suggested the terms by which his treatment of women characters might be compared with Hawthorne's. In an 1842 review of *Twice-Told Tales*, Poe praised "The Minister's Black Veil" as "a masterly composition" whose underlying meaning would probably be lost on most readers, for the "*moral* put into the mouth of the dying minister will be supposed to convey the *true* import of the narrative; and that a crime of dark dye, (having reference to the 'young lady') has been committed, is a point which only minds congenial with that of the author will perceive."[2]

Poe's use of the term "crime" was perceptive in this instance and virtually prophetic of the direction Hawthorne's tales would take in the next few years. Nina Baym has observed, for example, that in "most of the stories written before . . . 1842, the destruction or damaging of the woman seems to result accidentally as a by-product." The question of the male character's having a "covert intention" to cause such harm, however, "cannot be entirely absent," especially since in the years which followed, Hawthorne's stories "escalate" the male character's ambiguous intentions to "an attitude more clearly hostile."[3] In stories such as "The Birthmark" (1843), "Rappaccini's Daughter" (1844), "Drowne's Wooden Image" (1844), "The Artist of the Beautiful" (1844), and "Ethan Brand" (1849), "crimes" against women are indeed laid bare.

A chronology of Poe's women-centered tales written during these same years suggests a reason for his apparently inside knowledge of Hawthorne's "true import" in 1842. Having already published "Berenice" (1835), "Morella" (1835), "Ligeia" (1838) and "The Fall of the House of Usher" (1839), Poe had clearly established his own "congenial" interest in the fictional possibilities to be found in covert crimes against ladies. With the publication of "The Murders in the Rue Morgue" in 1841, he had begun to highlight such crimes and would continue to do so in the two subsequent detective stories in the Dupin series, "The Mystery of Marie Rogêt" (1842) and "The Purloined Letter" (1845). Thus the evolution of Hawthorne's women-centered tales followed the same pattern as Poe's: both authors gradually changed their fictional focus from covert to overt victimizations of women.

A brief look at individual works reveals more similarity between the authors, because the recurring crime in all of the above-mentioned tales is that one or more women have been criminally silenced; the speech that would allow them self-expression has been denied or usurped by male agents. Poe was especially prolific in creating images of violently silenced women, their vocal apparatus the apparent target of their attackers, who, in the earlier stories, are the storytellers themselves. One remembers the forcible removal of Berenice's teeth by her professed "lover"; the premature shroud that "lay heavily about the mouth" of Ligeia[4]—and of Madeline Usher, no doubt; and later, the throat-cutting and strangulations in "The Murders in the Rue Morgue" and "The Mystery of Marie Rogêt." The psychological violence in such tales is no less pre-emptive. Morella's narrator-husband comes to a point where he can "no longer bear . . . the low tone of her musical language," and after she dies she is denied a place in his own speech: "Morella's name died with her at her death. Of the mother I had never spoken to the daughter. . . ." (II, 231, 235). Even in "The Purloined Letter," the least violent of Poe's tales about women, the Queen who sees her "letter" stolen before her very eyes cannot speak to save herself for fear of jeopardizing her position with the King, who fails to understand the crime taking place.

In Hawthorne's tales about victimized women, silencing is most often effected by the artifices of male characters who are ostensibly obsessed with "perfecting" women according to their own ideas of what women should be. Georgiana in "The Birthmark" and Beatrice Rappaccini are imprisoned, both literally and figuratively in male fantasies, their self-expression limited and finally extinguished altogether. In "Drowne's Wooden Image," in which the process appears to be reversed and the image of a woman comes to life, the woman is still not allowed to speak for herself. This man-made creature is led silently away by another male character, which surely accounts for the broad gold chain around her neck: she is marked from first to last as a slave to male image-making. Hawthorne continued to explore the idea of the male artist's thinly veiled misogyny in "The Artist of the Beautiful." There, Owen Warland originally fantasizes Annie Hovenden as a fitting "interpreter" of his works to those of lesser sensibilities, but he eventually forecloses his own fantasy and any pronouncement she might have made by convincing himself that Annie "could never say the fitting word . . . which should be the perfect recompense of an artist."[5] Finally, in "Ethan Brand," the recurring crime against women is labeled as such—"the only crime for which Heaven could afford no mercy," and the prototypical victim of the Unpardonable Sin is Esther, the girl whom, "with such cold and remorseless purpose, Ethan Brand had made the subject of psychological experiment, and wasted, absorbed, and perhaps annihilated her soul, in the process."[6]

It is crimes of silencing such as these which have understandably fueled the feminist critical debate over Hawthorne's responsibilities as an artist. Judith Fetterley has argued of "The Birthmark" in particular that Hawthorne "is unwilling to do more with the sickness [of the male victimizer] than call it sick," and of such stories in general that they expose "the imaginative limits of our literature." This type of "storytelling and art," she claims, "can do no more than lament the inevitable"— the criminal nature of our culture's sexism—and the "lament is self-indulgent; it offers the luxury of feeling bad without the responsibility of change."[7] Baym has taken a more approving view of Hawthorne, basing her argument on the gradual evolution of his art which culminates, she maintains, in "the triumph of *The Scarlet Letter.*" Like Fetterley, she acknowledges "the responsibility of change": while condemning his male characters' crimes against women, he must nevertheless "represent them, and thus the question of his own motivation as an artist enters his discourse. He must hold himself responsible along with other men for injuries done to women; he inflicts imaginary injuries on imaginary women through the stories he creates, in which women are injured. To some degree, he has a higher degree of responsibility than other men, because he has an awareness that others lack. . . ." Baym argues, however, that Hawthorne's art accedes to that responsibility. His progression from the delineation of ambiguous or covert criminality to blatantly condemnatory portrayals of the injuries done to women by "warped" male mentality brings him at last to that ground-breaking moment in "The Custom House" when "the Hawthorne narrator accepts the woman's story as his subject and, putting her scarlet letter on his own breast, loses his identity in hers."[8] In *The Scarlet Letter* "the woman's story" is finally told, and in crossing gender boundaries Hawthorne thus goes beyond "the imaginative limits" of male-authored fictions.

What I propose to do in this essay is to bring Poe into the critical arena on Hawthorne's coat-tails, as it were. Given the similar progression of his fictional focus from covert to overt crimes against women, and given his similar understanding of what in fact constitutes such "crimes," Poe's women-centered tales raise the same issues as Hawthorne's: "the imaginative limits" of male-authored fictions and "the responsibility of change." What makes Poe an equally apt candidate for a feminist inquiry is that, like Hawthorne, he incorporates those issues into his own discourse, and his fictional response to both problems is also to cross gender boundaries in order to tell "the woman's story."

Poe's villainous narrators in tales like "Berenice," "Morella," and

"Ligeia" do indeed tell one-sided stories, and the warped nature of their sexual crimes has been well documented.[9] Poe's search for a solution to such crimes is my main subject here, and "The Fall of the House of Usher" marks the beginning of that search. Starting with Roderick Usher, Poe began his experiments with the androgynous male character whose developing empathy with a woman enables him to reject one-sided male-authored fictions and finally to engender a new fictional form—a second story that provides a text for female experience. In the Dupin tales that follow, in which the task of solving crimes against women calls for a detective with an awareness that other men lack, the androgynous Dupin becomes virtually a feminist critic. In Dupin, Poe created a new caretaker of social and political order, and Dupin fulfills these responsibilities by going beyond the imaginative limits of the male storytellers around him and recovering the second story—"the woman's story"—which has previously gone untold. Whether that act of recovery establishes Poe as a writer of feminist sensibility is an issue I will take up in my conclusion.

II

The crime against the Lady Madeline Usher is that she is prematurely entombed, and while Roderick has traditionally been considered solely responsible, he is but a character in the story himself, and his actions are at least in part the product of his narrator's construction. That is, while critics have credited him with a variety of personal motives for trying to kill his "tenderly beloved sister" (II, 404), including self-defense, euthanasia, and a vampiristic "creative impulse,"[10] the fact remains that he could not have incarcerated Madeline without the narrator's help, as Roderick himself comes to realize: "*We have put her living in the tomb!*" (II, 416). Thus it is the male narrator's actions in this story, his influence over Roderick and his misogynist strategies of textual control, that first warrant a reader's attention—and suspicion.

A boyhood friend of Roderick, the narrator arrives on the scene at the outset to bolster his friend's waning manhood, and from hints variously placed in his narration, it soon becomes clear that he views Roderick's acute nervous condition as arising from his sister's presence, perhaps from her overcloseness or her unmanly influence. The longstanding critical consensus regarding the narrator is that he is a well-intentioned man of reason, valiantly, albeit naively, trying to make sense of a world skewed by irrational forces.[11] His animosity towards Madeline, however, which is foreshadowed in his first description of the mansion upon his arrival, seems if anything unreasonable, irrational. The "vacant and eye-like windows" (II, 398), the "fine tangled web-work" of fungi "hanging . . . from the eaves" (II, 400), and the crack which runs from roof to foundation prefigure Roderick's "luminous" eyes, his "hair of a more than web-like softness and tenuity" (II, 401-02), and his oddly split personality, all of which seem ominous enough to the narrator. But he experiences "a shudder even more thrilling than before" when he looks at the reflection of the House in the tarn, the "remodelled and inverted images" (II, 398) which represent Madeline, Roderick's physical and psychological counterpart. In particular, the "silent tarn" (II, 400) foreshadows Madeline's ill-fated exclusion from the narrator's story, for she will be buried at a "great depth" (II, 410) in the House, in a chamber that lies beneath the surface of the tarn and of the narrative.

The narrator's first encounter with Madeline confirms the conflict between the male storyteller and the lady of the House, for he frames the encounter as one between mutually exclusive presences. "I regarded her with an utter astonishment not unmingled with dread. . . . A sensation of stupor oppressed me," he tells us, and the effect of his presence on her is equally oppressive: "on the closing in of the evening of my arrival at the house, she succumbed . . . to the prostrating power of the destroyer." What is of interest here is the periphrastic description of her lapse into a cataleptic-speechless-stupor and the narrator's passive construction in the phrasing that follows: "the lady, at least while living, would be seen by me no more." Without implicating himself as an agent in her immediate demise, the narrator uses language covertly to relegate Madeline to a passive position in relation to himself, and in the next sentence he tries to exclude her from the text altogether: "For several days ensuing, her name was unmentioned by either Usher or myself" (II, 404). Although he ostensibly remarks on this to demonstrate his concern and sensitivity for his friend's grief over his sister's deteriorating condition, the effect is to show the narrator making sure that Madeline has no place in their masculine language or in this male-authored fiction.

Similarly, on the verge of her return from the tomb, the narrator will try not to hear what he dismisses as her "indefinite sounds" (II, 411) as she breaks through steel and a copper-lined vault, sounds which emanate from the tomb "beneath . . . [his] own sleeping apartment" (II, 410) on a night when he tries unsuccessfully to sleep. The suggestion here of a guilty conscience, or more specifically, of a consciousness plagued by its repressed underpinnings, is heightened by the fact that the narrator is awakened to such ominous sounds by the nightmare vision of "an incubus," which he wants to believe is "of utterly causeless alarm" (II, 411). His word is ill-chosen, however, or at least revealing of the psychological processes he has previously tried to conceal, for "incubus" is the archaic name for a male spirit that visited women in their sleep and aroused female sexuality. If his word choice is a conscious misnomer, that is, if he has substituted "incubus" for "succubus," the female counterpart supposed to visit sleeping men, then the choice is but another narrative strategy intended to exclude any female agency from his text. If, as seems more likely, we are to take "incubus" as an authentic report of a mind that is losing conscious control (for on this night of nights the return of the repressed is imminent), then Poe would seem to be suggesting that the narrator's homoerotic attraction to Roderick has caused him to see himself in some way feminized. If this is the case, then the nightmare status of this identification with female sexuality is no less proof of the narrator's misogyny—of his fear and hatred of the female sexuality incarnate in Madeline Usher.

It is Roderick who finally admits to hearing Madeline, and it is Roderick's growing consciousness of the crime perpetrated against his sister that finally allows her back into the text. Before he can make such an admission, however, he has first to undergo a mighty transformation for a fictional character and free himself of his narrator's control. Essentially, the conflict between the male storyteller and the female character is internalized in the androgynous Roderick, whose dual gender is depicted in behavior that is "alternately vivacious and sullen" and in a voice that varies "rapidly from a tremulous indecision" to a "species of energetic concision" also described as a "guttural utterance" (II, 402). That he is Madeline's twin more obviously implies a merging of gender identities in this story, and there are other suggestions of his partly feminine nature. Given the year of publication for "The Fall of the House of Usher," for example, when the "feminization of American culture" was well under way, the fact that Roderick is an artist is itself enough to insure his effeminate status.[12] In addition, his composition of a musical ballad is reminiscent of Morella and Ligeia, who had been characterized by their musical language (II, 227, 311), which their male narrators had also found unsettling. Poe's physical description of Roderick is in fact, as D. H. Lawrence recognized, very similar to that of the beautiful Ligeia.[13] He has the same large, pale brow; eyes "large, liquid, and luminous beyond comparison"; lips of "a surpassingly beautiful curve"; and "a nose of delicate Hebrew model" (II, 401). Thus it is not surprising that the narrator speaks distastefully of his friend's "peculiar physical conformation and temperament" (II, 402) or that he will try to cure him of the effeminacy he denigrates as a "mental disorder" (II, 410).

We may speculate that it was the masculine side of Roderick's character, or rather, his desire for an exclusively masculine identity, that originally motivated him to summon the narrator to him, "with a view of attempting . . . some alleviation of his malady" (II, 398). Once the narrator is in authorial possession of the House, however, and Madeline's effeminizing influence has been dispatched, Roderick begins to have second thoughts about what he will finally come to see as the crime of masculine exclusivity, and his change of mind is imaged in his search for a narrative form that will allow him to express what the narrator has so artfully excluded.

Roderick's first attempt to communicate his inner turmoil after Madeline has been confined to her sick chamber, for example, is through a "perversion and amplification" of a waltz by Von Weber. That Roderick gives an unusual interpretation of this musical score suggests his desire to deviate from male-authored compositions. But the single-minded narrator characteristically refuses to confer such meaning on his friend's deviation from a masculine script and thus labels it merely a "perversion" (II, 405). The next of Roderick's creations we see, a small painting of an interior vault that suggests both Madeline's femaleness and her fate, is illuminated, the misogynous narrator would have us believe, with "inappropriate splendor," and again he resists assigning meaning to his friend's subversive attempt to communicate otherness, claiming that Roderick's subject may be "shadowed forth, [only] feebly, in words" (II, 405-06). Roderick's third formal experiment, the musical ballad of "The Haunted Palace," has its own verbal component, which implies Roderick's growing abilities as a storyteller in his own right. But here, perhaps sensing a rival narrative voice for the first time, our narrator escalates his textual control. Acknowledging that there is an "under or mystic current of . . . meaning," he nevertheless exerts editorial authority over Roderick's text in phrasing that hints at partial censorship: "The verses . . . ran very nearly, if not accurately, thus:" (II, 406).

"The Haunted Palace," like "The Fall of the House of Usher," tells the story of a mind ("Thought's dominion") assailed and enervated by nameless "evil things," and as in the prose narrative, where Madeline's enshrouded body is graced by "the mockery of a faint blush upon the bosom and the face" (II, 410), "the glory / That blushed and bloomed / Is but a dim-remembered story / Of the old time entombed" (II, 406-07). The narrator of "The Fall of the House of Usher" has used his narrative strategies to suppress the "story" of Madeline's victimization, and Roderick's ballad, while it is an improvement over the nonverbal suggestiveness of his music and his painting, is no more explicit about the crime perpetrated against his sister: it tells its tale in symbolism, metonymy, allegory—all misnomers sanctioned historically by a male-dominant literary tradition. It is Roderick's task finally to retrieve that "dim-remembered story" from the obfuscating language of male-authored fictions, and to do so he must become fully conscious of his own complicity in the crime of excluding-by-misnaming. It was Roderick after all who had first invited the narrator's misogynistic intrusion into the House of Usher by labelling his "sympathies" with his lady sister a "malady" (II, 410).

Roderick's reviving sympathies with and for his sister precipitate her return from the tomb to the text, and in the climactic closing scenes of this tale, where Roderick at last acknowledges and renounces his crime, the narrator struggles to maintain his textual control. As Madeline makes headway up from the lower regions of the House, the narrator, finally showing his true colors, tries desperately to shut out her noisy return with the language of another male-authored fiction, "the only book immediately at hand." Trying to hold Roderick's divided attention with "a gentle violence" (II, 413), he reads him the story of Ethelred, a manly hero and "conqueror," who is challenged by a dragon with "a shriek so horrid and harsh, and withal so piercing, that Ethelred had fain to close his ears with his hands against the dreadful noise of it" (II, 414). But Roderick here becomes virtually "a resisting reader." He rejects both the model of manliness the narrator has tried to impose upon him and the misnaming of the sound he hears, and he replaces the narrator's death-dealing text with a new, second story in a dramatic act of "re-vision"[14]:

Not hear it?—yes, I hear it, and *have* heard it. Long—long—long—many minutes, many hours, many days, have I heard it—yet I dared not—oh, pity me, miserable wretch that I am! I dared not—I *dared* not speak! *We have put her living in the tomb*! . . . And now—tonight—Ethelred—ha! ha! the breaking of the hermit's door, and the death-cry of the dragon, and the clangor of the shield!—say, rather, the rending of her coffin, and the grating of the iron hinges of her prison, and her struggles within the coppered archway of the vault! . . . MADMAN! I TELL YOU THAT SHE NOW STANDS WITHOUT THE DOOR! (II, 416)

By momentarily freeing himself of the narrator's control and authoring a second story that explicitly reveals the crime perpetrated against femaleness, Roderick has succeeded in bringing Madeline to the threshold of the narrator's tale. And indeed, the unmasked "MADMAN" in Poe's story is here forced to acknowledge in unambiguous words the irrefutable truth of Roderick's narrative: "without those doors there *did* stand the lofty and enshrouded figure of the lady Madeline of Usher. There was blood upon her white robes, and the evidence of some bitter struggle upon every portion of her emaciated frame" (II, 416; Poe's emphasis). The narrator is still not willing to admit his role in her long "struggle" for acknowledgment, however, any more than he is willing to wait around for her to speak her own mind. Claiming that Madeline and Roderick reunite only to die in each other's arms, this eminently unreliable narrator flees the chamber, the House, and his own misogynistic narrative endeavor.[15] "The Fall of the House of Usher" ends with the narrator's fragmented sentences, the last fragments of his control. But control, nevertheless, for his final act of "sentencing" is to dispatch Madeline and her too-familiar twin into the "silent tarn," out of mind and out of language one last time: "the deep and dark tarn at my feet closed sullenly and silently over the fragments of the '*House of Usher*'" (II, 417).

In this tale, Roderick's growing abilities as a storyteller are paralleled by his growing terror at the implications of what he must finally do: act as a free agent and virtually rupture the narrative proper with a second story that lays bare the crime of male-authored fictions. The rupture is momentary, lasting just long enough to allow the

---

woman character to get a foot in the door, but it is a significant moment in the evolution of Poe's artistry. Roderick Usher was a new character in Poe's repertoire, an androgynous spokesperson capable of giving voice to female experience and critiquing male-authored fictions which mute that experience, and despite what his madman-narrator must have hoped, his unusual talents were not so easily laid to rest. They would surface again two years later in the service of C. Auguste Dupin, Poe's great detective. The new genre that serves as a vehicle for this androgynous mastermind may be said to be Poe's own "second story," for it too is a new narrative form that critiques male-authored interpretive paradigms which fail to do justice to women. In the three detective stories published between 1841 and 1845, Poe moved from the timeless, dreamlike worlds of remote gothic mansions, turrets, and dungeons to the social realm of neighborhoods, shops, newspapers, and political intrigue, where the investigation of seemingly isolated crimes against women uncovers a network of covert gender-related "crimes" that pervades the entire social order. And Dupin, like Roderick Usher before him, is the detective-critic who brings such "crimes" to light.[16]

The epigraph to the first tale, "The Murders in the Rue Morgue," introduces the idea of crossing gender boundaries to recover the now "dim-remembered story" of female experience: "What song the Syrens sang, or what name Achilles assumed when he hid himself among women, although puzzling questions, are not beyond *all* conjecture" (II, 527). Like Roderick, Dupin exhibits a "Bi-Part Soul," which leads his narrator to imagine "a double Dupin," and he speaks in dual modes, his normal speaking voice "a rich tenor" which rises "into a treble" when he delivers his analysis of a crime, i.e., when he recounts the experience of a female victim (II, 533). That he represents a second draft of Roderick's character, however, is evident in his greater ability to speak, literally, for the silenced woman, to imagine her story in her own words. In "The Mystery of Marie Rogêt," for example, Dupin goes so far as to recreate the thought-pattern of the murdered Marie in the first-person: "We may imagine her thinking thus—'I am to meet a certain person. . . .'" (III, 756).

The most significant difference between Dupin's ability to recover the story untold by male-authored fictions and Roderick's, however, is that the detective's skill is presented as the desired model. Unlike Roderick's closed-minded narrator, for example, Dupin's narrator greatly admires his friend's mental powers (as do the police), and Dupin in fact tries to teach his lesser-skilled narrator how to read in a new way. In this, the evolution of his character may be traced back to Ligeia, whose deeper knowledge of texts had threatened her narrator-husband by revealing his lesser abilities. In "Ligeia," the narrator had described his attempt to attain to Ligeia's knowledge as being like "our endeavors to recall to memory something long forgotten": "we often find ourselves *upon the very verge* of remembrance, without being able, in the end, to remember" (II, 313-14). In "The Murders in the Rue Morgue," Dupin tells his narrator his own partial interpretation of a newspaper text reporting the grisly murders of two women and asks for the man's conclusion: "At these words a vague and half-formed conception of the meaning of Dupin flitted over my mind. I seemed to be upon the verge of comprehension, without power to comprehend—as men, at times, find themselves upon the brink of remembrance, without being able, in the end, to remember" (II, 555). One critic has claimed that readers rightly identify with this "ostensible dummy," rather than with the detective, whom he sees as "grotesquely naive" in this story. He argues in particular that the story is a lesson in the dangers inherent in sexual repression: while the overly intellectual Dupin fails to see the obvious sexual nature of the crime and thus tries to rationalize the evidence in a way that the narrator finds incomprehensible, the narrator, who represents "every reader," more naturally sees evidence of rape. "Every reader," this critic explains, knows that "he" is potentially "capable of such actions" and all-too-humanly "finds himself excited by—and identifying with—" the putative rapist-murderer.[17] The similar phrasings above, however, suggest that Poe conceived of Dupin as being like

Ligeia, or at least as thinking like her, and it seems unrealistic to fault a character who apparently thinks like a woman for failing to identify with or be excited by the idea of a rapist. Indeed, this seems to be the point of the similar phrasings, that men and women think and see things differently; specifically, that Dupin, like Ligeia, has mental abilities of which most "men" are unconscious, their conceptions merely "half-formed." He is thus able to read beyond the surface narrative of male-authored texts, to perceive the gap between text and reality, as we are shown in "The Mystery of Marie Rogêt," where he criticizes virtually point by point a newspaper journalist's attempted reconstruction of the crime. "The sentence in question has but one meaning, as it stands," Dupin instructs his narrator, "but it is material that we go behind the mere words, for an idea which these words have . . . failed to convey" (III, 739).

What I have called the gap between text and reality is, of course, a gender gap. In the Dupin tales, male-authored texts exclude femaleness because their authors are incapable of imagining women's experience; which is to say, they fail to recognize the various ways in which women are victimized. Such failures of imagination, recognition, and empathy are thus "crimes" in their own right, for although these male authors are less obviously misogynistic than Poe's earlier narrators, the texts they create continue to leave the woman's story untold, the overt crime unsolved. In "The Murders in the Rue Morgue," for example, Dupin is able to track down the murderer of the old woman and her daughter because he can recognize what has gone unnamed by the newspaper account of the crime: the strange "voice" of the attacker, which none of the "witnesses" could identify, is that of an orangutan. Once this fact is established, the detective is then able to recover the entire scenario—the second story, which reveals at last what the women actually suffered. Not surprisingly, that story presents a grim parody of what in Poe's tales constitutes normative masculine behavior. The trained animal had been acting out a masculine script, first flourishing a razor around the face of one of his victims, "in imitation of the motions of a barber"; then silencing both women when they put up a struggle; and finally trying to conceal all evidence of the crime (II, 566-67).

The issue of masculine norms, or rather, masculine conceptions of normative behavior, is continued in "The Mystery of Marie Rogêt." In this tale Dupin criticizes several conflicting newspaper articles on the grounds that they are indeed male-authored "fictions": "[I]t is the object of our newspapers rather to create a sensation—to make a point—than to further the cause of truth" (III, 738). Specifically, the "truth" of a woman's experience gets lost sight of because the language of each text is informed by a rigidly masculine perspective. In discussing attempts to identify Marie's body, for instance, one journalist had argued that the fact that garter clasps had been set back to accommodate smaller legs, as Marie was said to have done, was not admissible evidence that the corpse was the petite Marie, because after buying them, "most women find it proper to take a pair of garters home and fit them to the size of the limbs" (III, 745). "Here it is difficult to suppose the reasoner in earnest," Dupin comments, revealing the flaw in the male author's generalization: the "elastic nature of the clasp-garter is self-demonstration of the *unusualness* of the abbreviation" which Marie undertook (III, 746). That men cannot imagine what the life of a woman is like and that they thus define all experience in masculine terms is more explicitly demonstrated in Dupin's criticism of another newspaper's argument. "It is impossible," this text urges, "that a person so well known to thousands as this young woman was, should have passed three blocks without some one having seen her." But, Dupin explains, this

is the idea of a man long resident in Paris—a public man—and one whose walks to and fro in the city, have been mostly limited to the vicinity of the public offices. He is aware that *he* seldom passes so far as a dozen blocks from his own *bureau*, without being recognized and accosted. And, knowing the extent of his personal acquaintance with others, and of others with him, he compares his notoriety with that of the perfumery-girl, finds no great difference between them, and reaches at once the conclusion that she, in her walks, would be equally liable to recognition with himself in his. This could only be the case were her walks of the same unvarying, methodical character, and within the same *species* of limited region as are his own. (III, 749)

In the third and final tale in which Dupin appears, the "limited region" whose boundaries are set by masculine minds is shown to be the province of the Parisian police. Their failure to recover "the purloined letter" results, as Dupin explains, from the narrow "limits of the Prefect's examination—in other words, had the principle of [the letter's] concealment been comprehended within the principles of the Prefect . . . its discovery would have been a matter altogether beyond question" (III, 986). In this tale the plot-lines we have seen previously are reduced to their essence and the issue of gender conflict is in fact given a political dimension, for the crime is the theft of a text that rightfully belongs to the Queen; the thief is the Minister D——, "who dares all things, those unbecoming as well as those becoming a man" (III, 976); and "the power thus attained," as even the Prefect of police recognizes, "has . . . been wielded, for political purposes, to a very dangerous extent" (III, 977). Once again Dupin, acting according to his "political prepossessions" as "partisan of the lady" (III, 993), is able to recover the lost text (and replace it with a clever substitute) because he alone can decode the artifice by which the woman has been disempowered: the male criminal had merely disguised her "letter" to look as if it was his own. And once again this second story acts as a gloss upon the first. The Minister's conscious concealment of the Queen's letter is but the external manifestation of the police's interpretive paradigm, by which they unconsciously define all human action only according to "their *own*"—masculine—"ideas" of it. In Dupin's words, "They have no variation of principle in their investigations." Their unchanging principle is "based upon . . . one set of notions regarding human ingenuity"

(III, 985), and one set of notions, as the "double Dupin" demonstrates, is not enough to accommodate both halves of humanity.

This tale has a new ending, suggesting perhaps that Poe felt he had taken his critique of male-authored fictions to its logical conclusion: the victimized woman lives to benefit from Dupin's recovery of the second story, and the male criminal faces imminent retribution. As Dupin reveals at the end, for "eighteen months the Minister has had her in his power. She has now him in hers; since, being unaware that the letter is not in his possession, he will proceed with his exactions as if it was. Thus will he inevitably commit himself, at once, to his political destruction" (III, 993). Dupin's criticism of the police's interpretive paradigm, however, is obviously not new; it merely rounds out the metaphorical arguments begun in "The Fall of the House of Usher." The police's "one set of notions," like the earlier depictions of "half-formed conception" and male-authored texts which failed to convey "but one meaning," represents a blind spot in masculine interpretations of reality that keeps men from seeing how women are victimized. What the men in these tales cannot see, they cannot include in their own "story" of events, but the crime metaphor that provides the basis for Poe's detective tales insists on the criminal nature of such oversights. The death-dealing misogyny of Roderick Usher's narrator differs from the half-formed conceptions of Dupin's newspaper writers and police only in degree, not in effect. The second story, or perhaps finally, the second half of the human story, must be recovered by a mind capable of "looking back, of seeing with fresh eyes, of entering an old text from a new critical direction,"[18] and Poe's solution to the problem of such much-needed "re-vision" is the androgynous mind that had first so terrified Roderick Usher and had finally so distinguished C. Auguste Dupin.

III

I have twice referred to Adrienne Rich's definition of "re-vision" to help explain Roderick's and Dupin's recovery of the second story, so it seems only proper to repeat it here as she originally articulated it: "Re-vision—the act of looking back, of seeing with fresh eyes, of entering an old text from a new critical direction—is for women more than a chapter in cultural history: it is an act of survival. Until we can understand the assumptions in which we are drenched we cannot know ourselves. . . . We need to know the writing of the past, and know it differently than we have ever known it; not to pass on a tradition but to break its hold over us." Read in sequence, "The Fall of the House of Usher" and the three Dupin tales suggest that Poe was considering what Fetterley has called "the responsibility of change" and experimenting with the idea of the androgynous mind which would be capable of imaginative re-vision. The androgynous Dupin accomplishes what Roderick Usher so tentatively began, a fully-specified critique of "the imaginative limits" of one-sided male-authored fictions. The end-product of such a critique is the recovery of "the woman's story," which, in the last tale in the sequence, breaks the hold of male domination and finally insures the woman's survival by restoring her honor and her sociopolitical power.

There is no question that Poe's depictions of acts of physical violence committed against women are particularly gruesome, and some feminist readers might feel that having to encounter such grisly surface details is too big a price to pay to get to the final acts of recovery and restoration Poe seems to have had in mind. A greater stumbling block to any acceptance of Poe as an author capable of feminist sensibility must surely be his now infamous statement that "the death . . . of a beautiful woman is, unquestionably, the most poetical topic in the world." Certainly at first glance it would seem to contradict any argument that his tales show an evolving feminist ethos, a growing awareness and renunciation of death-dealing male-authored fictions, and indeed, it appeared a year after "The Purloined Letter," in "The Philosophy of Composition," published in 1846.

When feminist critics cite the statement, however, they tend to leave off the second half of the sentence: "—and equally is it beyond doubt that the lips best suited for such topic are those of a bereaved lover."[19] While I do not intend to justify the images of death which Poe habitually chose as a vehicle for his vision, I do believe that the halves of this statement constitute a conceptual whole which is not inconsistent with his use of the androgyny metaphor, and to argue this final point, I will extrapolate from Baym's reading of Hawthorne one last time: "The domain of his work is the male psyche, and throughout his writings 'woman' stands for a set of qualities which the male denies within himself and rejects in others. . . . The ability to accept woman—either as the 'other' or as part of the self—becomes in his writing a test of man's wholeness."[20]

The domain of Poe's work is also the male psyche, and the loss of "woman" throughout his writings represents a halving of "man's" soul, his human potential, and—for the male artist—his imagination. Telling the story of that loss seems to have been for Poe a compelling need, for he told it obsessively again and again and clearly derived a kind of perverse pleasure from doing so. Nevertheless, that such works are cautionary tales is confirmed by the heroic stature of his androgynous heroes. Roderick Usher does come to accept woman both as the "other" and as part of the self, but it is Dupin who stands finally as Poe's greatest achievement. "The double Dupin" represents his creator's fullest expression of the need for wholeness and the need to tell not only the story of loss, but the second story as well: the story of recovery and restoration, "the woman's story." I have to conclude that Poe's ability to tell both stories, or both halves of the human story, is—like Hawthorne's—the sign of what we would today call feminist revision.

Notes

1. Nina Baym has made the strongest and most persuasive case for regarding Hawthorne's treatment of women characters as feminist, in a series of articles, two of which will be cited below, and a full-length critical biography, *The Shape of Hawthorne's Career* (Ithaca: Cornell Univ. Press, 1976). For opposing views, see Wendy Martin, "Seduced and Abandoned in the New World," in *Woman in Sexist Society*, ed. Vivian Gornick and Barbara K. Moran (New York: Basic Books, 1971), pp. 329-46; and Judith Fryer, *The Faces of Eve: Women in the Nineteenth-Century American Novel* (New York: Oxford Univ. Press, 1976).

2. *Graham's Magazine*, May 1842; rpt. in *Hawthorne: The Critical Heritage*, ed. J. Donald Crowley (London: Routledge & Kegan Paul, 1970), p. 92.

3. "Thwarted Nature: Nathaniel Hawthorne as Feminist," in *American Novelists Revisited: Essays in Feminist Criticism*, ed. Fritz Fleischmann (Boston: G. K. Hall, 1982), pp. 64-65.

4. "Ligeia," in *Collected Works of Edgar Allan Poe*, ed. Thomas Ollive Mabbott (Cambridge: Harvard Univ. Press, 1978), II, 330. Subsequent references to this edition will appear parenthetically in the text.

5. In *Mosses from an Old Manse*, Volume X of *The Centenary Edition of the Works of Nathaniel Hawthorne*, ed. William Charvat et al. (Columbus: Ohio State Univ. Press, 1974), pp. 468, 472.

6. In *The Snow-Image and Uncollected Tales*, Volume XI of *The Centenary Edition of the Works of Nathaniel Hawthorne*, ed. William Charvat et al. (Columbus: Ohio State Univ. Press, 1974), pp. 88, 94.

7. *The Resisting Reader: A Feminist Approach to American Fiction* (Bloomington: Indiana Univ. Press, 1978), pp. xiv-xv.

8. "Thwarted Nature," pp. 63, 62, 61, 73.

9. Michael Davitt Bell has shown the narrators of "Berenice," "Morella," and "Ligeia" to be "lover-murderers," repulsed by sexuality, in *The Development of American Romance: The Sacrifice of Relation* (Chicago: Univ. of Chicago Press, 1980), pp. 101, 112-17. See also Terence J. Matheson, "The Multiple Murder in 'Ligeia': A New Look at Poe's Narrator," *Canadian Review of American Studies*, 13 (1982), 279-89.

10. J. O. Bailey, "What Happens in 'The Fall of the House of Usher'?" *American Literature*, 35 (1964), 445-66; Maurice Beebe, "The Universe of Roderick Usher," in *Poe: A Collection of Critical Essays*, ed. Robert Regan (Englewood Cliffs, N.J.: Prentice-Hall, 1967), pp. 129-30; and Daniel Hoffman, *Poe Poe Poe Poe Poe Poe Poe* (New York: Doubleday, 1972), pp. 310-11.

11. See, for example, Charles Feidelson, Jr., *Symbolism and American Literature* (Chicago: Univ. of Chicago Press, 1953), p. 35; Joel Porte, *The Romance in America: Studies in Cooper, Poe, Hawthorne, Melville, and James* (Middletown, Conn.: Wesleyan Univ. Press, 1969), p. 62; and Stefano Tani, *The Doomed Detective: The Contribution of the Detective Novel to Postmodern American and Italian Fiction* (Carbondale: Southern Illinois Univ. Press, 1984), p. 12.

12. I have borrowed the phrase from Ann Douglas' *The Feminization of American*

Culture (New York: Knopf, 1977), in which she discusses the feminized status of nineteenth-century American artists at length.

13. *Studies in Classic American Literature* (Garden City, N.Y.: Doubleday, 1923); rpt. in *The Shock of Recognition*, ed. Edmund Wilson (New York: Random House, 1955), p. 979.

14. Adrienne Rich, "When We Dead Awaken: Writing as Re-Vision," in *On Lies, Secrets, and Silence: Selected Prose 1966-1978* (New York: Norton, 1979), p. 35. I will give Rich's full definition of "re-vision" later in the text.

15. G. R. Thompson has also argued the unreliability of the narrator, but for different reasons. He claims that the narrator gradually comes to accept Roderick's mad interpretations and that the scene of Madeline's return is thus a dual hallucination. See *Poe's Fiction: Romantic Irony in the Gothic Tales* (Madison: Univ. of Wisconsin Press, 1973), pp. 68-104, and "Poe and the Paradox of Terror: Structures of Heightened Consciousness in 'The Fall of the House of Usher,'" in *Ruined Eden of the Present: Hawthorne, Melville, and Poe*, ed. G. R. Thompson and Virgil L. Lokke (West Lafayette, Ind.: Purdue Univ. Press, 1981), pp. 313-40.

16. Tani, p. 4, likens Dupin to Roderick Usher on the grounds that each is a poet-figure suffering from a "diseased" imagination. For other readings of Dupin as a poet-figure, see Leslie A. Fiedler, *Love and Death in the American Novel*, 2nd ed. (New York: Stein and Day, 1966), p. 497; and Hoffman, pp. 114-22.

17. J. A. Leo Lemay, "The Psychology of 'The Murders in the Rue Morgue,'" *American Literature*, 54 (1982), 177, 178, 187.

18. Rich, p. 35.

19. See, for example, Sandra M. Gilbert and Susan Gubar, *The Madwoman in the Attic: The Woman Writer and the Nineteenth-Century Literary Imagination* (New Haven: Yale Univ. Press, 1979), p. 25. Also, *The Complete Poems and Stories of Edgar Allan Poe, with Selections from his Critical Writings*, ed. A. H. Quinn (New York: Knopf, 1951), II, 982.

20. "Hawthorne's Women: The Tyranny of Social Myths," *Centennial Review*, 15 (1971), 250-51.

Absolute Poe:
His System of Transcendental Racism_____

Maurice S. Lee

A haunting image appears on the cover of the 1995 essay collection *The American Face of Edgar Allan Poe*. From a perspective slightly above the subject, we see a grainy, black-and-white figure with vaguely familiar features: disheveled hair, broad forehead, thin mustache, deep-set eyes. The picture is not unlike a still frame taken from a surveillance video, as if Poe had come back from the grave and was captured leaving a convenience store. The hazy image simultaneously suggests Poe's modern presence and historical alterity, a fitting introduction to an essay collection that signaled a shift in Poe studies from abstract, ahistorical universals toward "Poe's syncopated relation to American culture." Subsequent scholarship in this vein has rendered rich interpretation.[1] The problem is that Poe is becoming something of a divided figure, embedded in his era's material discourse but divorced from the metaphysics of his day. It may be possible, however, to bring into focus a more stubbornly historical Poe who not only participates in his era's political, economic, and mass cultural life but also uses historically available ideas to theorize his American world.

This world, as critics have increasingly found, was torn by slavery and race. Through varying degrees of interpretive will, blackness and bondage become powerfully political in a wide array of Poe's poetry, fiction, essays, and reviews. What is striking in these analyses is how often Poe's social proclivities appear to be beyond his control as ideology and unconscious desire determine textual meanings.[2] But what if Poe is a more self-conscious observer of slavery and race whose political vision is mediated by his philosophical beliefs? This is not to suggest that Poe achieves a coherent or commendable understanding of slavery. Far from it. The terror, disruption, and chaos that mark Poe's treatment of the institution originate from the tensions between his metaphysics and racism. On one hand, Poe maintains distinctions between black and white, slave and master, brutish object and reasoning subject. On the other, he indulges what *Eureka* (1848) calls "the appetite for Unity," the transcendental urge to synthesize dualities in an "absolute oneness."[3]

This essay traces Poe's divergent urges for metaphysical unity and racial difference. It begins with "Metzengerstein" (1832), an exemplary story that offers an early and surprisingly cogent position on the American slavery debate. However, the racist anti-abolitionism evident in "Metzengerstein" and beyond conflicts with transcendentalist concepts Poe borrows from Schelling and Coleridge. Here Enlightenment dualisms threaten to collapse into romantic absolutism as blackness and bondage are figured as dangers immanent in the unwitting white mind. For Poe, the slavery crisis is a crisis of the unconscious, which he dramatizes with a repetition more compelling than compulsive. Poe, that is, seems less an author bedeviled by buried racial fears than one who prejudicially enacts a strategic metaphysics of race.

*   *   *

The facts of Poe's politics are open to argument but can look something like this: Poe himself never owned a slave and was ambivalent about Southern plantation culture. In New York City, he was loosely affiliated with the literary wing of the Democratic Party, even as he resisted conscription by the nationalists of Young America. But while Poe learned to resent the aristocratic mores he enjoyed as a youth in Virginia, he also expressed reactionary ire against progressive causes in general and abolitionism in particular. Poe lambasted the antislavery movement in critiques of Lowell and Longfellow; his correspondence with proslavery thinkers can imply his concurring beliefs; and he may have condoned as writer or editor the disputed Paulding-Drayton review, a text that celebrates chattel bondage as a positive good. For the most part, Poe's literary practice and criticism support the racist stereotypes of plantation fiction. At the same time, Terence Whalen offers an important caveat. Aspiring to a national reputation and attuned to market forces, Whalen's Poe generally manages to avoid the slavery controversy, displaying instead an "average racism" that a range of readers could support. One might doubt, however, Poe's willingness and ability to pander consistently to popular tastes, especially given his lifelong penchant for self-destructive behavior. More crucially, a larger question looms: even if Poe eschews explicit discussion of the slavery conflict, to what extent might the crisis have influenced his literary work?[4]

There has been some study of racial ideology in Poe's poetry and poetic theory, although Poe's prose represents his most sustained engagement of slavery and race.[5] *The Narrative of Arthur Gordon Pym* (1838) and subsequent stories receive much notice, but the focus on Poe's middle and later writings obscures a formative tale. Poe's first published story, "Metzengerstein," describes the horrifying death of a Baron who becomes obsessed with a mystical horse that materializes out of a tapestry. The tale does not seem particularly political, nor are its interests overtly American. In his preface to *Tales of the Grotesque and Arabesque* (1840), Poe probably had "Metzengerstein" in mind when he wrote that only one story in the collection favors that "species of pseudo-horror which we are taught to call Germanic" (*PT*, 129). Here Poe associates "Metzengerstein" with E. T. A. Hoffmann's *phantasystück* tradition, a comparison scholars tend to accept if only to watch Poe burlesque such supernaturalism.[6] Yet by this token, Poe's slippery preface itself may be ironic, for despite "Metzengerstein"'s Hungarian setting and tongue-tying Teutonic names, its fantastical terror is not solely Germanic but also intensely American. Published five months after Nat Turner's revolt, "Metzengerstein" stands as Poe's first serious treatment of slavery and race, offered in the form of a cautious—and cautionary—political commentary.[7]

In the story, the families of Berlifitzing and Metzengerstein represent two "contiguous" and "mutually embittered" estates that had "long exercised a rival influence in the affairs of a busy government."[8]

This tense situation is analogous to political conditions in the United States as conflict between the North and South spiked in 1831, when South Carolina threatened to nullify Andrew Jackson's tariff on the dangerous grounds that states' rights superseded federal authority. Commentators of the time recognized that the nullification crisis bore heavily on the slavery conflict, which was entering a new and more militant phase.[9] In 1831, David Walker's "Appeal" (1829) and William Lloyd Garrison's *Liberator* outraged the South. That same year, John Calhoun renounced his ambitions for national office, pursuing instead a sectional course increasingly marked by secessionist rhetoric and aggressive defenses of slavery. Most dramatically, Nat Turner's revolt stoked the slavery controversy, unifying proslavery forces and engendering harsher slave codes even while convincing many observers that slavery needed to end. In 1831, chattel bondage was seen as a threat to the Union by Americans in both the North and South, including the twenty-two-year-old Poe, who that year crossed the Mason-Dixon line twice before settling near Frederick Douglass in Baltimore to begin a career in prose.[10]

Poe's first production was "Metzengerstein," a story that speaks to American sectionalism by exploiting regional stereotypes. In the antebellum era, hunting and horsemanship were standard features of the Southern cavalier, and by 1831, the South was depicted as a passionate, feudal, failing place.[11] The Berlifitzing house is headed by a count who possesses "so passionate a love of horses, and of hunting, that neither bodily infirmity, great age, nor mental incapacity, prevented his daily participation" ("M," 20). In stories such as "The Man That Was Used Up" (1839), "The Fall of the House of Usher" (1839), and "The Gold-Bug" (1843), Poe shows both fealty and resentment toward a South (and an adopted father) that was for him an occasional home in which he never felt fully welcome.[12] "Metzengerstein" expresses these turbulent feelings in the "loftily descended" but "infirm" Count Berlifitzing, whose "honorable" but "weaker" estate falls to its neighboring rival ("M," 20).

This rival, the Metzengerstein house, is headed by the young Baron Frederick who, among other immoral acts, purportedly sets fire to the Berlifitzing stables. Poe could be indulging a fantasy of vengeance against his adopted father, John Allan, and authority in general, but it is also at this point that race and slavery irrupt into the tale. As the Baron listens to the crackling stables, he fixates on an ancient tapestry featuring an "unnaturally colored horse" that once belonged to a "Saracen ancestor" of the neighboring Count. Against the backdrop of a Metzengerstein stabbing a fallen Berlifitzing, the horse's eyes glare with a "human expression" and its teeth show through "distended lips" ("M," 22-23). Spiritualist gambits and horrifying teeth are, of course, favorite Poe tropes, but the racial connotations of the "Horse-Shade" ("M," 18) increase when it takes physical form, seemingly emerging from the tapestry under the Baron's monomaniacal gaze. The origins of the beast are unclear, except that it is branded with Berlifitzing's initials, indicating to one servant that the animal belonged to the "old Count's stud of foreign horses" ("M," 23). The antebellum era linked horses and slaves as branded, bred, and brutish chattel—a fact decried on the masthead of the *Liberator*, which conflated slave and horse auctions—though this linkage stretched back in Southern thought from Thomas Jefferson to William Byrd, who warned as early as 1736 that African slaves require "tort rein, or they will be apt to throw their rider."[13] If, as "Metzengerstein" suggests, the horse represents a slave, then the Baron plays an abolitionist role, for just as Turner's Southampton revolt was blamed on "incendiary" abolitionists, the Baron is an "incendiary" villain implicated in the disastrous end of his neighbor's chattel institution.[14]

Poe's basic position is anti-abolitionist. Count Berlifitzing, decrepit though he is, dies attempting to rescue his horses. Like the loving masters of plantation fiction, he is too fond of his chattel. The tale also broaches what was for many the most troubling prospect of abolition: slavery may be undesirable, but what happens with masterless slaves? This question arises time and again in the American slavery debate,

particularly after Turner's revolt when the fear of free blacks made col-
onization a popular (albeit unworkable) scheme and states passed laws
more severely restricting the rights of free persons of color. In 1832,
Thomas Dew, an architect of proslavery thought, saw "[e]mancipation
without deportation" as the single greatest danger to the South. Dew
could only imagine black-white relations in which "[o]ne must rule the
other"; and he predicted that any "commingling of races" would inevitably bring about "barbarism."[15]

Like Dew, "Metzengerstein" worries over the control and ownership
of chattel. When the Baron first meets the mysterious steed, he immediately asks, "Whose horse?" to which a servant replies, "He is your own
property, . . . at least he is claimed by no other owner" ("M," 23). Despite
the "suspicious and untractable character" attributed to the brute, the
Baron then muses: "[P]erhaps a rider like Frederick of Metzengerstein,
may tame even the devil from the stables of Berlifitzing." This line
echoes a frequent complaint about abolitionists: Northern reformers
foolishly think that they can handle intractable slaves, an optimism
born of perfectionist ignorance, which leads to Metzengerstein's death.
Obsessed with the horse to the scandalous point that he "disdained the
company of his equals," Metzengerstein allows his "perverse attachment" to grow into a "hideous and unnatural fervor" exacerbated by
the horse's "peculiar intelligence" and "human-looking eye" ("M," 27,
28). In 1853 William Gilmore Simms wrote: "The moral of the steed is
in the spur of his rider; of the slave, in the eye of his master."[16] Such is
not, however, the case in "Metzengerstein" when the Baron is mastered
by his semihuman chattel and borne into his own burning palace. As
the "ungovernable fire" dies to a "white flame," Poe ends "Metzengerstein": "[A] cloud of smoke settled heavily over the battlements in
the distinct colossal figure of—*a horse*."

Responsibility for this terrible end falls on Baron Metzengerstein as
Poe takes up what was becoming a national anti-abolitionist stand.[17]
The Baron relishes the destruction of his neighbor and then slyly pos-
sesses his chattel, implying—as did some proslavery radicals—that the

North practiced its own form of bondage and coveted the labor of free blacks. Deadly to himself and his rivals alike, Metzengerstein prefers the company of a brute, a fact that Poe describes in sexualized language, thus voicing an anti-abolitionist jibe he repeats in subsequent works.[18] Of most importance, the Baron tragically discounts the savagery of the chattel he frees. Just as accounts of the Southampton revolt dwelled on Turner's "spirit of prophecy," Poe's story begins with an "ancient prophecy" predicting the fall of both houses ("M," 19).[19] Like an abolitionist fanatic, however, the Baron ignores all warnings. He fails to tame the devilish brute that survives the fire of Berlifitzing's stables, bringing to pass the darkest fears of anti-abolitionists—that the emancipation of African slaves would destroy both North and South, that blacks would come to rule over whites, and that the United States would go up in flames in the shadow of slaves without masters.

Such is one political subtext of "Metzengerstein" that may not come as a total surprise. The fear of incendiary slave revolt looms over much of antebellum literature, and slave rebellion potentially lurks in a number of Poe texts—from vague indications in "Silence—A Fable" (1835), "The Fall of the House of Usher," and "The Black Cat" (1843) to *Pym*, "The Murders in the Rue Morgue" (1841), "The System of Doctor Tarr and Professor Fether" (1844), and "Hop-Frog" (1849).[20] Like these later works, "Metzengerstein" takes a racist, anti-abolitionist stand at least insofar as Poe dwells on black savagery and the dangers of masterless chattel. Reflecting the anxieties of post-Turner America, "Metzengerstein" fits a familiar Poe profile, even as the story remains distinctive in at least two critical ways. First, "Metzengerstein" shows that Poe's fiction addresses slavery from the beginning. Poe did not discover the national sin as a literary topic during the writing of *Pym*, nor is his early political commentary limited to lesser satirical pieces such as "Four Beasts in One" (1833). Blackness and bondage are for Poe more than abstracted symbols of evil, as he treats the presence of Africans in America as a national problem.

"Metzengerstein" is also distinctive in that its political argument seems remarkably coherent and specific compared to Poe's later narratives. Racial horrors and slavery tropes run amok in many Poe texts, often collapsing allegorical structures into ideological chaos. "Metzengerstein" reaches its own frantic end, but its political logic is sustained, revealing subtle but recognizable patterns of anti-abolitionism and registering not only racial terror but also a position on civic events. This politicized reading need not entirely conflict with Whalen's account of Poe's career. Even if a savvier, market-driven Poe shied away from the slavery controversy, the partisan and provincial "Metzengerstein" comes at the outset of Poe's professional life—before he knew the publishing world and before he formulated ambitious plans for a national literary magazine.[21] There is no indication that "Metzengerstein" was criticized for its politics, yet Poe's subsequent fiction is more circumspect in that it lacks as discernible an opinion on the slavery conflict. For Whalen, such obscurity is governed by the strictures of political economy. But "Metzengerstein" suggests that Poe is not a passive conduit for racist ideology, nor is his racism, average or otherwise, so easily separated from the question of slavery. There remains another explanation for Poe's tortured treatment of blackness and bondage: Poe struggles to assimilate his politics and metaphysics, an antinomy evident in "Metzengerstein," if only in nascent form.

* * *

To read "Metzengerstein" in light of the slavery crisis is not to say that the story is philosophically flat. Joan Dayan has written on both Poe's metaphysics and his politics, and although these lines of inquiry do not often cross, Dayan links Poe's writings on color and servitude to "the mysteries of identity" and "the riddle of body and mind."[22] Can one ever know one's self? Is the self a stable entity? To what extent does the subject's mind constitute objective reality? Such questions are manifest in Poe's discussions of American race and slavery, just as race and slavery help generate his explorations of subjectivity. This dialectical relationship, so fundamental to American romanticism before the Civil War, points Poe toward a synthesis in which subject and object, white and black, master and slave become one. "Metzengerstein"'s metaphysics of race broach this troubling prospect as the story exposes the political threat of a horrible absolutism. Here again the tale's ambiguous steed plays a central role, for among its many manifestations, the horse can be a creature of transcendental idealism representing a dangerous blackness hiding in the white mind.

Famously, Kant posits a subjectivity that constitutes objective reality in that the structures of the mind organize, reveal, and—in this sense—make up the phenomenological order. This seems the case when Baron Metzengerstein, "buried in meditation," fixates on the tapestry horse, seemingly bringing it into the natural world ("M," 21):

> The longer he gazed, the more absorbing became the spell—the more impossible did it appear that he could ever withdraw his glance from the fascination of that tapestry. . . . To his extreme horror and astonishment, the head of the gigantic steed had, in the meantime, altered its position. The neck of the animal, before arched, as if in compassion, over the prostrate body of its lord, was now extended, at full length, in the direction of the Baron. ("M," 22-23)

Simply considered, this summoning scene can enact a general transcendentalist claim: reality is not passively perceived by the subject but actively constructed by it. As we shall see, Poe's theory of race relies on this Kantian conviction, particularly as extended by Schelling and disseminated by Coleridge, who together propound two ideas that are of special importance to Poe: absolute identity, a reality concept that synthesizes subject and object, and unconscious production, the means by which subjects unknowingly create the phenomenological world. First, however, some words on history and sources are needed, for Poe's relation to transcendentalism is complicated.

Poe is most often seen as a detractor of transcendental idealism who satirizes the cant of Kant and the croaking of the Concord "Frog-pondians."[23] Poe certainly has fun with romantic philosophy, and he feuds with Emerson and his circle. However, some scholars find strong affinities between Poe and transcendentalism, in part because they go directly to Europe without passing through the confines of Concord.[24] Which sources one studies makes a difference when looking for Poe's philosophy, although how Poe got his transcendentalism is difficult to say, especially in 1831—prior to Frederic Hedge's essays on Kant and the stirrings of the Frogpondians, prior to Poe's occasional and at times misinformed direct references to German romanticism. Poe probably lacked the skill and opportunity to read German philosophy in its original. However, by 1831 he was reading Coleridge and may have learned some version of transcendentalism from Carlyle, Cousin, de Quincey, and de Staël.[25] There is also another possible source indicated by "Metzengerstein," for as the story itself suggests by footnoting "D'Israeli," Poe may have taken some philosophical direction from Benjamin Disraeli's *Vivian Grey* (1826).[26]

In Disraeli's novel, Grey meets a German Prince who wars with a bordering estate and obsesses over a painting of a horse that seems to spring into life. Parallels to the plot of "Metzengerstein" are evident enough, but what has not been discussed is another scene in which Grey attends a party where he refers to the German states as the "country of Kant." His host then points to a fellow guest:

> The leader of the Idealists, a pupil of the celebrated Fichte! To gain an idea of his character, know that he out-Herods his master. . . . The first principle of his school is to reject all expressions which incline in the slightest degree to substantiality. . . . Some say that he dreads the contact of all real things, and that he makes it the study of his life to avoid them. Matter is his great enemy.[27]

The joke is that the student of Fichte is gorging himself on beer soup, showing that even committed idealists must live in the material world.

Baron Metzengerstein suffers from a similar kind of double consciousness, for though prone to reflective meditation, he is also a "temporal king" whose appetites, like those of Disraeli's idealist, have "out-heroded" Herod. At the same time, the Baron avoids touching the horse to whom he is so passionately attached, and none of his servants can recall having "placed his hand upon the body of the beast" ("M," 21). In one sense, then, the horse is unreal, a phenomenon of the Baron's subjectivity, but in another, the horse is too real, embodying a savage materiality that proves the great enemy of Metzengerstein's mind. Is the horse an objective brute or a subjective nightmare? How does Poe mediate the dialectic of materialism and idealism, a dialectic that Plato's *Phaedrus* compares to being torn apart by two horses?[28]

By eliding potentially determinative evidence with disclaimers and narrative gaps, "Metzengerstein" refuses to settle the metaphysical status of the steed. This has the familiar Poe effect of collapsing Enlightenment dualisms as the spectral horse-shade seems simultaneously objective and subjective, natural and supernatural. David Leverenz attributes such ambiguity to Poe's "mind-body crossings," though what Poe hopes to accomplish with them remains of much concern.[29] Poe does more, I think, than only gratify the iconoclastic urge to cast the shadow of dark romanticism over Enlightenment order. For Poe, such skepticism is the obverse of a serious transcendentalist effort to imagine the synthesis of subject and object in an absolute truth. In this way, Poe resists Enlightened duality, not with a materialist critique that Jonathan Elmer associates with Adorno and Horkheimer, and not with an African epistemology hinted at by Dayan and Toni Morrison but, rather, with the available logic of a specific type of transcendentalism.[30]

The hungry idealist of *Vivian Grey* is a caricature of Schelling, the pupil of Fichte who during his phase of so-called "identity philosophy" sought to incorporate the material world into his transcendental system. For de Staël, "Schelling refers every thing to nature." Hedge calls him "the ontologist of the Kantian School." More recently, Emil Fackenheim describes Schelling as an idealist "who has been struck, almost physically, by brute facticity."[31] This description is eerily appropriate for Poe, whose writings respond to both material and metaphysical modes of interpretation, and whose tales careen between idealism and a brute facticity often figured as race. It makes sense that Schelling, more than any other German philosopher, had an early influence on Poe.[32] "Loss of Breath" (1832) and "How to Write a Blackwood Article" (1838) refer to Schelling by name. Poe's resistance to dualistic order in "Metzengerstein" and beyond dramatizes what in "Morella" (1835) is called "*Identity* as urged by Schelling" (*PT*, 235)—that is, identity not only as self but also as an absolute truth that Schelling's *System of Transcendental Idealism* (1800) formulates as "the coincidence of an objective with a subjective."[33]

Poe probably learned such absolutism from Coleridge. As early as 1831, Poe knew *Biographia Literaria* (1817), a book that praises Schelling's massive influence and pays homage to the point of plagiarism. Citing Schelling, Coleridge discusses absolute identity: "All knowledge rests on the coincidence of an object with a subject. . . . During the act of knowledge itself, the objective and subjective are so instantly united, that we cannot determine to which of the two the priority belongs."[34] This is an abiding dilemma for Poe and precisely the challenge of Metzengerstein's steed. Because the horse is both a phenomenon produced by the mind of Frederick Metzengerstein and a brutish, material beast from the stables of William Berlifitzing, subjectivity and objectivity are joined in an inseparable union that can represent the absolute identity of Friedrich Wilhelm Schelling.

But whereas Schelling and Coleridge see such synthesis as harmonious, beautiful, and true, for Poe the union of subject and object is a horse of a different color:

[T]he Baron's perverse attachment to his lately-acquired charger—an attachment which seemed to attain new strength from every fresh example of the animal's ferocious and demon-like propensities—at length became, in the eyes of all reasonable men, a hideous and unnatural fervor. In the glare of noon—at the dead hour of night—in sickness or in health—in calm or in tempest—the young Metzengerstein seemed riveted to the saddle of that colossal horse, whose intractable audacities so well accorded with his own spirit. ("M," 26-27)

Poe cannot celebrate a transcendentalism that synthesizes black and white. Just as the narrator of "William Wilson" (1839) murders himself and the twin whose "absolute identity" nearly "enslaved" him (*PT*, 355-56), "Metzengerstein" recoils from a master-slave pairing by killing both subject and object. Eschewing the ecstatic, lyrical flights that characterize synthesis in Schelling and Coleridge, Poe renders the union of subject and object in an idiom of racial horror as absolute identity becomes an analog for amalgamation and slave revolt.

Even worse, Poe hints that this hideous synthesis originates in Metzengerstein's unwitting mind, a possibility also theorized by transcendentalist thought. The concept of unconscious production was first explored by Fichte, for whom the subjective production of phenomena precedes the subject's knowledge of it. This explains why radical subjectivity is so counterintuitive to the uninitiated. Because our minds do not know that they spontaneously make up reality, only guided philosophical reflection can discover the truth-making process. Absolute identity is thus revealed when unconscious production becomes conscious, when subjectivity finally recognizes that it is indistinguishable from objectivity, a realization that effectively abolishes subject-object dualism.[35]

For Schelling and Coleridge, art is the means for discovering this absolutism. Or as Schelling writes in *System of Transcendental Idealism*, "[A]rt is at once the only true and eternal organ and document of philosophy, which ever and again continues to speak to us of what philosophy cannot depict in external form, namely the unconscious element in acting and producing, and its original identity with the conscious."[36] Following Schelling, Coleridge posits "a *philosophic* (and inasmuch as it is actualized by an effort of freedom, an *artificial*) con-

sciousness, which lies beneath or (as it were) *behind* the spontaneous consciousness natural to all reflecting beings." By thus extolling the role of art as an aid to freely willed reflection, Schelling and Coleridge conflate metaphysics, psychology, and aesthetics, for the creation and appreciation of beauty bring unconscious production to light, revealing absolute identity through what Coleridge calls art's "synthetic and magical power."[37]

For Poe, however, the unconscious-made-conscious-through-art is finally horrific, not so much because the Kantian and Burkean sublimes can be implicated in race but because a deadly blackness emerges from the unsuspecting white mind.[38] When Metzengerstein first glances at the tapestry horse, he does so "without his consciousness," and he cannot quell the "overwhelming anxiety" that makes it "impossible" to avert his gaze as he "mechanically" stares at the object of art that becomes the "uncontrollable" horse-shade ("M," 22, 29). Here the monomaniacal subject unconsciously produces the object of its demise, creating a self-generated, self-annihilating nightmare that culminates in the Baron's last ride. Schelling calls the unconscious-made-conscious "the holy of holies" that "burns in eternal and original unity, as if in a single flame."[39] "Metzengerstein" ends with the unholy union of white master and black slave, a pairing that perishes in an inferno of unnameable absolutism. "Metzengerstein" can play upon the horror of slave revolt, but absolute identity and unconscious production turn the screw once more. Distinctions of color and servitude become metaphysically untenable when an irrepressible, bestial blackness lives in the white subject, ready to spring into hideous synthesis through an uncontrollable and distinctly transcendental coming-to-consciousness.

This blurring of black and white subjectivity may recall another pupil of Fichte, Hegel, whose dialectic of lord and bondsman frames the celebrated argument that the subject can only know itself through a subordinate or dominant other.[40] Yet as sensitive as Poe is to the dynamics of power and selfhood, Schelling and Coleridge remain more likely philosophical forerunners than Hegel. Calvin Stowe, Harriet

Beecher's husband, suggested as much in 1845 when he reviewed the *"four great pillars of the Modern Transcendentalism"*—Kant, Fichte, Schelling, and Hegel. Stowe writes of Schelling: "It was from him immediately that Coleridge drew, and the transcendentalism of this country probably owes its existence to a great extent to the influence of his writings." Stowe then offers what he believes to be the first American translation of Hegel, adding: "I have never been able, I must frankly confess it, to find out what the man means by any thing which he says."[41] Stowe is right to doubt his expertise, but his confusion is indicative. In antebellum America, particularly during the formation of transcendentalism in the early 1830s, Schelling was more accessible, better understood, and more influential than Hegel, despite an early interest in Hegel by a handful of American thinkers and despite the growing popularity of Hegel that would culminate after the Civil War.[42]

Antebellum philosophical contexts, thematic affinities, and textual allusions all suggest that "Metzengerstein" treats subjectivity in the logic of Schelling and Coleridge. The tale probably errs by pursuing this interest in a third-person voice, for like many precocious works of fiction, "Metzengerstein" tells but does not show its protagonist's state of mind. For this reason, however, the story is instructive—and also powerfully predictive—as a kind of component tasting in which political commentary and transcendental idealism are not formally integrated. Later, Poe's distasteful politics are more carefully blended in first-person texts characterized by racist aspersions and wild transcendental imaginings. Such narratives are often more dramatic and psychologically nuanced than "Metzengerstein," even though slavery and race refuse to be entirely assimilated as transcendental subjectivity unconsciously creates the blackness it fears most.

Critics have shown how *Pym* reveals the social constructedness of race, but the novel also subtly describes its phenomenological production. As Pym drifts from a unified white subjectivity to the subjectivity of a prisoner, of a cannibal, and finally of a fugitive slave, he is repeatedly lost in the depths of his mind, figured by Poe in scenes of drunkenness, insanity, and interment. The generative power of the unconscious becomes terrifyingly clear when a cliff-hanging Pym discovers his "fancies creating their own realities" (*PT,* 1170). Pym attempts to define a more stable subjectivity over and against the jet-black Tsalalians, and he appears to succeed when escaping their island and sailing toward an all-white South Pole. This seems especially true when his Tsalalian captive dies from overexposure to whiteness, suggesting that black people have no place in the "perfect whiteness" at the end of the book (*PT,* 1179). And yet the corpse of the Tsalalian remains in the bottom of the boat. Inassimilable and inescapable, it shows that racial others are fundamental to Pym's subjectivity, which is terrorized by dark bodies it spontaneously creates and thus cannot leave behind. As the novel concludes with Pym's canoe careening toward an unknown absolutism, the presence of blackness makes the looming synthesis an occasion more of horror than joy.

A similar dynamic is at work in "Ligeia." Ligeia is a maven of "transcendentalism" and also a figure of amalgamation, whose physical features conjure images of Africa and Arabia (*PT,* 266). Like Metzengerstein's steed, Ligeia can symbolize the possibilities of absolute identity insofar as she is both a material other and a product of the narrator's mind. Synthesizing subjectivity and objectivity under the narrator's transcendentally influenced eye, Ligeia's struggle to return from the dead models a process of unconscious production when her resurrection as dark phenomenon is dialectically enacted in the natural world and in the narrator's irrepressibly associative mind. In the end, his white subjectivity is subsumed by the gaze of Ligeia, whose "black" eyes are "far larger than the ordinary eyes of [his] own race" (*PT,* 264). Is Ligeia an embodied black figure or the figment of a racist unconscious? The transcendentalism of Schelling and Coleridge suggests that the answer is *yes.*[43]

Even an aggressively satirical piece like "How to Write a Blackwood Article" does not eschew race when trying to "[s]ay something about objectivity and subjectivity" (*PT,* 282). The story's narrator, Psyche Zenobia, is told to adopt "the tone transcendental" and shun "the tone heterogeneous," and to praise the harmony of "Supernal Oneness" while avoiding "Infernal Twoness" (*PT*, 283). Poe associates such absolutism with both "Coleridge" and a "pet baboon" (*PT*, 281), and he further conflates transcendentalism and race mixing in Zenobia's tale, "A Predicament." Not only is the bluestocking Zenobia a reformer in the Frogpondian mode but Poe links her philosophy to amalgamation when her grotesque black servant crashes into her breasts. Poe responds to this bawdy union by decapitating Zenobia, which she describes in sensational detail as she wonders whether her head or body represents her "proper identity" (*PT*, 295). Faced with an absolute identity entailing the threat of racial unity, Poe retreats to an epistemology in which the division of subject and object is explicitly, violently demarcated. "How to Write a Blackwood Article" is clearly a burlesque, yet Poe's caricature of transcendental writing aptly describes some of his best work. Under the influence of Schelling and Coleridge, Poe desires the supernal truth and beauty of absolute oneness. At the same time, he does not let go of dualistic formulations of slavery and race, making transcendence a philosophically attractive but politically threatening prospect.[44]

Teresa Goddu has shown how Cold War critics took the blackness of classic antebellum texts not as an indication of race but as a metaphysical cipher.[45] The pendulum has swung in the opposite direction as race and slavery now seem everywhere in Poe, though the politics and philosophy of blackness seem to me inextricably tied. In the case of Poe, dark romanticism is appropriately named. Hawthorne, Melville, and Dickinson know how to pit Calvin against Concord. For Poe, race and slavery remain fearsome facts that resist any blithe absolutism. This is not to say that transcendental idealism cannot accommodate racism. Kant maintained a racist taxonomy, as did Coleridge and Emerson, and romanticism—European and American—can be profoundly implicated in racialist thought.[46] This did not prevent almost all transcendentalists from supporting abolitionism, from thus becoming both part of the racism problem and part of the emancipation solution. In Poe, however, the power of blackness is too threatening a concern. Poe retains a racist anti-abolitionism that mars his potentially transcendental plots, pushing his idealism toward a hideous synthesis in which absolute identity and unconscious production undermine the mastery of white subjectivity, an embattled political and philosophical formation after Nat Turner.

*   *   *

Poe reportedly once leapt twenty feet in the running broad jump. To move from "Metzengerstein" to the end of Poe's career may require a similar stunt. The preceding discussion schematically offers some sense of the long middle ground. Poe's formal technique matures; his aspirations for a national magazine swell; in 1845 the Longfellow War and Poe's disastrous reading at the Boston Lyceum bring a more personal, polemical hostility to his views of New England reform. The vagaries of Poe's career make for a tragic and fascinating story. Yet it is hard to index his fictions according to the shifting fortunes of his life, in part because he tends to revisit earlier topics and narrative strategies, prompting some scholars to organize his texts thematically, not chronologically. This makes sense in the matter of slavery and race, for Poe's literary treatment is in many ways consistent. Although the political subtext of "Metzengerstein" appears to me exceptionally cogent, absolute identity and unconscious production when combined with color and servitude continue to cause ungovernable horror, not only in "Ligeia," *Pym,* and "How to Write a Blackwood Article" but also in such texts as "The Fall of the House of Usher," "The Murders in the Rue Morgue," "The Black Cat," "The System of Doctor Tarr and Professor Fether," "The Raven" (1845), and "Hop-Frog." These works need not be explicitly about the American slavery crisis to show unconscious white subjectivities rising toward a terrible, self-generated blackness. Race and transcendental philosophy are frequently entangled in Poe's imagination, though a singular departure may be *Eureka*, his challenging, seldom-loved "Prose Poem" whose rhapsodic cosmology potentially invokes an absolutism free from the anxiety of race (*PT*, 1257). How sustainable such freedom is for Poe is the subject of this final section, which ultimately explores the extent of Poe's political intentions.

In his "Marginalia" of 1849, Poe celebrated his skeptical prowess: "It is laughable to observe how easily any system of Philosophy can be proved false" (*ER*, 1458). Poe, however, immediately betrays a lingering desire for belief: "[I]s it not mournful to perceive the impossibility of even fancying any particular system to be true?" For all his doubting, Poe never abjures the Enlightenment dream of metaphysical coherence, and nowhere is this clearer than in *Eureka*, his best effort to expound a philosophical system. Poe announces at the start of the text: "I design to speak of the *Physical, Metaphysical and Mathematical— of the Material and Spiritual Universe:—of its Essence, its Origin, its Creation, its Present Condition and its Destiny*" (*PT*, 1261). The hubris here may rival that of some university mission statements. But if Poe becomes increasingly unbalanced toward the end of his life, there is no reason to take *Eureka* less seriously than any other Poe text. Indeed, considering Poe's long-standing commitment to speculation, and considering the metaphysical maxims of his "Marginalia" (1844-49) and "Fifty Suggestions" (1849), his attempt at a major work of philosophy comes as no surprise.

Eureka draws from a dizzying number of thinkers, including Newton, Laplace, Leibniz, Kepler, and Alexander von Humboldt. Much of the text discusses the physical sciences, which Poe's rage for total coherence pushes to metaphysical extremes. In this way, *Eureka* is a work of synthesis, for although the treatise dismisses "Transcendentalists" as canters and "divers for crotchets" (*PT*, 1263), its larger dialectal structure is recognizably transcendental. Poe begins by positing "Material" and "Spiritual" aspects of the universe (*PT*, 1261), and he mocks the division of object and subject that vexes the history of Western thought. Poe's goal is to formulate what he variously calls "*absolute truth*" (*PT*, 1269), "absolute oneness" (*PT*, 1280), and "absolute homogeneity" (*PT*, 1279). He seeks what he calls a "return into unity" (*PT*, 1278), which is reached through the "tranquility of self-inspection" and the "cool exercise of consciousness" (*PT*, 1356). The unity of object and subject in reflection sounds precisely like Schelling and Coleridge, as absolute truth reveals itself in an ecstatic coming to consciousness.[47] This process serves as a climactic synthesis of *Eureka*'s argument. For Poe, "conscious Intelligences" learn "proper identity" through self-knowledge and, in doing so, recur to an "identity with God" in which "myriads of individual Intelligences become blended . . . into One" (*PT*, 1358). Here Poe moves toward absolute identity with an emphasis on conscious reflection, showing that the subject must be reunited with its original, unconscious productions.

What is stunning is how happy this synthesis is: for once, Poe is not shaken but stirred. In the vast majority of his writings, self-inspection is not tranquil, nor is self-consciousness cool, nor is the absolute blending of egos cause for transcendental joy. When the narrator in "Loss of Breath" is lynched, Poe mocks romantic absolutism: "Schelling himself would have been satisfied with my entire loss of self-identity."[48] In *Eureka*, however, there is "*perfection* of plot" (*PT*, 1342), and even evil is "intelligible" and "endurable" (*PT*, 1357). The union of self and other in God is not a violation of the personal mind, for although *Eureka* admits "[t]he pain of the consideration that we shall lose our individual identity," assurance arrives with the conviction that "*each* must become God" (*PT*, 1359). In *Eureka*, absolute oneness is "agglomeration," not amalgamation (*PT*, 1306), and Poe's predicted "revolution" of knowledge is not figured as a revolt (*PT*, 1262). Thus Poe seemingly frees transcendentalism from the trammels of race, for to come to ecstatic consciousness and realize absolute identity is to leave behind the dualistic vision that *Eureka* calls "mental slavery" (*PT*, 1269).

And yet the very mention of slavery can summon the specter of the national sin. Given the intense racialist fears that appear in so much of

Poe's work, *Eureka* and its inset text—supposedly lifted from a "Nubian geographer"—only tenuously banishes political fear from the paradise of absolutism (*PT*, 1263). Unity is a crucial concept in transcendental philosophy, but it also had significant meaning in ethnologic debate. In the antebellum era, monogenesists argued that all races spring from a single origin, a conclusion that was readily adapted to abolitionist ends. For their part, polygenesists and slavery advocates denied the unity of races, often citing the pseudoscientific work of Samuel George Morton. Morton's writings on mummies and skulls form a background for *Pym* and "Some Words with a Mummy" (1845).[49] *Eureka*, however, is dedicated to Alexander von Humboldt, whose influential opus, *Cosmos* (1845), refuted Morton's polygenesist views.[50] Following Humboldt, *Eureka* holds that all matter comes from a "common parentage" (*PT*, 1286), and so if the text speaks to slavery at all, it appears to speak against it, even as Poe forecloses this possibility in a subsequent tale, "Mellonta Tauta" (1849).

Presented as a series of letters from a balloonist in the year 2848, "Mellonta Tauta" quotes copiously from *Eureka* as it mocks the double consciousness of previous eras and celebrates the "absolute truth" recognized in the twenty-ninth century (*PT*, 878). The difference is that "Mellonta Tauta" is an overt political satire that takes "Amriccans" to task for reformist ignorance and government by mob (*PT*, 879). The heavy-handed politics of the story are combatively conservative, sending up such republican practices as voting and the "queerest idea" that "all men are born free and equal" (*PT*, 879). The commentary can be so extravagant as to seem at times capricious, yet Poe's complaint about equality has poignant political relevance. From Thomas Dew, Robert Montgomery Bird, and William Harper in the 1830s to James Henry Hammond, John Calhoun, and George Fitzhugh in the decades that followed, proslavery thinkers repeatedly denied that "all men are born free and equal," mainly because the phrase was a rallying cry in abolitionist discourse.[51] Questions about the freedom and equality of black people dominated antebellum political debate, and in "Mellonta

Tauta," Poe's narrator stakes a popular proslavery claim. Unable or unwilling to keep race and slavery out of *Eureka*'s transcendental speculations, "Mellonta Tauta," like so many Poe texts, cannot reconcile race and absolutism. In an 1847 article, "Bad News for the Transcendental Poets," an author in the *Literary World* crowed: "The transcendental balloon is rapidly suffering collapse."[52] "Mellonta Tauta" ends when the narrator announces that her "balloon has collapsed" (*PT*, 884-85). As it plummets toward the sea, Poe presents a familiar (if sanguinely reported) apocalypse in which transcendentalism yet again cannot bear the burden of antebellum politics. *Eureka*, then, is the exception that proves the rule represented by "Mellonta Tauta": Poe's ambivalence toward transcendentalism constitutes and is constituted by his views on slavery and race. What remains unclear is why Poe continues to tangle metaphysics and politics. Why do his writings so stubbornly dwell on so disruptive an antinomy?

In 1923, D. H. Lawrence hinted at a powerful explanation: "Moralists have always wondered helplessly why Poe's 'morbid' tales need have been written. They need to be written because old things need to die and disintegrate, because the old white psyche has to be gradually broken down before anything else can come to pass." Lawrence recognized that "Poor Poe" subverts white subjectivity, and although he sometimes described Poe as performing this work "consciously," he also attributed this impulse to a primitive, irresistible, and almost pathological "need."[53] Harry Levin and Leslie Fielder saw this need as an unconscious "racial phobia," a view that continues to predominate Poe scholarship in more sophisticated forms.[54] John Carlos Rowe, Dana Nelson, David Leverenz, and J. Gerald Kennedy are among those critics who see Poe as both in and out of control insofar as the vision of his "semiconscious" texts remains obscured by his racism. Even Whalen, who ascribes to Poe a larger amount of intention, does not consistently theorize Poe's conscious relation to political conditions. Whether the method is Marxist or psychoanalytic, whether the agency is ideology or id, for scholars who entertain questions of intention, Poe's literary treatment of slavery and race seems to operate beyond his authorial will.[55]

There is always space for the unconscious, politically or psychoanalytically understood. There is surely some truth to the picture of Poe as a man at the mercy of some hidden perversity. Henry James, no stranger to the dramatic potential of coming to consciousness, associated the vulgar pleasures of Poe with a "primitive stage of reflection."[56] Perhaps we like Poe best this way. Bodies under the floorboards, beasts in the jungle, madwomen in the attic—it is gripping to watch a subject in the throes of the unconscious, especially when the unconscious threatens to stun us by degrees. And Poe knows. For him, as for Schelling and Coleridge, the dialectical process of coming to consciousness is a necessary element of art premised on an aesthetic theory based in transcendental subjectivity.

In 1842, a British critic in the *American Eclectic* wrote of German romantics: "They consider, that as Art is a production, a creation of the mind of man, the real way to set about its examination must be the investigation of those laws of the mind from whence it proceeds. . . . Thus it becomes itself a branch of psychology. . . . *They* [the Germans] examine the producing mind; *we* the work produced."[57] Poe's aesthetics often focus on the form of the object of art, a tendency that can align him with high modernists and New Critics. However, as much as any antebellum thinker, Poe follows the Germans in taking an interest in the subjectivity of the artist. As Poe suggests when calling *Biographia Literaria* "an important service to the cause of psychological science," his aesthetics are closely related to his sense of the operations of the mind (*ER*, 188).

Part of Poe's fame as a cryptologist and critic came in 1842 when his review of Dickens's *Barnaby Rudge* correctly predicted some features of the ending before the novel was entirely serialized. In playing prognosticator, Poe also pronounced on the unconscious production of literature: "This is clearly the design of Mr. Dickens—although he himself may not at present perceive it. In fact, beautiful as it is, and strikingly original with him, it cannot be questioned that he has been led to it less by artistical knowledge and reflection, than by that intuitive feeling for the forcible and the true" (*ER*, 222-23). Here Poe's theory of artistic production relies not on conscious "knowledge" or "reflection" but on an "intuitive" mental faculty of which the author remains unaware. Such claims undermine the omnipotent intention Poe ascribes to the poet in "The Philosophy of Composition" (1846), a work that seems especially specious in light of other Poe texts. In "MS. Found in a Bottle" (1833), the narrator "unwittingly" paints "DISCOVERY" on a sail, suggesting in both production and product that writing uncovers the unconscious (*PT*, 195). And in an 1836 review, as well as in later critical pieces, Poe further celebrates artistic effects that "arise independently of the author's will" (*ER*, 263).[58]

Thus, unconscious production is a consciously theorized aspect of Poe's thought—both in his metaphysics of race and in his thinking on art. This does not, of course, exclude psychoanalytic or ideological readings of Poe, but it does suggest that Poe can be a remarkably canny subject whose texts are acutely self-aware of the play between the known and unknown mind. Considering the political position presented in "Metzengerstein," and considering Poe's continued attention to the unconscious production of beauty and blackness, texts that may seem haunted by Poe's lurking racial phobias can be taken as complex dramatizations of a psychology of mastery and racism, dramatizations driven by Poe's abiding refusal to integrate the differences of racial others into an absolute oneness. In this way, Poe rises from the couch and moves toward the analyst's chair. The story of many of his stories—and a narrative in the history of Poe criticism—is the gradual coming to consciousness of chattel bondage and race.

The problem is that such self-consciousness fails to raise Poe's moral conscience. How can an author so committed to the issue of race and subjectivity deny the subjectivity of racial others who become, for Poe, literal images of blackness in the white mind? Clearly, theoretical sophistication need not lead to convincing truth-claims or humanist convictions. Clearly, Poe can be placed within a tradition of transcendental racism, even if there is no necessary equivalence between romanticism and egregious racial views. One might also read Poe's philosophy of race as a kind of sublimation or ideological formation, thus reinscribing Poe's psychological system within an unconscious plot. Such claims might invoke some version of the intentional fallacy, although there are more specific, more historical grounds for retaining what Nelson calls "psychopolitical imperatives" as an explanatory factor in the structure and practice of antebellum racism.[59]

Addressing the fear of slave revolt in the post-Turner South, Alexis de Tocqueville wrote that the white man "hides it from himself."[60] Douglass, Melville, and Jacobs all notice this white repression of blackness, but the fact that these writers ascribe a "deep" psychology to the slavery crisis suggests that Poe himself had access to similar conclusions. There is always space for consciousness when the evidence interpreted by the analyst is available to the subject of analysis, even if the subject's sense of psychology is not phrased in the same modern idiom. One way to determine authorial intention is to look for patterns of reflection and recognition that indicate an extended look into the recesses of the mind. If my reading of Poe is right, Poe knows that race operates unconsciously. The difference between Poe and his savvy contemporaries is that he does not follow this insight toward a more progressive politics. A reason for this is that Poe's thinking is so aggressively phenomenological that for him to conclude that the horror of blackness is "only" a mental construction may not serve to subvert that construction as such but, rather, to establish it as the most convincing account of a reality maintained only through fierce denials of intersubjectivity that mark the limits of Poe's truth-claims, psychology, ethics, and art. In the end, the unconscious in Poe combines two implications of the word: the modern sense of the unrecognized mind and the etymological meaning that signals the negation ("un") of shared ("con") knowledge ("science").[61]

As morally suspect as Poe's writings can be, their outcome is often affective. Applying Jonathan Elmer's theory of sensationalism, one might formulate race in Poe's work as an inassimilable and therefore compelling Lacanian "leftover" or "slag."[62] Slavoj Žižek supports such claims in a general discussion of American racism when he calls race an "unfathomable remainder" that simultaneously drives and defies the search for absolute unity. That Žižek makes this point while forging connections between Schelling and Lacan suggests that Poe's appeal to both transcendental and psychoanalytical criticism may not be entirely coincidental or inherently at odds.[63] Most histories of modern American psychology begin with either William James or the arrival of Freudian thought.[64] However, transcendental idealism helped invent the modern unconscious when it located the source of absolute truth beyond the subject's immediate mind. This claim is borne out by the deep psychology of British romanticism, and the philosopher Paul Redding has argued that "Schelling's development of Fichtean ideas . . . gave rise to pre-Freudian ideas about the nature of unconscious mental function."[65] In this sense, Poe can be a stop on the road from Kant to Lacan. Influenced by unconscious production and intensely attentive to psychological states, Poe writes about the fraught relation between the hidden and recognized mind. Which is to say that Poe is less an uncanny predictor of psychoanalysis and more a thinker who participates in a history of subjectivity.

In 1800, Coleridge first used "unconscious" to indicate what the self does not know of itself. In 1822, he coined "subjectivity" to signify the consciousness of one's mind engaged in the act of perception. Coleridge did not invent these concepts, but he brought them to the United States with the help of other romantics who impressed, among others, Poe. In 1831, Carlyle proclaimed: "Unconsciousness is the sign of creation." In 1832, De Quincey coined the related term "subconscious."[66] In that same year, Poe published "Metzengerstein," commencing a prose career that would use romantic theories of the mind to explore the metaphysics of race and art. Poe's thinking is not exactly systematic, coherent, or analytically rigorous. Yet as Stanley Cavell has argued, Poe is perversely attuned to the skeptical potential of romantic philosophy, showing us "the recoil of a demonic reason, irrationally thinking to dominate earth . . . not to reject the world but rather to establish it."[67] More specifically, Poe's creativity lies in the application of romantic idealism to antebellum culture, particularly the issue of slavery and race that was tearing the United States apart.

The slavery crisis thus helps to explain Poe's anomalous standing in antebellum literature. On the margins of Southern gentility, his racial views are too radically vexed for pastoral plantation fiction. Fearing transcendence, he could not join in the perfectionist projects of Concord. Such skepticism can leave Poe in the familiar company of Hawthorne and Melville, though an important difference is that Poe is a more insistent idealist, returning repeatedly to the troubling prospects of transcendental unity, particularly in *Eureka*'s vigorous, if ultimately tenuous, synthesis. When Hawthorne and Melville harass transcendentalism, they are overly conscious of Concord, and as a result, they tend toward satiric, reactive, and derivative critique. Emerson and his circle would pay some heed to the unconscious production of oneness.[68] Poe, however, pursued romantic absolutism before the founding of the Transcendental Club. He would eventually meet the Frogpondians in polemical, defensive, and not always earnest ways, but this was long after he established an original relation to transatlantic transcendentalism. Poe's sense of absolute truth is not premised on a transparent eye, for his dramatic depictions of absolute identity are occluded by slavery and race, and his thinking is intensely attentive to the productive opacity of the unconscious mind. Poe's terror is of Germany. It is carried through England. And unrelieved from political anxiety, it is shaped by the American slavery crisis as Poe pursues a metaphysic, an aesthetic, and a psychology that for all his sophistication form a conscious and unconscionable system of transcendental racism.

It may be tempting to think of racism as irrational, unconscious, unenlightened, and therefore open to reform through reflection and education. However, to take this too much for granted is to make the mistake of Poe: to maintain a separate, masterful subjectivity by radically distancing others. It is probably easier to think of Poe as culturally, morally, and philosophically distant. It is easy to be swayed by his popular image—wine bottle in one hand, opium pipe in the other, lusting after relatives and shamelessly plagiarizing while muttering racial slurs and dying in the gutter. Poe may be a pathological figure, but the point that his writings make so well is that perversity is never far from reason. Enlightenment thinking, including its resistant relative transcendentalism, certainly can lead to liberating views and progressive political ends. Poe reminds the rational reader that this conclusion is by no means foregone, especially in the antebellum United States where plenty of racists thought hard about race and where the project of emancipation remained as yet unfinished.

Notes

I want to thank John Evelev, Tom Quirk, and Noah Heringman for their help with this essay.

1. Shawn Rosenheim and Stephen Rachman, introduction to *The American Face of Edgar Allan Poe*, ed. Shawn Rosenheim and Stephen Rachman (Baltimore: Johns Hopkins Univ. Press, 1995), xii. Subsequent scholarship includes Jonathan Elmer, *Reading at the Social Limit: Affect, Mass Culture, and Edgar Allan Poe* (Stanford, Calif.: Stanford Univ. Press, 1995); Terence Whalen, *Edgar Allan Poe and the Masses: The Political Economy of Literature in Antebellum America* (Princeton, N.J.: Princeton Univ. Press, 1999); and J. Gerald Kennedy, ed., *A Historical Guide to Edgar Allan Poe* (New York: Oxford Univ. Press, 2001).

2. For a sense of the diversity of Poe scholarship on race that nonetheless offers a kind of consensus regarding Poe's lack of intention, see J. Gerald Kennedy and Liliane Weissberg, eds., *Romancing the Shadow: Poe and Race* (New York: Oxford Univ. Press, 2001).

3. Edgar Allan Poe, *Eureka*, in *Edgar Allan Poe: Poetry and Tales* (New York: Library of America, 1984), 1280; further references to this collection are to this edition and will be cited parenthetically as *PT*.

4. See Terence Whalen, "Average Racism: Poe, Slavery, and the Wages of Literary Nationalism," in *Romancing the Shadow*, ed. Kennedy and Weissberg, 3-40. On

Poe's ambivalence about plantation culture, see David Leverenz, "Poe and Gentry Virginia," in *The American Face*, ed. Rosenheim and Rachman, 210-36. On Poe's relationship with the Young America movement, see Meredith McGill, "Poe, Literary Nationalism, and Authorial Identity," in *The American Face*, ed. Rosenheim and Rachman, 271-304. For Poe and slavery, see Whalen, *Edgar Allan Poe and the Masses*, 111-46. Here and elsewhere, I rely for biographical information on Kenneth Silverman, *Edgar A. Poe: Mournful and Never-Ending Remembrance* (New York: HarperCollins, 1991).

5. See John Carlos Rowe, *At Emerson's Tomb: The Politics of Classic American Literature* (New York: Columbia Univ. Press, 1997), 42-62; and Betsy Erkkila, "The Poetics of Whiteness: Poe and the Racial Imaginary," in *Romancing the Shadow*, ed. Kennedy and Weissberg, 41-74.

6. See Edward H. Davidson, *Poe: A Critical Study* (Cambridge: Belknap Press of Harvard Univ. Press, 1957), 138; and G. R. Thompson, *Poe's Fiction: Romantic Irony in the Gothic Tales* (Madison: Univ. of Wisconsin Press, 1973), 39-44.

7. Because "Metzengerstein" came soon after Turner's revolt, specific dates matter. Turner's uprising began 23 August 1831, with coverage in the popular press appearing quickly thereafter. Poe had been writing short fiction in Baltimore from as early as April 1831. On May 28, the *Saturday Courier* of Philadelphia announced the short-story contest for which Poe would submit "Metzengerstein," though details for the contest were not provided until July 9. We do not know when Poe submitted "Metzengerstein," but the deadline for the contest was December 1 and Poe had a history of procrastination. It is thus possible, and in my mind quite likely, that Poe did not finish his "Metzengerstein" manuscript until after he heard of Turner's revolt through various available sources (see Dwight Thomas and David Jackson, eds., *The Poe Log: A Documentary Life of Edgar Allan Poe, 1809-1849* [Boston: G. K. Hall, 1987]), 120-24).

8. "Metzengerstein," in *Edgar Allan Poe: Tales and Sketches, 1831-1842*, vol. 2 of *Collected Works of Edgar Allan Poe*, ed. Thomas Ollive Mabbott (Cambridge: Belknap Press of Harvard Univ. Press, 1978), 19; further references to "Metzengerstein" are to this edition and will be cited parenthetically as "M."

9. See Richard E. Ellis, *The Union at Risk: Jacksonian Democracy, States' Rights, and the Nullification Crisis* (New York: Oxford Univ. Press, 1987), 187-94.

10. For the geographical proximity of Douglass and Poe, see J. Gerald Kennedy, "'Trust No Man': Poe, Douglass, and the Culture of Slavery," in *Romancing the Shadow*, ed. Kennedy and Weissberg, 225-57.

11. See William Taylor, *Cavalier and Yankee: The Old South and American National Character* (New York: George Braziller, 1961), 51-55.

12. See Silverman, *Edgar A. Poe*, 26-68; and Leverenz, "Poe and Gentry Virginia," 210-36.

13. William Byrd II to John Perceval, 12 July 1736, *The Correspondence of the Three William Byrds of Westover, Virginia, 1684-1776*, ed. Marion Tinling, 2 vols. (Charlottesville: Univ. of Virginia Press, 1977), 2:488. I am grateful to Albert Devlin for pointing out Byrd's letter. See also Thomas Jefferson, *Notes on the State of Virginia* (1785; reprint, New York: Harper, 1964), 133.

14. "Incendiary Publications," *National Intelligencer*, 15 September 1831; reprinted in Eric Foner, ed., *Nat Turner* (Englewood Cliffs, N.J.: Prentice-Hall, 1971), 87-89.

15. Thomas Roderick Dew, "Abolition of Negro Slavery" (1832), in *The Ideology of Slavery: Proslavery Thought in the Antebellum South, 1830-1860*, ed. Drew Gilpin Faust (Baton Rouge: Louisiana State Univ. Press, 1981), 50, 47.

16. William Gilmore Simms, *Egeria: Or, Voices of Thought and Counsel for the Woods and Wayside* (Philadelphia: E. H. Butler, 1853), 15.

17. See Larry Tise, *Pro-Slavery: A History of the Defense of Slavery in America, 1701-1840* (Athens: Univ. of Georgia Press, 1987).

18. See, for instance, "How to Write a Blackwood Article" (*PT*, 291-92) and Poe's 1845 review of Longfellow in *Edgar Allan Poe: Essays and Reviews* (New York: Library of America, 1984), 762; further references to *Essays and Reviews* will be cited parenthetically as *ER*. It should also be noted that these insults accuse white female abolitionists of sexual desire for black male slaves. In "Metzengerstein," the horse is male, recalling Eric Lott's claim that antebellum racist anxiety is marked by the conflicted attraction and repulsion of white men for black male bodies (*Love and Theft: Blackface Minstrelsy and the American Working Class* [New York: Oxford Univ. Press, 1993], 53-55, 120-22, 161-68).

19. See *Constitutional Whig*, 29 August 1831; reprinted in Henry Irving Tragle, ed., *The Southampton Slave Revolt of 1831: A Compilation of Source Material* (Amherst: Univ. of Massachusetts Press, 1971), 53.

20. On the fear of slave revolts in antebellum literature, see Eric Sundquist, *To Wake the Nations: Race in the Making of American Literature* (Cambridge: Belknap Press of Harvard Univ. Press, 1993), 27-221. On this fear in Poe's "Silence—A Fable," see Joan Dayan, "Amorous Bondage: Poe, Ladies, and Slaves," in *The American Face*, ed. Rosenheim and Rachman, 194-96; in "The Fall of the House of Usher," see David Leverenz, "Spanking the Master: Mind-Body Crossings in Poe's Sensationalism," in *A Historical Guide to Edgar Allan Poe*, ed. Kennedy, 112-14; in "The Black Cat," see Lesley Ginsberg, "Slavery and the Gothic Horror of Poe's 'The Black Cat,'" in *American Gothic: New Interventions in a National Narrative*, ed. Robert K. Martin and Eric Savoy (Iowa City: Univ. of Iowa Press, 1998), 99-128; in *Pym*, see Toni Morrison, *Playing in the Dark: Whiteness and the Literary Imagination* (New York: Vintage, 1992), 31-59; Rowe, *At Emerson's Tomb*, 42-62; and Dana Nelson, *The Word in Black and White: Reading "Race" in American Literature, 1638-1867* (New York: Oxford Univ. Press, 1993), 90-108; in "The Murders in the Rue Morgue," see Elise Lemire, "'The Murders in the Rue Morgue': Amalgamation Discourses and the Race Riots of 1838 in Poe's Philadelphia," in *Romancing the Shadow*, ed. Kennedy and Weissberg, 177-204; in "The System of Doctor Tarr and Professor Fether," see Louis Rubin, *The Edge of the Swamp: A Study of the Literature and Society of the Old South* (Baton Rouge: Louisiana State Univ. Press, 1989), 162-67; and in "Hop-Frog," see Leland S. Person, "Poe's Philosophy of Amalgamation: Reading Racism in the Tales," in *Romancing the Shadow*, ed. Kennedy and Weissberg, 218-20.

21. In *Poe and the Masses*, Whalen argues that Poe's writings were governed by political economy before Poe entered the publishing industry. This may be so, although such claims seem stronger to me when applied to Poe's later career.

22. Joan Dayan, "Poe, Persons, and Property," in *Romancing the Shadow*, ed. Kennedy and Weissberg, 121.

23. Silverman, *Edgar A. Poe*, 265. See also Evan Carton, *The Rhetoric of American Romance: Dialectic and Identity in Emerson, Dickinson, Poe, and Hawthorne* (Baltimore: Johns Hopkins Univ. Press, 1985), 36-42, 101-5.

24. See Thompson, *Poe's Fiction*; Leon Chai, *The Romantic Foundations of the American Renaissance* (Ithaca, N.Y.: Cornell Univ. Press, 1987), 367-75; and Richard Gravil, *Romantic Dialogues: Anglo-American Continuities, 1776-1862* (New York: St. Martin's, 2000), 128-38.

25. See Thomas Hansen and Burton Pollin, *The German Face of Edgar Allan Poe: A Study of Literary References in His Works* (Columbia, S.C.: Camden House, 1995).

26. Poe's reference to Disraeli was probably not added until 1849 (*Tales and Sketches*, ed. Mabbott, 2:17). Poe mentions Disraeli and *Vivian Grey*, both positively and negatively, in multiple reviews of the 1830s.

27. Benjamin Disraeli, *Vivian Grey: A Romance of Youth*, 2 vols. (New York: M. Walter Dunne, 1904), 2:251.

28. See Plato, *Phaedrus*, trans. R. Hackforth (New York: Bobbs-Merrill, 1952), 69.

29. Leverenz, "Spanking the Master." See also Joan Dayan, *Fables of the Mind: An Inquiry into Poe's Fiction* (New York: Oxford Univ. Press, 1987), especially 199.

30. See Elmer, *Reading at the Social Limit*, 187-92; Dayan, "Amorous Bondage," 206-7; and Morrison, *Playing in the Dark*, 31-59. A possible purchase for African influence in "Metzengerstein" is the story's use of metempsychosis (see Helen Thomas, *Romanticism and Slave Narratives: Transatlantic Testimonies* [Cambridge, Eng.: Cambridge Univ. Press, 2000], 167-200).

31. Madame de Staël, *Germany* (1810; reprint, Boston: Houghton Mifflin, 1859), 196; Frederic Henry Hedge, "Coleridge's Literary Character" (1833), in *Transcendentalism: A Reader*, ed. Joel Myerson (New York: Oxford Univ. Press, 2000), 92; and Emil L. Fackenheim, *The God Within: Kant, Schelling, and Historicity*, ed. John Burbidge (Toronto: Univ. of Toronto Press, 1996), 51.

32. For Poe's references to Schelling and the availability of Schelling in English, see Hansen and Pollin, *The German Face of Edgar Allan Poe*, 80.

33. F. W. J. Schelling, *System of Transcendental Idealism*, trans. Peter Heath (1800; reprint, Charlottesville: Univ. of Virginia Press, 1978), 5.

34. Samuel Taylor Coleridge, *Biographia Literaria; or, Biographical Sketches of My Literary Life and Opinions*, in *The Collected Works of Samuel Taylor Coleridge, Vol. 7*, ed. James Engell and W. Jackson Bate, 16 vols. (Princeton, N.J.: Princeton Univ. Press, 1983), (I):252, (I):255.

35. My sense of unconscious production has been aided by Roger Hausheer, "Fichte and Schelling," in *German Philosophy since Kant*, ed. Anthony O'Hear (New York: Cambridge Univ. Press, 1999), 1-24; Andrew Bowie, *Schelling and Modern European Philosophy: An Introduction* (New York: Routledge, 1993), 45-54; and Paul Redding, *The Logic of Affect* (Ithaca, N.Y.: Cornell Univ. Press, 1999), 123-26.

36. Schelling, *System of Transcendental Idealism*, 231.

37. Coleridge, *Biographia Literaria*, (I):236, (II):16.

38. See Laura Doyle, "The Racial Sublime," in *Romanticism, Race, and Imperial*

Culture, 1780-1834, ed. Alan Richardson and Sonia Hofkosh (Bloomington: Indiana Univ. Press, 1996), 15-39. See also Erkkila, "Poetics of Whiteness," 65-67.

39. Schelling, *System of Transcendental Idealism*, 231.

40. On Poe and Hegel, see Carton, *The Rhetoric of American Romance*, 15-18. Carton doubts that Poe studied Hegel but argues that this "only enhances the significance" of their relationship (15), a position from which I dissent.

41. Calvin Stowe, "The Teutonic Metaphysics, or Modern Transcendentalism," *Biblical Repository and Classical Review*, January 1845, 65, 75, 79.

42. For Hegel in America, see Bruce Kuklick, *A History of Philosophy in America, 1720-2000* (New York: Oxford Univ. Press, 2001), 75-94; and William H. Goetzmann, introduction to *The American Hegelians: An Intellectual Episode in the History of Western America*, ed. William H. Goetzmann (New York: Knopf, 1973), 3-11. Poe's only explicit references to Hegel are neither early nor particularly telling: an 1842 review of Rufus Dawes (*ER*, 495) and "Marginalia," June 1849 (*ER*, 1459).

43. Dayan discusses race and "Ligeia" in "Amorous Bondage," 200-207.

44. For a compatible reading of "How to Write a Blackwood Article," see Leverenz, "Spanking the Master," 116-17.

45. See Teresa Goddu, *Gothic America: Narrative, History, and Nation* (New York: Columbia Univ. Press, 1997), 7-8.

46. For more on Kant's racist taxonomy, see Charles W. Mills, *The Racial Contract* (Ithaca, N.Y.: Cornell Univ. Press, 1997), 69-72; on Coleridge and racism, see Thomas, *Romanticism and Slavery Narratives*, 89-104; and on Emerson and racism, see Anita Haya Patterson, *From Emerson to King: Democracy, Race, and the Politics of Protest* (New York: Oxford Univ. Press, 1997), 129-38. Recent transatlantic studies of romanticism and race include Thomas, *Romanticism and Slavery Narratives*; and Debbie Lee, *Slavery and the Romantic Imagination* (Philadelphia: Univ. of Pennsylvania Press, 2002).

47. On Coleridge and *Eureka*, see Chai, *Romantic Foundations of the American Renaissance*, 132; and Gravil, *Romantic Dialogues*, 129-32. Carton associates *Eureka* with transcendentalism but as an ironic subversion of Emerson (*Rhetoric of American Romance*, 36).

48. This line does not appear in the Library of America version of "Loss of Breath" (see *Tales and Sketches*, ed. Mabbott, 2:79).

49. See Jared Gardner, *Master Plots: Race and the Founding of an American Literature, 1787-1845* (Baltimore: Johns Hopkins Univ. Press, 1998), 125-59; and Dana D. Nelson, *National Manhood: Capitalist Citizenship and the Imagined Fraternity of White Men* (Durham, N.C.: Duke Univ. Press, 1998), 206-16.

50. See Louis Menand, *The Metaphysical Club* (New York: Farrar, Straus and Giroux, 2001), 144.

51. See Dew, "Abolition of Negro Slavery," 28; Robert Montgomery Bird, *Sheppard Lee* (New York: Harper, 1836), 187; William Harper, "Memoir on Slavery" (1837), in *Ideology of Slavery*, ed. Faust, 83; James Henry Hammond, "Letter to an English Abolitionist" (1845), in *Ideology of Slavery*, ed. Faust, 176; John Calhoun, *"A Disquisition on Government" and Selections from the "Discourse,"* ed. C. Gordon Post (1853; reprint, New York: Liberal Arts Press, 1953), 44; and George Fitzhugh, *So-*

ciology for the South, or The Failure of Free Society (1854; reprint, New York: Burt Franklin, 1965), 177-79. Abolitionists and proslavery thinkers often misattributed the claim that "all men are born free and equal" to the Declaration of Independence ("all men are created equal"). "All men are born free and equal" is from the Massachusetts state constitution. It is worth noting that in an 1836 review in *The Southern Literary Messenger*, Poe referred to the "iniquities" of Jefferson's progressive tendencies (*ER*, 565).

52. "Bad News for the Transcendental Poets," *Literary World* 20 (February 1847): 53. Based on content, style, and Poe's friendly relationship at the time with the *Literary World*'s editor, Evert Duyckinck, Poe seems a plausible author of this piece.

53. D. H. Lawrence, *Studies in Classic American Literature* (New York: Viking, 1923), 65, 71.

54. Harry Levin, *The Power of Blackness: Hawthorne, Poe, Melville* (New York: Knopf, 1958), 121. See also Leslie Fiedler, *Love and Death in the American Novel* (1960; reprint, New York: Anchor, 1992), 391-400.

55. See John Carlos Rowe, "Edgar Allan Poe's Imperial Fantasy and the American Frontier," in *Romancing the Shadow*, ed. Kennedy and Weissberg, 75-105; Nelson, *The Word in Black and White*, 90-108; Leverenz, "Spanking the Master"; and Kennedy, "'Trust No Man,'" 253. Meredith McGill points out inconsistencies in Whalen's treatment of Poe's "authorial agency" in "Reading Poe, Reading Capitalism," *American Quarterly* 53 (March 2001): 145.

56. Henry James, *French Poets and Novelists* (1878; reprint, New York: Macmillan, 1893), 60.

57. "Hegel's Aesthetics: The Philosophy of Art, Particularly in Its Application to Poetry," *American Eclectic: or, Selections from the Periodical Literature of All Foreign Countries* 4 (July 1842): 71.

58. See also Poe's 1836 review of Daniel Defoe (*ER*, 202); and his 5 April 1845 installment in the Longfellow War (*ER*, 759).

59. Nelson, *National Manhood*, 206.

60. Alexis de Tocqueville, *Democracy in America*, ed. J. P. Mayer and Max Lerner (1835; reprint, New York: Harper & Row, 1966), 329.

61. For the connotations of *conscience*, see Jean Hagstrum, *Eros and Vision: The Restoration to Romanticism* (Evanston, Ill.: Northwestern Univ. Press, 1989), 3-28.

62. Elmer, *Reading at the Social Limit*, 125.

63. Slavoj Žižek and F. W. J. von Schelling, *The Abyss of Freedom: Ages of the World: An Essay by Slavoj Žižek with the Text of Schelling's Die Weltater (second draft, 1813)*, trans. Judith Norman (Ann Arbor: Univ. of Michigan Press, 1997), 27.

64. See, for instance, John Demos, "Oedipus in America: Historical Perspectives on the Reception of Psychoanalysis in the United States," in *Inventing the Psychological: Toward a Cultural History of Emotional Life in America*, ed. Joel Pfister and Nancy Schnog (New Haven: Yale Univ. Press, 1997), 63-64. One exception to this interpretation is James Hoopes, *Consciousness in New England: From Puritanism and Ideas to Psychoanalysis and Semiotic* (Baltimore: Johns Hopkins Univ. Press, 1989).

65. Redding, *The Logic of Affect*, 4.

66. All references to first usages are based on the *OED*. See Thomas Carlyle,

"Characteristics," in *John Stuart Mill and Thomas Carlyle*, ed. Charles W. Eliot (New York: P. F. Collier, 1909), 347. For helpful accounts of *subjectivity* and *unconscious*, see Raymond Williams, *Keywords: A Vocabulary of Culture and Society* (New York: Oxford Univ. Press, 1976), 259-64, 270-73.

67. Stanley Cavell, *In Quest of the Ordinary: Lines of Skepticism and Romanticism* (Chicago: Univ. of Chicago Press, 1988), 138.

68. See, for instance, Frederick Henry Hedge's selection and translation of a telling passage from Schelling: "It was long ago perceived that, in Art, not everything is performed with consciousness; that, with the conscious activity, an unconscious action must combine; and that it is of the perfect unity and mutual interpenetration of the two that the highest in Art is born" (*Prose Writers of Germany* [1840; reprint, Philadelphia: Porter and Coates, 1847], 512). The passage is from Schelling's "On the Relation of the Plastic Arts to Nature" (1807).

RESOURCES

1809	Edgar Poe is born in Boston on January 19 to David Poe, Jr., and Elizabeth Arnold Poe (née Hopkins).
1810	Poe's sister, Rosalie, is born on December 20.
1811	On December 8, Elizabeth Arnold Poe dies in Richmond, Virginia. David Poe dies a few days later. Orphaned, Edgar is taken into the home of John and Frances Allan of Richmond. Rosalie is taken in by Mr. and Mrs. William Mackenzie. Poe's brother, Henry (born 1807), remains with his grandparents in Baltimore.
1812	Poe is christened as "Edgar Allan Poe."
1815	The Allan family, with Poe, travel to England.
1815-1820	Poe attends the schools of Misses Dubourg and later Manor House School.
1820	Poe and family return to Richmond, Virginia.
1821-1823	Poe continues his education at the school of Joseph H. Clarke and then the school of William Burke.
1824	Poe serves as a lieutenant of the Richmond Junior Volunteers.
1825	John Allan inherits some money and moves the family into a mansion called Moldavia. Poe is engaged to childhood sweetheart Elmira Royster.
1826	Poe enters the University of Virginia in Charlottesville. Elmira, at her parents' insistence, breaks off her engagement with Poe and is engaged to Alexander B. Shelton.
1827	After arguing with John Allan over gambling debts, Poe leaves and heads to his family in Baltimore. Poe eventually enlists in the United States Army under the name Edgar A. Perry. His battery is sent to Fort Moultrie in Charleston, South Carolina. Poe publishes *Tamerlane and Other Poems*.

1829	Poe is promoted to sergeant-major. Frances Allan dies. Poe is granted leave from the army and returns to Richmond. His second book, *Al Aaraaf, Tamerlane, and Minor Poems*, is published.
1830	John Allan marries Louisa Patterson. Poe enters West Point.
1831	Poe is court-martialed and dismissed from service. He publishes *Poems*. Henry Poe, Edgar's older brother, dies in Baltimore.
1833	Poe moves in with his aunt Maria Clemm in Baltimore. Poe receives a prize for "Ms. Found in a Bottle."
1834	John Allan dies in Richmond. Left out of Allan's will, Poe inherits nothing.
1835	Poe moves to Richmond and becomes editor of Thomas W. White's *The Southern Literary Messenger*. Poe publishes critical reviews, poems, and stories.
1836	Poe marries cousin Virginia Clemm (age thirteen) in Richmond.
1837	Poe leaves his position as editor of *The Southern Literary Messenger* and moves to New York.
1838	Poe moves to Philadelphia. He publishes *The Narrative of Arthur Gordon Pym* with Harper & Brothers.
1839	*The Conchologist's First Book* is published. Poe becomes editor of *Burton's Gentleman's Magazine*.
1840	*Tales of the Grotesque and Arabesque* is published. "The Journal of Julius Rodman" is published in *Burton's Gentleman's Magazine* and is mistaken as an actual account of an expedition.
1841	"The Murders in the Rue Morgue" is featured in *Graham's Magazine*.
1842	Poe meets Charles Dickens as the latter tours America. Poe leaves his position at *Graham's Magazine*; he is replaced by Rufus W. Griswold.
1843	Poe publishes "The Gold-Bug" and *Prose Romances*. Poe begins his lectures on American Poetry.

1844	Poe moves to New York, where he begins working as member of the staff of the *Evening Mirror*.
1845	"The Raven" is published in the New York *Evening Mirror*. Poe becomes an editor of *The Broadway Journal*, eventually becoming owner as well. *Tales* and *The Raven, and Other Poems* are published.
1846	*The Broadway Journal* ceases publication. Poe publishes "The Literati of New York City: Some Honest Opinions at Random Respecting Their Authorial Merits, with Occasional Words of Personality" in *Godey's Lady's Book*. Poe moves to Fordham.
1847	Virginia Poe dies of tuberculosis.
1848	Poe's prose poem *Eureka* is published. Poe is engaged to Sarah Helen Whitman. Whitman later calls off the engagement.
1849	Poe begins a southern lecture tour and meets up with the now widowed Elmira Royster Shelton; the two eventually become engaged. On October 7, Edgar Allan Poe dies in Baltimore. He is buried in his grandfather's lot in the Westminster Burying Ground.

Works by Edgar Allan Poe

Drama
Politian, pb. 1835-1836

Long Fiction
The Narrative of Arthur Gordon Pym, 1838

Nonfiction
The Letters of Edgar Allan Poe, 1948
Literary Criticism of Edgar Allan Poe, 1965
Essays and Reviews, 1984

Poetry
Tamerlane, and Other Poems, 1827
Al Aaraaf, Tamerlane, and Minor Poems, 1829
Poems, 1831
The Raven, and Other Poems, 1845
Eureka: A Prose Poem, 1848
Poe: Complete Poems, 1959
Poems, 1969

Short Fiction
Tales of the Grotesque and Arabesque, 1840
The Prose Romances of Edgar Allan Poe, 1843
Tales, 1845
The Short Fiction of Edgar Allan Poe, 1976

Miscellaneous
The Complete Works of Edgar Allan Poe, 1902 (17 volumes)

Bibliography

Ackroyd, Peter. *Poe: A Life Cut Short*. New York: Doubleday, 2008.

Alexander, Jean. *Affidavits of Genius: Edgar Allan Poe and the French Critics, 1847-1924*. Port Washington, NY: Kennikat Press, 1971.

Allen, Michael. *Poe and the Magazine Tradition*. New York: Oxford University Press, 1969.

Baudelaire, Charles. *Baudelaire on Poe*. Translated and edited by Lois and Francis E. Hyslop, Jr. State College, PA: Bald Eagle Press, 1952.

Bloom, Harold. "The Inescapable Poe." *New York Review of Books* 31, no. 15 (October 11, 1984).

_____, ed. *The Tales of Poe*. New York: Chelsea House Publishers, 1985.

Bonaparte, Marie. *The Life and Works of Edgar Allan Poe: A Psycho-analytic Interpretation*. Translated by John Rodker. London: Imago, 1949.

Buranelli, Vincent. *Edgar Allan Poe*. New York: Twayne, 1961.

Burluck, Michael L. *Grim Phantasms: Fear in Poe's Short Fiction*. New York: Garland, 1993.

Campbell, Killis. *The Mind of Poe and Other Studies*. Cambridge: Harvard University Press, 1933.

Carlson, Eric. W., ed. *A Companion to Poe Studies*. Westport, CT: Greenwood Press, 1996.

_____. *Critical Essays on Edgar Allan Poe*. Boston: G. K. Hall, 1987.

_____. *The Recognition of Edgar Allan Poe: Selected Criticism Since 1829*. Ann Arbor: University of Michigan Press, 1966.

Davidson, Edward. *Poe: A Critical Study*. Cambridge: Harvard University Press, 1957.

Fisher, Benjamin Franklin, IV, ed. *Poe and His Times: The Artist and His Milieu*. Baltimore: Edgar Allan Poe Society, 1990.

_____, ed. *The Cambridge Introduction to Edgar Allan Poe*. New York: Cambridge University Press, 2008.

Fletcher, Richard M. *The Stylistic Development of Edgar Allan Poe*. The Hague: Mouton, 1973.

Hayes, Kevin J., ed. *The Cambridge Companion to Edgar Allan Poe*. Cambridge: Cambridge University Press, 2002.

Hoffman, Daniel. *Poe Poe Poe Poe Poe Poe Poe*. Baton Rouge: Louisiana State University Press, 1998.

Hutchisson, James M. *Poe*. Jackson: University Press of Mississippi, 2005.

Irwin, John T. *American Hieroglyphics: The Symbol of the Egyptian Hieroglyphics in the American Renaissance*. New Haven, CT: Yale University Press, 1980.

_____. *The Mystery to a Solution: Poe, Borges, and the Analytical Detective Story*. Baltimore: The Johns Hopkins University Press, 1994.

Jacobs, Robert D. *Poe: Journalist and Critic*. Baton Rouge: Louisiana State University Press, 1969.

Kennedy, J. Gerald. *Poe, Death, and the Life of Writing*. New Haven, CT: Yale University Press, 1987.

_____. *A Historical Guide to Edgar Allan Poe*. New York: Oxford University Press, 2001.

Ketterer, David. *The Rationale of Deception in Poe*. Baton Rouge: Louisiana State University Press, 1979.

Krutch, Joseph W. *Edgar Allan Poe: A Study in Genius*. New York: Russell and Russell, 1926.

Kumar, Satish. *Edgar Allan Poe: Style and Structure of His Short Stories*. New Delhi: Bahri Publications, 1989.

Lawrence, D. H. "Edgar Allan Poe." First published in 1923. *Studies in Classic American Literature*. New York: Penguin, 1977, 83-88.

Levin, Harry. *The Power of Blackness: Hawthorne, Poe, Melville*. New York: Knopf, 1958.

Ljungquist, Kent. *The Grand and the Fair: Poe's Landscape Aesthetics and Pictorial Techniques*. Potomac, MD.: Scripta Humanistica, 1984.

Mabbott, Thomas Ollive, ed. *Collected Works of Edgar Allan Poe, I: Poems*. Cambridge, MA: Harvard University Press, 1969.

Martin, Terry J. *Rhetorical Deception in the Short Fiction of Hawthorne, Poe and Melville*. Lewiston, NY: Edwin Mellen Press, 1998.

May, Charles. *Edgar Allan Poe: A Study of the Short Fiction*. Boston: Twayne, 1991.

Meyers, Jeffrey. *Edgar Allan Poe: Life and Legacy*. New York: Macmillan, 1992.

Mills, Bruce. *Poe, Fuller, and the Mesmeric Arts: Transition States in the American Renaissance*. Columbia: University of Missouri Press, 2006.

Peeples, Scott. *Edgar Allan Poe Revisited*. New York: Twayne, 1998.

Phillips, Elizabeth. *Edgar Allan Poe, an American Imagination: Three Essays*. Millwood, NY: Associated Faculty Press, 1986.

Quinn, Patrick F. *The French Face of Edgar Poe*. Carbondale: Southern Illinois University Press, 1957.

Regan, Robert, ed. *Poe: A Collection of Critical Essays*. Englewood Cliffs, NJ: Prentice-Hall, 1967.

Rosenheim, Shawn, and Stephen Rachman, eds. *The American Face of Edgar Allan Poe*. Baltimore: The Johns Hopkins University Press, 1995.

Silverman, Kenneth. *Edgar A. Poe: Mournful and Never-Ending Remembrance*. New York: HarperCollins, 1991.

Sova, Dawn B. *Edgar Allan Poe, A to Z: The Essential Reference to His Life and Work*. New York: Facts On File, 2001.

Sucur, Slobadan. *Poe, Odoyevsky, and Purloined Letters: Questions of Theory and Period Style Analysis*. New York: Peter Lang, 2001.

Thompson, G. R. *Poe's Fiction: Romantic Irony in the Gothic Tales*. Madison: University of Wisconsin Press, 1973.

Whalen, Terence. *Edgar Allan Poe and the Masses: The Political Economy of Literature in Antebellum America*. Princeton, NJ: Princeton University Press, 1999.

Zimmerman, Brett. *Edgar Allan Poe: Rhetoric and Style*. Montreal and Kingston: McGill-Queen's University Press, 2005.

_____. "Sensibility, Phrenology and 'The Fall of the House of Usher.'" *The Edgar Allan Poe Review* 8, no. 1 (2007): 47-56.

CRITICAL INSIGHTS

About the Editor

Steven Frye is Professor of English at California State University, Bakersfield. He served as the guest editor (with Eric Carl Link) of a double issue of *Poe Studies/Dark Romanticism: History, Theory, Interpretation* in honor of the journal's founder, G. R. Thompson. He is the author of *Historiography and Narrative Design in the American Romance: A Study of Four Authors* (Edwin Mellen, 2001) and *Understanding Cormac McCarthy* (University of South Carolina Press, 2009). In addition, he is the author of numerous essays on the American fiction and short fiction of the nineteenth and twentieth centuries, in journals such as *American Literary Realism*, *Studies in American Naturalism*, *American Studies*, *The Southern Quarterly*, *The Centennial Review*, *Leviathan*, *The Midwest Quarterly*, and *The Kentucky Review*. His work in the American romance tradition deals primarily with the relationship of history, religion, aesthetics, and narrative technique.

About *The Paris Review*

The Paris Review is America's preeminent literary quarterly, dedicated to discovering and publishing the best new voices in fiction, nonfiction, and poetry. The magazine was founded in Paris in 1953 by the young American writers Peter Matthiessen and Doc Humes, and edited there and in New York for its first fifty years by George Plimpton. Over the decades, the *Review* has introduced readers to the earliest writings of Jack Kerouac, Philip Roth, T. C. Boyle, V. S. Naipaul, Ha Jin, Jay McInerney, and Mona Simpson, and published numerous now classic works, including Roth's *Goodbye, Columbus*, Donald Barthelme's *Alice*, Jim Carroll's *Basketball Diaries*, and selections from Samuel Beckett's *Molloy* (his first publication in English). The first chapter of Jeffrey Eugenides's *The Virgin Suicides* appeared in the *Review*'s pages, as well as stories by Edward P. Jones, Rick Moody, David Foster Wallace, Denis Johnson, Jim Shepard, Jim Crace, Lorrie Moore, Jeanette Winterson, and Ann Patchett.

The Paris Review's renowned Writers at Work series of interviews, whose early installments include legendary conversations with E. M. Forster, William Faulkner, and Ernest Hemingway, is one of the landmarks of world literature. The interviews received a George Polk award and were nominated for a Pulitzer Prize. Among the more than three hundred interviewees are Robert Frost, Marianne Moore, W. H. Auden, Elizabeth Bishop, Susan Sontag, and Toni Morrison. Recent issues feature conversations with Salman Rushdie, Joan Didion, Stephen King, Norman Mailer, Kazuo Ishiguro and Umberto Eco. (A complete list of the interviews is available at www.theparisreview.org.) In November 2008, Picador will publish the third of a four-volume series of anthologies of *Paris Review* interviews. The first two volumes have received acclaim. *The New York Times* called the Writers at Work series "the most remarkable and extensive interviewing project we possess."

The Paris Review is edited by Philip Gourevitch, who was named to the post in 2005, following the death of George Plimpton two years earlier. Under Gourevitch's leadership, the magazine's international distribution has expanded, paid subscriptions have risen 150 percent, and newsstand distribution has doubled. A new editorial team has published fiction by Andre Aciman, Damon Galgut, Mohsin Hamid, Gish Jen, Richard Price, Said Sayrafiezadeh, and Alistair Morgan. Poetry editors Charles Simic, Meghan O'Rourke, and Dan Chiasson have selected works by Billy Collins, Jesse Ball, Mary Jo Bang, Sharon Olds, and Mary Karr. Writing published in the magazine has been anthologized in *Best American Short Stories* (2006, 2007, and 2008), *Best American Poetry*, *Best Creative Non-Fiction*, the Pushcart Prize anthology, and *O. Henry Prize Stories*.

The magazine presents two annual awards. The Hadada Award for lifelong contribution to literature has recently been given to William Styron, Joan Didion, Norman Mailer, and Peter Matthiessen in 2008. The Plimpton Prize for Fiction, given to a new voice in fiction brought to national attention in the pages of *The Paris Review*, was presented in 2007 to Benjamin Percy and to Jesse Ball in 2008.

The Paris Review won the 2007 National Magazine Award in photojournalism, and the *Los Angeles Times* recently called *The Paris Review* "an American treasure with true international reach."

Since 1999 *The Paris Review* has been published by The Paris Review Foundation, Inc., a not-for-profit 501(c)(3) organization.

The Paris Review is available in digital form to libraries worldwide in selected academic databases exclusively from EBSCO Publishing. Libraries can contact EBSCO at 1-800-653-2726 for details. For more information on *The Paris Review* or to subscribe, please visit: www.theparisreview.org.

Contributors

Steven Frye is Professor of English at California State University, Bakersfield. His books include *Historiography and Narrative Design in the American Romance: A Study of Four Authors* (2001) and *Understanding Cormac McCarthy* (2009), and he has published essays in *American Literary Realism*, *Studies in American Naturalism*, *American Studies*, *The Southern Quarterly*, *The Centennial Review*, *Leviathan*, *The Midwest Quarterly*, and *The Kentucky Review*.

Charles E. May is Professor Emeritus of Literature at California State University, Long Beach. He is the author and editor of seven books and more than five hundred articles and reviews in books, reference works, journals, and newspapers.

Nathaniel Rich, a senior editor at *The Paris Review*, has written for *The New York Review of Books*, *Vanity Fair*, *The New York Times*, and *Slate*. He is the author of two books: *San Francisco Noir: The City in Film Noir from 1940 to the Present* and a novel, *The Mayor's Tongue*. He can be found on the Internet at www.nathanielrich .com.

Jeff Grieneisen is Assistant Professor of English at Manatee Community College in Bradenton, Florida. He has published work as a contributing editor in *Edgar Allan Poe* in Harold Bloom's BioCritiques series, and his poetry has appeared in *Pennsylvania English*, *Sylvan Review*, and *Red Raven Review*. In addition to writing poetry, he is a founding editor of the literary journal *Florida English*. He continues to research the work of Ezra Pound and delivered a paper at the twenty-second Ezra Pound International Conference in Venice, Italy. His first book of poetry, *Good Sumacs*, appeared in 2009.

Courtney Ruffner is Assistant Professor of English at Manatee Community College in Bradenton, Florida. She has published work as a contributing editor in *Edgar Allan Poe* in Harold Bloom's BioCritiques series. She has contributed to the volume *Teaching Italian American Literature, Film, and Popular Culture* and has published an article on John Donne that has been translated into Portuguese and published in the Brazilian journal *Revisto Espaço Académico*. She is a founding editor of the literary journal *Florida English* and is finishing her dissertation regarding postcoloniality and the negative depictions of Italian Americans in film and television.

Susan Amper is Assistant Professor at Bronx Community College/CUNY. Her essays have appeared in *Poe Studies: Dark Romanticism* (for which she has served as a guest editor), the *Journal of the Association for the Interdisciplinary Study of the Arts*, and *Studies in Short Fiction*. Her book *How to Write About Edgar Allan Poe* was published in 2007.

Matthew J. Bolton is an English teacher and the academic dean of Loyola School in New York City. Bolton earned his Ph.D. in English literature in 2005 from the Graduate Center of the City University of New York, where he wrote his dissertation on Robert Browning and T. S. Eliot. He received the T. S. Eliot Society's Fathman Young Scholar Award for work related to his dissertation. In addition to his doctorate, Bolton holds master's degrees in teaching and in educational administration from Fordham University. His research and writing center on connections between Victorian and Modernist literature.

Santiago Rodríguez Guerrero-Strachan teaches in the Department of English at the University of Valladolid in Spain and served as a Fulbright Fellow at the University of Colorado. He has contributed chapters to *Evolving Origins, Transplanting Cultures: Literary Legacies of the New Americans* (2002), *World Wide Eliot* (2007), *Romantic Prose Fiction* (2008), *Native Shakespeares: Indigenous Appropriations on a Global Stage* (2008), and *The Reception of Percy Bysshe Shelley in Europe* (2009).

John Cleman is a Professor of English at the California State University in Los Angeles. He has published essays in American literary realism, early American literature, and American literature. His book *George Washington Cable Revisited* was published in 1996.

J. Gerald Kennedy is William A. Read Professor of English at Louisiana State University. He is the author of *The Narrative of Arthur Gordon Pym and the Abyss of Interpretation* (1995), *Imagining Paris: Exile, Writing, and American Identity* (1993), and *Poe, Death, and the Life of Writing* (1987). He served as editor for *The Portable Edgar Allan Poe* (2006) and *Oxford Historical Guide to Edgar Allan Poe*. He has received a NEH Senior Fellowship and a Guggenheim Fellowship.

J. O. Bailey was a professor of literature at the University of North Carolina at Chapel Hill. He wrote and published on a wide variety of topics. His books include *Poe's "Stonehenge"* (1941), *Sources for Poe's Arthur Gordon Pym, "Hans Pfaal," and Other Pieces* (1942), *Hardy's "Imbedded Fossil"* (1945), *Pilgrims Through Space and Time: Trends and Patterns in Scientific and Utopian Fiction* (1947), *Proper Words in Proper Places* (1952), *The Poetry of Thomas Hardy: A Handbook and Commentary* (1970), and *Thomas Hardy and His Cosmic Mind: A New Reading of the Dynasts* (1977).

Robert Shulman is Professor of English at the University of Washington. His books include *Social Criticism and Nineteenth-Century American Fictions* (1987) and *The Power of Political Art: The 1930s Literary Left Reconsidered* (2000). He has also edited editions of Charlotte Perkins Gilman's *The Yellow Wall-Paper, and Other Stories* (1995) and Owen Wistar's *The Virginian: A Horseman of the Plains* (1998).

Elena V. Baraban is Assistant Professor of Russian at the University of Manitoba. She has contributed articles to the *Encyclopedia of Contemporary Russian Culture* (edited by Tatiana Smorodinskaya, Karen Evans-Romaine, and Helena Goscilo, 2006). She has also published essays in *The International Fiction Review* and *The Rocky Mountain Review of Language and Literature*.

J. Woodrow Hassell, Jr., taught at the University of Georgia and at the University of South Carolina. In addition to his numerous essays, his books include *The Mirrour*

---

of Mirth and Pleasant Conceits (translated in the sixteenth century by "T. D.," 1959), *Medieval Studies in Honor of Robert White Linker* (edited with Brian Dutton and John E. Keller, 1973), *Amorous Games: A Critical Edition of "Les Adevineaux amoureux"* (1974), and *Middle French Proverbs, Sentences, and Proverbial Phrases* (1982).

Ronald Bieganowski is Associate Professor at Marquette University. His essays have appeared in *Literature and Belief, College Literature, American Literature*, and *The South Carolina Review*, among others.

Cynthia S. Jordan has published essays in *American Literature, American Quarterly*, and *Early American Literature*. Her book *Second Stories: The Politics of Language, Form, and Gender in Early American Fictions* was published in 1989.

Maurice S. Lee is Assistant Professor at Boston University. His book *Slavery, Philosophy, and American Literature: 1830-1860* was published in 2005, and his essays have appeared in *American Literature, Raritan, ESQ, African American Review*, and *PMLA*.

Acknowledgments

"The *Paris Review* Perspective," by Nathaniel Rich. Copyright © 2008 by Nathaniel Rich. Special appreciation goes to Christopher Cox and Nathaniel Rich, editors for *The Paris Review.*

"Irresistible Impulses: Edgar Allan Poe and the Insanity Defense," by John Cleman. From *American Literature* 63, no. 4 (December 1991), pp. 623-640. Copyright © 1991, Duke University Press. All rights reserved. Used by permission of the publisher.

"The Limits of Reason: Poe's Deluded Detectives," by J. Gerald Kennedy. From *American Literature* 47, no. 2 (May 1975), pp. 184-196. Copyright © 1975, Duke University Press. All rights reserved. Used by permission of the publisher.

"What Happens in 'The Fall of the House of Usher'?" by J. O. Bailey. From *American Literature* 35, no. 4 (January 1964), pp. 445-466. Copyright © 1964, Duke University Press. All rights reserved. Used by permission of the publisher.

"Poe and the Powers of the Mind," by Robert Shulman. From *English Literary History* 37, no. 2 (June 1970), 245-262. Copyright © 1970, The Johns Hopkins University Press. Reprinted with permission of The Johns Hopkins University Press.

"The Motive for Murder in 'The Cask of Amontillado' by Edgar Allan Poe," by Elena V. Baraban. From *Rocky Mountain Review of Language and Literature* 58, no. 2 (Fall 2004), pp. 47-62. Copyright © 2004, *Rocky Mountain Review of Language and Literature*. Reprinted with permission of *Rocky Mountain Review of Language and Literature*.

"The Problem of Realism in 'The Gold Bug,'" by J. Woodrow Hassell, Jr. From *American Literature* 25, no. 2 (May 1953), pp. 179-192. Copyright © 1953, Duke University Press. All rights reserved. Used by permission of the publisher.

"The Self-Consuming Narrator in Poe's 'Ligeia' and 'Usher,'" by Ronald Bieganowski. From *American Literature* 60, no. 2 (May 1988), pp. 175-187. Copyright © 1988, Duke University Press. All rights reserved. Used by permission of the publisher.

"Poe's Re-Vision: The Recovery of the Second Story," by Cynthia S. Jordan. From *American Literature* 59, no. 1 (March 1987), pp. 1-19. Copyright © 1987, Duke University Press. All rights reserved. Used by permission of the publisher.

"Absolute Poe: His System of Transcendental Racism," by Maurice S. Lee. From *American Literature* 75, no. 4 (December 2003), pp. 751-781. Copyright © 2003, Duke University Press. All rights reserved. Used by permission of the publisher.

Index

"Ethan Brand" (Hawthorne); Esther in, 214; psychological experiment in, 214

Eureka (Poe), 148, 153, 160; apocalyptic vision of, 100; origin of all things, 11; personal identity in, 145; transcendental speculation, 254

"Facts in the Case of M. Valdemar, The" (Poe), 48

Fagin, N. Bryllion, 182

"Fall of the House of Usher, The" (Poe), 10, 13, 15, 38, 45, 47, 106; concealment of terror, 119, 122; corpse of Madeline in, 121, 128, 130, 132-133, 135, 220; covert crimes against women in, 213; crime solution in, 216; dark tendencies of the mind in, 156; death-dealing misogyny in, 228; delusion in, 5; destruction of the House, 119; eye-like windows, 124, 128, 217; ideal reader in, 201; imagination in, 206-208; language of, 201, 208; Madeline Usher in, 32, 76, 119-121, 123, 125, 127, 130-134, 137, 139-143, 205, 207; madness in, 32, 119-121; psychic and supernatural influences on, 119, 122-123; publication, 120, 143; Roderick Usher in, 5, 32, 71, 76, 78, 115, 119-135, 139-143, 205-207; self-consuming narrator in, 198, 207; slave rebellion in, 239; South in, 236; storm imagery in, 121, 132-134, 138, 141-142; superstitions in, 205; twins, 131-132, 141-142, 219, 222; ungovernable horror in, 250; vampire lore in, 42, 123, 125, 129, 135-136

Fantastic (Poe's notion of), 69-72, 74, 77-79. *See also* Psychological fantastic

Fantasy themes, 104, 109, 111

Feidelson, Charles, 152

Feminist criticism; on Hawthorne, 214; on Poe, 212; re-vision, 230; sensibility, 216, 229

Fetterley, Judith, 214, 229

Fichte, Johann Gottlieb, 242, 245, 258

"Fifty Suggestions" (Poe), 251

Fish, Stanley, 198

Fisher, Benjamin Franklin, 44

Fletcher, Richard M., 69, 167

Fleurs du Mal, Les (Baudelaire), 54

Flowers of Evil. See *Fleurs du mal, Les*

Formalism, 3, 43, 50, 56, 163

Fortunato ("The Cask of Amontillado"), 28, 44; disrespect of Montresor, 64, 65, 168; freemason, 168; inadequacy, 170, 173; murder of, 64, 66, 164-165, 167, 176; physical condition, 173; prank, 174; social role, 168, 173; screams, 167

"Four Beasts in One" (Poe); and slavery, 239

Foye, Raymond, 22, 32

French; aesthetic movement, 3

French Revolution, 171

French Symbolist poets. *See* Symbolist poets

Freud, Sigmund, 29, 32, 40, 60, 78, 144, 152

Gaines, Helen F., 186, 189, 197

Gargano, James W., 44, 75, 108

Garrison, William Lloyd, 236

"Giaour, The" (Lord Byron), 122, 131, 140

"Gold Bug, The" (Poe), 11, 50, 236; Charlestonian in, 184, 191; concealed conflict in, 183; cryptography in, 182, 186, 189, 195; insect in, 185, 193; invisible ink in, 185, 195; Jupiter in,

184, 191-192; Kidd in, 183-184; mistakes in, 186, 189, 193, 195; narrative, 183, 186, 194; parchment theme in, 182, 184-185; problem of realism in, 185-186, 189, 192, 194-195; ratiocination in, 104; skull in, 183, 185, 190, 192, 195; structure of, 194, 196; Sullivan's Island in, 192, 194; William Legrand in, 104, 188, 194; Wolf in, 184

Good vs. evil, 4

Gothic tales, 69; British, 77; German, 3, 31, 37, 70; narrative, 70; realism, 22; romance, 4, 6-7; sensationalism, 37; tradition, 4, 16, 21, 23, 27, 30, 33

Goulet, Andrea, 25

Graham, J. Lorimer, 187-188

Graham's Magazine, 10, 17, 182

Grantz, David, 31

Griffith, Clark, 45, 70

Griswold, Rufus, 37-38

Grotesque. *See* Horror and grotesque themes

Halliburton, David, 164

Hammond, J. R., 69, 166, 168

Hammond, James Henry, 253

Hartley, David, 74

Haslam, John, 73

"Haunted Palace, The" (Poe), 33, 119, 146, 205; symbolism of, 123

"Haunted Palace, The" (Poe); symbolism of, 128

Hawthorne, Nathaniel, 4, 6, 10, 13, 23, 40-41, 45, 56, 68, 147, 249, 259; treatment of women characters, 212, 214, 231

Hegel, Georg Wilhelm Friedrich, 246

Histoires extraordinaires (Baudelaire), 39

Hoaxing, 45, 48-49

Hoffman, Daniel, 104

Hoffmann, E. T. A., 235

"Hop Frog" (Poe); alienated artist in, 150; hostility and drinking in, 150; justice in, 100; obsession and self-punishment in, 155; slave rebellion in, 239; ungovernable horror in, 250

Horkheimer, Max, 243

Horror and grotesque themes, 3, 5, 23, 37, 43, 49, 63, 104, 106, 154, 174, 235; and racism, 240, 245, 257

Houses, 78

"How to Write a Blackwood Article" (Poe), 5, 49, 244, 248

Humboldt, Alexander von, 251

Humor, 45, 47

Huxley, Aldous, 15, 23, 45

Imagination, 79. *See also* Fantastic (Poe's notion of)

Immorality, 28

"Imp of the Perverse, The" (Poe); confession in, 198-199; insanity defense in, 86, 88, 98; language of, 198-200; murder plot in, 199; narrator in, 98-100, 198-200; perverseness in, 198, 200, 205; rough voice of, 198; structure of, 98, 208

Insanity, 28, 55-56, 58, 61, 70. *See also* Madness

Insanity defense, 25; cases, 86-88, 90, 102; controversy over the use of, 86, 88; political nature of, 86; public consciousness of, 88; scientific/medical accounts, 98

Irony, 44

Irwin, John, 51

"Israfel" (Poe); music in, 6

Italian, The (Radcliffe), 33

James, Henry, 23, 45
Jay, Gregory S., 75
"Journal of Julius Rodman, The" (Poe), 48

Kant, Immanuel, 241-243, 246, 249, 258
Keats, John, 59, 68
Kennedy, J. Gerald, 71, 78, 165, 175, 177
Kennedy, John Pendleton, 9, 13
Krutch, Joseph Wood, 40, 105
Kunitz, Stanley, 54

Lacan, Jacques, 50
Lawrence, D. H., 15, 73, 219, 254
"Legends of the Province House" (Hawthorne), 45
Levin, Harry, 104
Levine, Stuart, 85, 167, 174
Lewis, Matthew, 33
Liberator, The (Garrison), 236-237, 250
Libraries, 78
"Ligeia" (Poe), 3, 5, 106; covert crimes against women, 213; eyes and vision in, 71, 76, 158; incantation in, 201, 206; ironic structure of, 108; Joseph Glanvill in, 202; Lady Rowena in, 71, 76; language of, 201-203, 209, 211; Ligeia in, 72, 201-203, 207, 211, 213, 248; memories in, 201-204; musical language in, 219; narrator of, 71, 75; obsession in, 76; opium fantasy in, 5; as parody, 45; psychological fantastic, 72; ratiocinative principle in, 70; return from the dead, 248; Rowena in, 201, 203; ruby-colored drops in, 109; self-consuming narrator in, 115, 198, 201, 204, 208-209; setting of, 77; shroud in, 213; ungovernable horror in, 250;

vampire lore in, 42, 122, 137; villainous narrator in, 216, 224
"Lionizing" (Poe), 5
Lippard, George, 88
Literary canon, 21
Longfellow, Henry Wadsworth, 10, 37, 40, 234; review of, 144, 146, 162
"Loss of Breath" (Poe), 244, 252
Love stories, 30
Lowell, James Russell, 45
Lyrical Ballads (Wordsworth), 54

Mabbott, Thomas O., 131, 187
MacLeish, Archibald, 43
McNaughton, Daniel, 25, 87, 90, 102
Madness, 55, 58, 70, 72-73, 77. *See also* Insanity
Madness tales, 27
"Maelzel's Chess-Player" (Poe), 105
Mallarmé, Stéphane, 3, 15, 22, 39
Man in the Iron Mask, The (Dumas), 64
"Man of the Crowd, The" (Poe), 51; bedeviled detective in, 106, 111, 114; ironic structure of, 111; man of reason in, 105, 111; narrator of, 107-108, 113; principles of investigation in, 106, 108; publication of, 106; terror and hypersensitivity in, 114
"Man That Was Used Up, The" (Poe), 236; comic voice in, 5
"Ms. Found in a Bottle" (Poe), 9; narrator, 256; narrator of, 75; setting, 79
Marginalia (Poe), 32, 251
"Masque of the Red Death, The" (Poe), 11, 45; language of, 146; obsession and madness in, 146, 155; Prince Prospero in, 146; publication, 148
May, Charles E., 13, 69, 74
Medical literature, 21
Melanchology, 73

"Mellonta Tauta" (Poe), 253
Melville, Herman, 4, 6, 56, 68, 78, 110, 249, 257, 259
Mercer, Singleton, 87-88, 98, 102
"Mesmeric Revelation" (Poe), 150
Mesmerism, 74
Metaphysics, 240, 254
"Metzengerstein" (Poe), 49; American slavery debate in, 234, 237; dualism in, 234, 243, 245; fire in, 237-238; Frederick, Baron of Metzengerstein in, 237-238, 244; horse in, 235-236, 238, 241, 243, 246, 262; Hungarian setting, 235; obsession in, 235, 238, 242; plot of, 242; politics in, 240; racist anti-abolitionism in, 234, 239, 250; rivalry in, 236, 239; setting of, 77; Teutonic names in, 235; William von Berlifitzing in, 236-237, 244
Mills, Bruce, 74
"Minister's Black Veil, The" (Hawthorne); review of, 212
Modernism, 32, 39
Monk, The (Lewis), 33
Monomania, 25, 28-29, 75
Montresor ("The Cask of Amontillado"), 28-29; confession, 66, 163, 165, 176; deathbed, 165, 177; escape from punishment, 67, 166, 175; heartsickness, 165; humanity, 165; insanity, 65, 163, 167, 175; insults to, 166, 167, 169, 175, 177; last words, 176; murder of Fortunato, 64, 66; narration, 63, 66, 164, 166-167, 176; noble ancestry, 169; philosophy of revenge, 64, 164; punishment, 64; roquelaire, 171, 173; screams, 167; self-awareness, 67-68; tone, 166; troubled conscience, 165
Moore, Thomas, 45
Moral themes, 85

"Morella" (Poe), 149, 244; covert crimes against women, 213; musical language in, 219; narrator in, 213; vampire lore in, 122, 137; villainous narrator in, 215
"Ms. Found in a Bottle" (Poe), 150, 153
Murder on the Orient Express (Christie), 27
Murderers, 55, 58, 60, 64
"Murders in the Rue Morgue, The" (Poe), 154; C. Auguste Dupin in, 5, 10, 85, 104, 107, 111, 114, 153; covert crimes against women, 213; crime story in, 85-86, 213; lack of moral issues in, 85; narrator of, 115, 224; orangutan in, 85, 225; process of detection in, 85; rational analysis in, 10, 104, 115; slave rebellion in, 239; ungovernable horror in, 250
Music, 7
"Mystery of Marie Rogêt, The" (Poe), 11, 13; C. Auguste Dupin in, 104, 111, 118, 223; covert crimes against women, 213; crime story in, 85, 213; newspapers in, 225-226; rational analysis in, 104
"Mystification" (Poe), 50

Narrative of Arthur Gordon Pym, The (Poe), 10, 42, 51, 235; creation of own reality in, 248; forces in, 160; slave rebellion in, 239; ungovernable horror in, 250
Narrative strategies of Poe, 28, 44, 54, 70, 75; double-voiced, 56, 62-63; first-person, 42, 55, 59, 68, 73
Neoclassical period, 5
New Criticism, 3, 43
New York Mirror, 11
Nickerson, Catherine, 24

"Oblong Box, The" (Poe); Cornelius
    Wyatt in, 112-114; corpse of
    Mrs. Wyatt in, 112, 114; crime
    story in, 85; detective in, 113-114;
    irony in, 112, 114; man of reason
    in, 105; motif of self-deception in,
    111; narrator of, 112-113, 115;
    parody of the ratiocinative tale
    in, 111; Poesque Paul Pry in,
    112
On the Interpretation of Dreams (Freud),
    61
Opium, 5, 72, 79, 120, 136
"Oval Portrait, The" (Poe), 77; vampire
    lore in, 122, 137

Pahl, Dennis, 51
Parodies, 45, 48
Peeples, Scott, 69, 76, 165, 177-178
Peithman, Stephen, 167
Perversity, 16, 44, 60
Philadelphia, Pennsylvania; insanity
    cases, 87-88, 102
Philadelphia Saturday Courier, 9
Phillips, Elizabeth, 92
"Philosophy of Composition, The"
    (Poe), 17, 163, 229, 256
"Pit and the Pendulum, The" (Poe), 15;
    metaphysical dread in, 4
Planche, J. R., 122, 137
Plath, Sylvia, 33
Poe, David, Jr. (father), 8
Poe, Edgar Allan; aesthetics, 3, 6, 144,
    158, 160; alcoholism, 22, 153;
    American reception, 40; cosmology,
    144, 146, 148-149; criticism, 36, 45,
    144, 148, 154, 158, 162; death, 9, 11,
    15, 22, 33, 38; early life, 8; egotism,
    212; European reception, 22, 39;
    financial problems, 8-9; hair, 124;
    humor, 5; imagination, 125; influence

of, 3, 22; influences on, 235, 244,
    249, 258; inner conflicts, 41; interest
    in science, 70, 79; lectures, 11, 37;
    moral conscience, 256; neurotic
    personality, 40, 73; poetics, 69-70,
    74; politics, 37, 234, 240, 247, 254,
    257; reputation, 11, 22, 36-37, 40;
    scandals, 11, 22; search for identity,
    136; self-destructive behavior, 235;
    and the supernatural, 119, 134; vision
    of human condition, 5, 116; writing
    process, 17; writing style, 45; youth,
    234
Poe, Elizabeth Arnold (mother), 8
Poe, Virginia Clemm (wife), 31; death,
    11
Poems by Edgar A. Poe, Second Edition
    (Poe), 9
Poe's Fiction (Thompson), 44
"Poetic Principle, The" (Poe), 6, 11, 144,
    162
Poetry (Poe on), 9-10
Poets and Poetry of America, The
    (Griswold), 37
"Poet's Vision, The" (Poe), 18
Point of view, 54
Polidori, John William, 122, 126, 138-
    142
Pollin, Burton R., 170, 178
Poststructuralism, 50
"Power of Words, The" (Poe), 209-210
Powers of the mind; intellect, 144-145,
    147, 161; moral sense, 145, 147, 161;
    taste, 145-147, 161
"Predicament, A" (Poe), 249; Zenobia
    in, 49
"Premature Burial, The" (Poe), 48, 149
Prichard, J. C., 27
Prichard, James, 73
Pruette, Lorine, 40
Psychoanalysis, 21, 29; of Poe, 40

Psychological fantastic, 70, 72
Public Ledger, 87-88, 103
"Purloined Letter, The" (Poe), 50; covert
	crimes against women, 213;
	doppelgänger motif in, 24;
	C. Auguste Dupin in, 5, 24-25, 104,
	115; imagination, 154, 160; King in,
	213; narrator's self-deception in, 114;
	Prefect in, 25; publication of, 104,
	117; Queen in, 213; rational analysis
	in, 24, 104, 153

Quaker City, or The Monks of Monk Hall
	(Lippard), 88
"Question of Poe's Narrators, The"
	(Gargano), 75
Quinn, Arthur Hobson, 31, 136
Quinn, Patrick F., 104, 106

Rabelais and His World (Bakhtin), 172,
	179
Rachman, Stephen, 50
Racism, 233, 235, 240, 245, 249, 254,
	256-259
Radcliffe, Ann, 3, 33, 71
"Rappaccini's Daughter" (Hawthorne),
	41, 212; Beatrice in, 214
Ratiocination, 24, 70, 79
Rational analysis theme, 104, 115
Rauter, Herbert, 106
"Raven, The" (Poe), 11, 16, 18, 37;
	ungovernable horror in, 250
Ray, Isaac, 28; authority on medical
	jurisprudence, 90, 92-93, 97
Rea, John, 175
Reader as accomplice, 54
Realism, 22, 78
Reason, 69
Rees, Abraham, 122
Regan, Robert, 45
Repetition and embellishment, 15

Revenge tales, 29, 64
Rich, Adrienne, 228
Robertson, John, 40
Romanticism, 3, 22, 39, 44, 55, 59, 68,
	71, 78; absolutism, 234, 252, 259;
	American, 241, 249; dark, 243, 249;
	German, 242, 255; philosophy, 242,
	259
Rosenheim, Shawn, 27, 50
Rossetti, Dante Gabriel, 39
Rovner, Marc Leslie, 44
Rowe, John Carlos, 51
Russian Formalists, 43, 56, 163. *See also*
	Formalism

Scarlet Letter, The (Hawthorne), 215
Schelling, Friedrich Wilhelm, 234, 241,
	243-244, 246, 248, 252, 255, 258
Schlegel, August Wilhelm, 6, 9, 69
Schlegel, Friedrich, 6
Science, 70, 79
Settings, 77
Sexton, Ann, 33
Shaw, George Bernard, 40
Shelley, Mary, 4
Shelley, Percy Bysshe, 23, 59, 68
Ships, 79
Short fiction (Poe's theory of), 9, 23
Shulman, Robert, 29
"Silence—A Fable" (Poe), 48; slave
	rebellion in, 239
Sin themes, 96
"Some Words with a Mummy" (Poe),
	253
Southern Literary Messenger, The, 9, 37,
	39, 119
Stauffer, Donald Barlow, 75
Steele, Charles W., 174
Structuralism, 43
Studies in Classic American Literature
	(Lawrence), 40

Whitman, Walt, 59, 68
"Why the Little Frenchman Wears His Hand in a Sling" (Poe), 48
Wilbur, Richard, 32, 153, 208
Wilde, Oscar, 3, 39
"William Wilson" (Poe), 10, 13, 106, 245; doppelgänger motif in, 106; narrator of, 44, 115; setting of, 77
Williams, Valentine, 106
Williams, William Carlos, 40

Willis, Thomas, 73
Wimsatt, W. K., 182, 186, 189, 196
Wood, James, 87, 93-94, 102
Wordsworth, William, 54, 59, 68

Yeats, William Butler, 15, 23, 45

Zenobia, Psyche ("How to Write a Blackwood Article"), 49
Zimmerman, Brett, 75